Also by Lolo Houbein

ONE MAGIC SQUARE

VEGETABLE GARDENING

The Easy, Organic Way to Grow Your
Own Food on a 3-Foot Square

EXPANDED SECOND EDITION
NOW WITH OVER 40 PLOT DESIGNS

LOLO HOUBEIN

THE EXPERIMENT

NEW YORK

ONE MAGIC SQUARE VEGETABLE GARDENING: *The Easy, Organic Way to Grow Your Own Food on a 3-Foot Square*—Expanded Second Edition

Text and photographs copyright © 2008, 2010, 2016 Lolo Houbein

First published in Australia in 2008 as *One Magic Square* by Wakefield Press. With excerpts from *Outside the Magic Square*, first published in 2012 by Wakefield Press.

The Experiment, LLC
220 East 23rd Street, Suite 301
New York, NY 10010-4674
www.theexperimentpublishing.com

This book contains the opinions and ideas of its author. It is intended to provide helpful and informative material on the subjects addressed in the book. It is sold with the understanding that the author and publisher are not engaged in rendering medical, health, or any other kind of personal professional services in the book. The author and publisher specifically disclaim all responsibility for any liability, loss, or risk—personal or otherwise—that is incurred as a consequence, directly or indirectly, of the use and application of any of the contents of this book.

The Experiment's books are available at special discounts when purchased in bulk for premiums and sales promotions as well as for fund-raising or educational use. For details, contact us at info@theexperimentpublishing.com.

Library of Congress Cataloging-in-Publication Data

Names: Houbein, Lolo, author.
Title: One magic square : vegetable gardening : the easy, organic way to grow your own food on a 3-foot square / Lolo Houbein.
Other titles: Vegetable gardening
Description: Second edition. | New York, NY : The Experiment, [2016] | Includes bibliographical references and index.
Identifiers: LCCN 2015041550 | ISBN 9781615193257 (pbk.)
Subjects: LCSH: Organic gardening. | Vegetable gardening. | Kitchen gardens.
Classification: LCC SB453.5 .H68 2016 | DDC 635/.0484--dc23
LC record available at http://lccn.loc.gov/2015041550

ISBN 978-1-61519-325-7
Ebook ISBN 978-1-61519-335-6

Cover design by Sarah Smith
Author photograph by Laura Smith
Text design by Sarah Smith

Manufactured in the United States of America
Distributed by Workman Publishing Company, Inc.
Distributed simultaneously in Canada by Thomas Allen & Son Ltd.

First printing February 2016
10 9 8 7 6 5 4 3 2 1

For my grandchildren Paul, David, Uaan, and Ty.
This is a book for their future. And for Burwell, for putting up.

In memory of Hendrik Houbein (1796–1874), grower of cabbages,
carrots, onions, and potatoes in North-West Frisia, and Uncle Wim Schild,
who taught me about vegetables, fruits, and chickens in his
magic food garden at Laren, North Holland.

A

Contents

PART 4: DESCRIPTIONS OF FOOD PLANTS

Preface

MY UNDERSTANDING of food gardening comes from deep time, from my great-great-grandfather who was an estate gardener in Fryslân, the Netherlands, where Friesian cows hail from. In later life he was registered as a *kooltjer*, a grower of four main vegetable crops: potatoes, cabbages, carrots, and onions. Maybe he became a market gardener because socioeconomic changes caused people to give up growing the family's food in favor of working for wages. Food had to be purchased and someone else had to grow it. His son operated a vegetable shop as well as teaching school, and his grandson, my grandfather, owned a vegetable shop and wholesale business. One of my grandfather's sons, my uncle, grew oranges in California. On my mother's side, Uncle Wim took me for walks from the time I toddled through his pride-and-joy food garden in Laren, North Holland.

Yet, just as surely as I carry this joyous history of food growing and harvesting, I suspect that my ongoing concern with hunger and food shortages also comes from deep time and from both sides of the family, as well as my personal experience of famine.

During 1944 and 1945, I endured a famine and, at 5 feet 8 inches tall, was reduced to 75 pounds of bone and sinew. I carry the memories of my hometown, Hilversum (population 80,000 in the 1940s), breaking down as war action cut off the region. All trees became firewood, as did doors, cupboards, furniture, and fences. Cats, dogs, and rabbits disappeared. I starved rather than eat our rabbit Trudy. Mice, rats, and birds went into the pot. Rivers were fished out. We ate chard—normally reserved for pig fodder—and tulip bulbs, which made me ill. I dug for grass roots under the snow to steady my stomach. A long winter of famine ensued during which 24,000 people died of starvation. Now, I witness the world's food-producing regions declining again through wars, landmines, and farmers' deaths. All famines are caused by war. In peacetime, crop failures through natural calamities, usually local and short-term, can be met by rapid food aid.

I became a food gardener after I immigrated to Australia, in my first backyard. My daughter, son, and grandson now grow their own herbs, fruits, and vegetables. Yet I know people with no food-growing history whatsoever who produce impressive vegetables at first try! The time is here for everyone to get in touch with food at a grassroots level. Even if you do not have a garden, you can start or join a community garden in your neighborhood.

By growing some of your own food and starting a pantry collection of staples, you take control of your food needs if times of chaos should arrive. Meanwhile, you eat healthier, fresher, tastier food, enjoy gentle exercise, and make new friends. Nothing unites people more congenially than eating, swapping, and comparing locally grown good food. Food gardening is the most intelligent adult endeavor on earth and ought to be understood by anyone who eats.

Lolo Houbein

Introduction

MANY TIMES I have been asked: "Why a 3-foot square?" Each time, I seem to give a different answer. Finally, I dug back in my memory to 1945 and the last months of World War II. It seems 3-foot square garden plots have dotted my life ever since.

At the age of eleven, I was evacuated with many other children from the starving western provinces of the Netherlands. I landed in a small canal village in southeast Drenthe bordering Germany. The village had a tiny school of two classrooms and an office.

Our teacher was an enlightened young man from Amsterdam. He may have felt fortunate to have escaped that starving city in time, for he prepared a long strip of ground in the school yard and divided it into as many plots as there were children. I remember my plot well, probably 3 × 1.5 feet. The teacher handed out the seeds. I think I grew radishes and some flowers, maybe marigolds. The summer was all too short for me and my plot, because convoys of children were being returned to the west after the country was liberated on May 5, 1945. My truck rolled up on July 4th, and I said goodbye to my foster parents and my teacher and was delivered home in the late afternoon of that same day to my very surprised mother.

We had no garden at home. Our workman's cottage stood a little more than 3 feet from the pavement that adjoined the road. At the back of the house was a concrete place for the laundry, to tinker and store bikes, and a small shed. Our only plants were indoor plants, looked after by Mother and me.

When I arrived in Australia, I was hoping to have a garden. It took a few years before we qualified for a State Bank loan and had a simple house built on a block in what was then still countryside. I adored the wide views of the Adelaide Hills and the Aldinga Range. Although we could not afford fences, I started to dig some ground for a vegetable garden, but due to my ignorance and the poor quality of former grazing land, nothing grew and I gave up. Deciding on tough geraniums and succulents, I was constantly prevented from developing a garden because of plans to terrace the sloping site with concrete retaining walls. And so the best memory I have is of a quarter circle drawn in a 3-foot square corner where two walls met. Here, I made a miniature garden, building a hill with excavated soil, retained with rocks, planted with succulent cuttings I picked here and there. This became the only delightful little corner, full of tiny starry flowers in the summer. I'd lay flat on the grass looking up my little hills and imagine it to be a landscape.

In the '80s, my partner, Burr, and I set up a trailer and shed on a hill in the Adelaide Hills, where we lived in primitive comfort. Burr began building an environmentally sound house, and I started to make a garden on top of the plateau in the forest. It would eventually spread across an acre. But the plots began by Burr picking over 9 square feet at my request, from which I removed rocks, stones, and roots. The soil was then dug, given compost, and planted with herbs. I remember a huge electricity truck with two men coming up the long driveway, looking fruitlessly for an electricity meter—we were not connected—as I sat on my bank of clay raking out gravel for yet another plot. "Making a little garden, luv?" asked the driver from his great height behind the wheel, a note of pity in his voice. They circled the rainwater tank and left the property, shaking their heads.

On the plateau, we built planter boxes with second-hand bricks to grow vegetables. These were approximately 3 × 6 feet—convenient to cultivate, plant, and reach across.

After fifteen years in the forest, we moved to a level 2.5 acres where we planted a mixed native forest on more than half of it. The house gardens sprawled over an acre and were developed in the same way as the Hills garden, square foot by square foot, cultivated and planted before going on to the next plot. You can have an overall plan in your head of what will go where, but to enjoy gardening, you best take it one square step at a time.

So there you have it. I am but a round peg standing proudly in a square plot. And since *One Magic Square* appeared, thousands of people have discovered how much fun, food, and satisfaction can be had from such small spaces.

Abbreviations

B&B	blood and bone
CM	compost topped with mulch
CMC	composted manure with a topping of compost
COF	compost and organic fertilizer
GE	genetically engineered
GM	genetically modified
Half a square	one 3-foot square divided in half lengthwise or diagonally
Half row	1.5 feet, or half a yard
LS	liquid seaweed
OF	organic fertilizer
Plot	the same as square, a 3-foot square plot
Plugs	plants plugged in
Quarters	a 3-foot square divided into four equal squares or triangles
Row	3 feet long, or one side of the square
Season	either spring/summer or autumn/winter, spring, and early autumn/late summer (depending on your climate) being sowing seasons, and summer and autumn (and even winter in some places!), growing seasons
Singles	single seeds
Square	1 square yard, or 3 × 3 feet

PART 1

TOWARDS
SUSTAINABLE
and
SELF-SUFFICIENT
FOOD GROWING

The TERRIFYING IMPORTANCE of GROWING FOOD

THIS BOOK has been inspired by the chaotic times we live in. It aims to put you in control of the production of at least part of the food you need. Food economists say it is now urgent that consumers start growing some of their own food, before shortages become the norm and prices hit the roof.

The book starts with a 3-foot-square plot of soil to grow your chosen vegetables, providing about one tenth of your food needs. An Australian food producer acknowledged on ABC Radio in 2004 that world food reserves in storage periodically drop to less than one month's supply. Additionally, supplies are becoming increasingly potential or virtual supplies. Another expert revealed that more fish is fed to fish in aquaculture than comes on the market, and that oceans will get fished out in the foreseeable future. In "first world" countries, more grain is fed to animals—those we eat, those that work, and those that run the races—than is consumed by humans.

Although the world population keeps increasing, food production is decreasing. Only about two percent of Australians, Britons, and Americans are food producers. Countries at war cannot produce sufficient food or invest in agricul-

ture. Their resources are destroyed or used to feed non-productive armies.

Since globalization took hold, the USDA reports that 32 percent of fruits and nuts and 16 percent of vegetables consumed in the United States are imported. Produce is purchased in places where labor is cheap or forced or growers are subsidized. While supermarkets sell imported food, local and small-scale growers are forced out of the industry.

In the United States, along with most other industrialized countries, the number of farms and farmers has steadily decreased since 1934, even as the demand for agricultural products continues to grow.[1] To make up for this discrepancy, farmers have been forced to turn to engineered seed and chemical fertilizers and pesticides to force the most food from tired land. Additionally, the Bureau of Labor Statistics reports that more than 40 percent of America's farmers are 55 years or older. The number of acres per farm worker has grown exponentially from 27.5 in 1890 to 740 in 1990. The global farming industry continues to dictate competition by lowering prices in supermarkets and raising shareholders' profits. All factors combine to increasingly threaten what was once a quintessential American institution: the family farm.

Some people still believe that genetically modified (GM) foods will feed the world. But GM food has not been discussed enough, nor is it supported by long-term testing. Meanwhile, the better policy is to foster food plant diversity, preserve the inherently good qualities of reproducible food plants, and maintain extensive local seed banks in case of regional crop failures due to war, weather, or new space-age weevils. See Useful Addresses (page 317) for seed sources and seed banks.

Professor Julian Cribb of the University of Technology in Sydney foresees growing populations needing to increase food production by 110 percent over the next four decades while facing decreasing resources of water, farmland, and soil fertility and a global decline in agricultural research.[2] Even aquaculture—meant to feed us as the oceans get fished out—is in trouble due to contamination from the land. Frequent droughts are to be expected as the norm, and some countries will grow more biofuel crops than food crops. Professor Cribb regards adapting to greenhouse conditions as urgent, but not nearly as urgent as working toward doubling world harvests with fewer resources.

During half a lifetime of food gardening, in four locations with different soils and climates, I found that books with illustrations of perfect aspects, lush black earth, plentiful water, and beauty-parlor vegetables did not match my own experience. Hence, illustrations of my own vegetable jungles and cabbages with holey leaves. But I learned that healthy food can be grown anywhere. Food will grow where you are. The best agricultural land is being covered by suburbs; therefore we should grow our food in the suburbs.

Scientists calculate that if food crops are consumed by people instead of being fed to livestock, one person can, in theory, live on the produce of 100 square yards.[3] That is 30 × 30 feet per person, intensively cultivated. A family of four would need four such plots, covering 60 × 60 feet (not counting paths) with one rotating plot growing grain, and another peas and beans to dry and freeze.

A 3-foot square garden gives you a fair idea how far you want to go. The labor required is minimal and pleasurable because you don't start off with a big project only to find you have over-reached yourself, throwing the garden fork away and running to the supermarket for half a sprayed cauliflower and two pale tomatoes.

In the year 1500, the globe supported approximately 400 million people of whom some 80 million lived in the Americas. Of these, Mexico had 25 million people who were fed on corn, beans, and squash. In 1999, the populations of the United States (258,233,000), Argentina (33,778,000), Chile (13,813,000), and Puerto Rico (3,620,000) alone totaled just over 400 million.[4] In 500 years, the world population has risen to approximately 6.3 billion, taking up all arable land for sustenance, and is expected to increase to approximately 10 billion by the middle of the twenty-first century.

Important reasons for growing your own food keep mounting. The same multinational corporations that gave us global warming—by using fossil fuels in industry, cutting forests around the globe, robbing millions of people of self-sufficiency, and causing man-made disasters that force untold millions to lose their land, homes, and belongings (if not their lives) through floods, droughts, and climate change—are now bringing us genetically modified foods because they profess to have a new mission "to feed a hungry world."

The corporations are as compassionate about hungry humanity as giant pharmaceutical companies are about poor children with AIDS or malaria. These corporations have switched from mining, logging, and manufacturing to seed and food production because these are globally consumed commodities they don't yet control. Moreover, it's time to get out of manufacturing cigarettes and logging. They will want to get out of oil before it runs out.

Genetically modified foods are unknown quantities because manufacturers do not want to label them correctly, which would allow consumers to check contents, make informed choices, avoid substances that may cause allergies, or give the foods a miss altogether. Governments buckle at the knees because these food companies are also major investors in raw materials—from mining to wood pulping—and are potential investors in our mining, railways, and armament industries. That's why they won't legislate for adequate labeling. No long-term safety trials have been done either, so we don't even know how GM and genetically engineered (GE) foods will affect our future health.

The best way to feed a hungry world is to return to poor people the security of an average plot of land with a water source and control over their own seeds, enabling them to grow their own food and sell the surplus in local markets. But corporations want to control the world's seeds in order to insert terminator genes, meaning the next generation of seeds will be unable to germinate. The company can then sell farmers and gardeners new seeds every year, combined with the fertilizer and herbicides needed by these hybrids. Thus, they protect their investment in the "improved" seeds, which came from a farmer in the first place and whose ancestors saved them over centuries. Selling seeds has been identified as having a vast, as yet untapped, global market. See Saving Seed (page 129).

You and I are fortunate to have private plots of soil, however small, and should not waste a day to get stuck into these and avail ourselves of earth's bounty. Nature will surprise us by conducting its own biodiversity maintenance as long as we feed, mulch, and water. It's that simple. We only play at being conductors of a green symphony composed at the beginning of time on earth. The music starts slowly to end in a crescendo of delectable tones, tastes, and colors.

People who do not currently regard themselves as poor, who can afford to buy fruits and vegetables, are increasingly finding some produce becoming luxury items. Farmers have to pass on their increased costs to the consumer. Corporations are always "improving" seeds and want to be paid handsomely for their efforts—more handsomely than any farmer ever is—and water restrictions, droughts, and climate changes are making food crops scarcer and more expensive.

During 2001, the hottest summer in 95 years in the part of Australia where I make my home, zucchinis and cucumbers doubled in price, tomatoes and celery almost doubled, and potatoes went up by a third. Only onions, lettuce, cauliflower, and broccoli remained the same price, but were smaller and fewer. Patty pan squash, prolific in the garden, went from $5.00 to $7.00 a kilogram (in Australian dollars); by 2006, it was $9.50, and garlic stood at $10.00. By 2015, our hottest year on record, I have given up comparing prices.

In the recent past, people grew their own vegetables to avoid toxic sprays on their food, to get that lovely freshness and superb taste of a sun-ripened tomato, and because it saved a little money. Now, it's becoming more serious.

In 1996, the USDA reported that a "conventionally grown" apple could test positive for up to 14 different pesticides and that 73 percent of all conventional produce showed significant pesticide residues. The Australian Government

Analytical Laboratory reported organically grown vegetables can contain an average of up to ten times more nutrients than chemically fertilized vegetables.[5] These facts are disturbing, but pale compared with other major forces that threaten our food supplies. We must start taking responsibility for producing some of our daily food.

Hunger is caused less by failure of food production than by failure of distribution, interruption from wars and regional conflicts, political chicanery, robbery, or plain apathy. Now distribution is being interrupted by the withholding of viable, reproducible seeds and exacerbated by years of drought. It would be foolish to think that a famine periodically happens somewhere else and could not happen where we live.

Even though the world has space, much is not arable. Underground water resources are being overused, and rivers have stopped flowing. Alarmingly, our wildernesses have shrunk and our forests are still being axed.

However, there is one place that can still be a biodiverse wilderness. That is our garden. Not just the backyard—that utility area for bins, barbecues, dogs, kids, and the washing—but the front yard, side yard, and the strip along the driveway: all are private domains. Privacy and wilderness are important to you. To almost walk into a giant spider web hung with dew on a path between two shrubs, to see brilliantly colored beetles at work, to find stick insects, lizards, frogs, and tiny birds skating between plants you have given the freedom to reach for the sun, is hugely satisfying and elevates the spirit. The only wilderness you can access daily, whose gates do not keep you out or charge a fee, is your garden. Make it beautiful. Make it a place of increase. Your own wilderness can feed your body and soul.

As urban food growing becomes a necessity instead of a hobby, it's good to know there are millions upon millions of backyards in North America. Imagine squares of green edibles in every backyard that doesn't grow vegetables yet! Globally, more than half of all people now live in urban areas, and urban food farming is bound to increase.

Naturalist Sir David Attenborough said in his television series *State of the Planet* that the decisions we humans make in the next fifty to 100 years will determine what happens to all life on earth thereafter. Sadly, what happens to all life on earth hereafter may have little to do with decisions you and I make and more with decisions by our and other people's governments.

For decades, small producers have gone out of business due to competition from government-subsidized agribusiness. Agribusiness, in the language of the World Trade Organization (WTO), concerns soy bean, corn, rice, wheat, and canola, some of which go into processed foods that sit on supermarket shelves for years without going bad, but most of which feeds animals raised for meat to feed the humans who can afford to buy it.

Moreover, just one company, Monsanto, is responsible for 94 percent of all GM seeds planted across the globe. To have the world's staple food crops narrowed to so few varieties, and to have ownership of practically all commercial seed for these major crops in the hands of one corporation, is an unprecedented and frightening situation—especially when you know that this company is also developing the technology for terminator seeds. The company wants the 1999 United Nations moratorium on this technology lifted. So do the US, Australian, New Zealand, and Canadian governments. Can they all be wrong? You bet they can.

Crops can fail. When they are big crops, they are big failures, causing famines. Corporations can fail, too—especially those that make huge mistakes incurring liability and causing the loss or disappearance of all assets. Meanwhile, the pollen of crops with terminator seeds, once let loose, will out-cross with normal crops, endangering their seed-producing viability. There is no known method to prevent this. In time—no one knows how long or short a time—seed stocks could be perpetually compromised until self-replicating seeds are a thing of the past.

Therefore, what we can do in the coming years with our part of the globe has already been decided by those who went before—which is how things work, of course. Or fail to work. Water shortages, the gradual death of river systems, the salinization of soils through irrigation and tree removal, and the droughts blowing away tens of thousands of tons of topsoil—these and many local land issues caused by lack of good governing are going to determine what we can or can no longer do, never mind what we had wanted to do.

For the home gardener, this means the garden becomes the last resource. As agricultural lands keep shrinking and water supplies dry up, it's a piece of land not yet saline that, with care, can yield sustainable food production. The home garden will also increasingly be a place where biodiversity is preserved on a small scale.

As the best agricultural land around cities and towns is urbanized and put under concrete, it is an inescapable fact that the best land on which to grow our food lies at the back door. Even in a concrete jungle, you can grow food with some care. There may be minerals waiting to be unlocked, and like all other worlds, the plant world is one of entrepreneurs waiting for opportunities; all they need is a hand up.

Industrialized food is sometimes claimed to be cheap, but as India's food activist Vandana Shiva has pointed out, it uses ten times more energy to be produced and ten times more water than food grown in organically maintained soil. She includes in the cost the technologists, producers of pesticides and farm machinery, truck drivers, the cost of diseases contracted by mono crops, environmental destruction in the name of agricultural expansion, government subsidies, and the cost of wars fought over the indispensable oil that drives the food industry. What you produce behind your home is dirt cheap by comparison.

Having used up in one century half of all oil resources—the halfway point, or peak oil, was reputedly reached in 2006, earlier than even the pessimists expected—we will now have to scale back our usage. Oil has given rise to previously unimaginable mining of resources from rivers, forests, seas, and soils, and the shipping of these resources around the globe. As a result, the carbon dioxide level of Planet Earth's atmosphere has increased more than a third since the start of the industrial revolution.

It is now inescapable that every individual must scale down their oil consumption. By growing your own food, you save not only the petrol for driving to the supermarket, but also the oil the industry uses to place food on supermarket shelves.

There are times when really cheap food is on offer, just as the multinational corporations promised. But we ought to investigate the true cost of "cheap food." It may be a dumping. In Britain, the question was posed at the start of this century during outbreaks of mad cow and foot-and-mouth disease. Both spread far beyond what would normally have been contained locally due to the globalization of trade and transport, the centralization of slaughterhouses, and a variety of animal husbandry measures intended to drive production up and prices down. Once the diseases broke out and spread rapidly, entire herds were destroyed, businesses went broke, and families became destitute. Now, many people live under a death sentence from diseases formerly not known to affect humans. Add that to the cost of your cheap food. Something similar could happen with vegetables and fruits.

There is no free lunch. There is no cheap food. The cheapest and best food is the food you grow yourself—food that does not accumulate added costs for transport from other states or continents, needs no refrigeration because you pick it minutes before preparing it, does not add to pollution because it only travels from garden to back door, is free of costly chemicals, and needs no packaging. Consider the real cost of a cucumber in a plastic jacket, grown in a temperature-controlled poly tunnel, refrigerated, put in the jacket, transported a great distance, and displayed in an air-conditioned supermarket under burning lights. The cucumber you grow yourself just has to be fresher, tastier, and healthier than that, doesn't it?

By growing your own organic vegetables, you make unnecessary all the spraying, heating, cooling, and transport—from state to state and continent to continent—needed to stock greengrocers and supermarkets. Heed the warnings of outspoken oil experts. Without oil, transporting food over vast distances becomes prohibitive. We ought to start shortening as much as possible the distance between our fork and the farm.

All it takes on your part is a seasonal pick-up of a packet of straw and some organic fertilizer or manure. If you don't have a car, buy compressed straw cubes and organic fertilizers in small bags that fit in your shopping cart. If the garden center doesn't have what you need, persuade them to order it in. Buy seed as you do other shopping, or by mail order—see Useful Addresses (page 317). Find a hand trowel and fork. Yes, there is some transport involved, but the reduction is enormous.

As your food ripens a few steps from the back door, the environment is spared clouds of toxic fumes and run-off because you turned a sod one Saturday and wielded a hand-held hose as you watched the sunrise. You are doing Planet Earth a service, as well as yourself and those you provide for. More so if you frequent local growers' markets for what you cannot grow yourself.

As part of this process, we simply have to change our expectations of how vegetables ought to look. The horticultural industry achieves those sleek good looks by toxic means. With your own plot, you will eat vegetables and fruits in season and adjust menu planning to what the garden offers. Whereas a shopper muses, "Shall we have cauliflower or green beans?", the gardener lifts up leaves and discovers that it is bean day, cauliflower day, or a zucchini emergency. If there's nothing but chard and tomatoes in quantities, it may be a stir-fry day with small pickings: beans, broccoli, a patty pan, the biggest rutabaga, or maybe two carrots and an Asian radish.

Add a handful of pick-and-come-again greens and herbs and you will still have a feast of flavors!

Therein lies an enormous plus for the home grower. The selection in shops is limited to varieties that have shelf life. If a shop provides vegetables with short shelf life, you pay a price that has quick wastage calculated into it (plastic bags of mixed salad greens, for example). So grow a dozen salad greens on one square, pick daily, and grow them for months.

You can grow fifty varieties of fresh beans and peas in your garden if you so choose, but buy only two at the shop. You can experiment with pumpkins in all colors and patterns, grow exotic cucumbers, or a dozen different chilies and black tomatoes. There are many vegetables that never even reach the shops, not even the markets, so read a catalog of organic non-hybrid seeds and let your imagination take flight.

HOW *to* GET STARTED

T**O START GROWING** your own food without delay, put down this book, go out in the garden, and select a spot in the sun. Dig over a 3-foot square with a garden fork and remove all the weeds by hand. If digging up lawn, cut out the sod with a spade, roots and all, and stack them upside down under a tree as mulch.

Come inside again and thoroughly wash your hands and clean your nails, as you must always do after working with soil. Pick up this book and in Part One (page 1) find all the information you need to make your magic square flourish. Then turn to Part Two (page 23) to select what you want to grow in your first Salad Plot. This book presents plot designs graded from the easiest and most robust to the complex and tender, starting with five plans for salads and leading you in easy stages to the degree of food self-sufficiency you decide on. The sequence presented takes care of crop rotation to keep the soil healthy. However, you can grow plots in a different sequence by feeding plants regularly.

You can read descriptions and helpful tips about the vegetables you'll be getting in List of Common Vegetables (page 230) in Part Four. While you're at it, put a bookmark at every vegetable you would like to grow down the road. It's easy to grow your own spuds. No more lugging home ten-pound bags—lug manure instead. Love corn on the cob? That's easy, too. So are artichokes, asparagus, and rhubarb. Make a list and go out to buy seedlings or seeds for your chosen vegetables and one small bag of blood and bone (B&B), since you don't yet have compost and composted manure. If you dug a square hole in the lawn, you may need to fill it with a bag of potting soil and plan to put in deep edgings to keep the grass roots out. There must be something you can recycle!

Go outside again and rake a few handfuls of B&B through the square, loosening the soil to a depth of 6 inches. Water it in. Now plant your seeds and seedlings according to your chosen Salad Plot plan (page 147). Water again. Go indoors to scrub your hands and nails as a surgeon would.

You are now a food gardener!

Having done the hard work, sit back and read this chapter and all of Part Two (page 23) that you didn't get to earlier, gathering ideas for your own little food paradise. Maybe you settle for gourmet vegetables or expensive delectables such as artichokes, asparagus, baby squash, garlic, or green onions. Easy and rewarding. Make notes on the back of an envelope. Don't make it more complex than need be! If you never go beyond the Salad Plots, but maintain your square through the seasons by practicing crop rotation with peas or fava beans in the cool seasons, you could double your good health and well-being.

Each plot has suggestions for follow-up crops to avoid plant diseases that build up from growing the same vegetables season after season. Follow the plots list to become familiar with growing a variety of vegetables over several seasons on just a 3-foot square. If you grow all plots in succession, as presented in Part One (page 1), your square will remain healthy and productive. Or choose a Stir-Fry Plot, Pasta/Pizza Plot or Soup Plot, then grow green or bean crops in between (see Part Three on page 145). And if some vegetables fail to produce, there are many things to blame: climate change, freak weather, a scorcher, snap-freezes, dud seeds, or the neighbor's cat. It's not your fault. Flops happen to the experts. They just don't publicize them!

Each plot is charted to start in the season best suited to the vegetables it grows, then carries through the year with other options for crop rotation. You can therefore start your square at any time of the year. Many vegetables are sown repeatedly through summer, while others are harvested to be replaced by cool-weather plants in autumn. The majority of plots grow a multiplicity of vegetables, so intercropping occurs naturally. Companion-planting principles and nitrogen-fixing plantings govern the plot designs. When the season and the spirit is upon you, check out other plot plans in Part Three (page 145) and roam through the lists of common vegetables, herbs, and easy-care fruit trees in Part Four (page 221).

Some plots are sown like a jungle with mixed seeds, such as the Horta Plot for lovers of wild herbs and vegetables.

There are certain things you will want to know before you turn your second square, even if you are going to lay out that food garden in annual increments over ten years.

Horta can be sown any season. You could make it your first plot as it grows fast, provides variety, and can be resown on one quarter each season thereafter.

It's so easy to make mistakes that may be long regretted. One vital ingredient of a food garden is your choice of watering system. This should determine the layout of the beds, not the other way around. Read Water and Watering (page 55).

Another point to consider is the garden's aspect. Where does the sun strike, the wind blow, the shade fall? Where is the garden bordered by walls, fences, trees, or buildings that function as windbreaks or heat reflectors? Think infrastructure and make a sketch.

Not all vegetables need so many adjustments, but a few minutes' attention can mean the difference between a puny cauliflower and a snowy head. Placing wood or a tile under a pumpkin to prevent rot takes little effort. So does placing a shade cloche over seedlings or lettuces.

Of course, you can't be self-sufficient in cabbages on a 3-foot square; the big drumheads feel crowded at four to a square. But you can be self-sufficient in one vegetable or another on one square. Plant compact sugar cabbages four to a quarter, with another four on a quarter not adjoining. That's eight cabbages for coleslaw, with two quarters for lettuce, carrots, radishes, and a tomato. Check out mini cauliflowers.

Such density does not suit rambling pumpkin vines, but drape two cucumber plants over an old chair, trellis, or wire tower on a quarter. Go vertical with peas, beans, and mini pumpkins draped over the edge. With trellises on two sides you are in clover, but in summer, don't place them against hot fences or walls. But in early spring or late autumn, a plot dug close to a fence or wall benefits from reflected warmth.

Everyone likes salads. Supermarket lettuces—too big for singles and couples—are often crisp from overwatering, but not always tasty. Yet a 3-foot square of soil makes you self-sufficient for months in pick-and-come-again salad greens, up in six weeks. Grow half a dozen varieties of non-hearting lettuces and radicchio close together, with chives and radishes in between, and cucumber and giant red mustard hanging around on the corner of the block.

Such a bed keeps going if you plug in more seed. If meanwhile you prepare another square, you will have salad greens all year on two 3-foot squares. For soil health, grow a bonus of beans in summer and peas or fava beans in winter on the finished plot. What is 9 square feet in most backyards in return for daily fresh salads and seasonally fresh peas and beans?

A Salad Plot showing six varieties of pick-and-come-again lettuces and a broccoli seedling and shallots around an onion setting seed. A dozen new lettuce seedlings have been plugged in between with fresh compost.

Do you love garlic, nature's antibiotic that adds such a kick to pastas and soups, salads and stir-fries? It is no longer a cheap knob because it takes the better part of a year to mature, tying up the commercial producer's soil longer than other crops. Yet, if you deep dig one square, or one quarter of reasonable soil in a corner of the backyard, fork in composted animal manure, plant the cloves of garlic bulbs, and mulch thickly, you will have the joy of seeing green sprigs turn into edible straps until drying tops announce that new bulbs are ready for harvest. Plant plenty for cooking, pickling, and replanting. Enjoy the luxury of whole roasted garlic knobs, artichoke hearts in garlic sauce, or baby squash with garlic butter. Present a trio of knobs braided together to your best friends, who wouldn't be your best friends unless they also loved garlic!

To recap:

1. Choose your first plot from the Contents (page viii).

2. Read the section on your chosen plot.

3. Choose which vegetables and herbs to grow.

4. Read up on the vegetables and herbs of your choice in Part Four (page 221). If you don't see a vegetable in the first list, it may be an herb.

5. Read the section Starting and Maintaining (page 24) to learn everything of immediate concern.

6. Prepare soil as described for your chosen plot.

7. Plant seedlings and sow seeds; water in well and daily.

Now, sift your desires and visions splendid, clarify your aims, and postpone a few ideas. By the end of Part Three (page 145), you will know just what you want and be able to find any description you need through the Contents or Index.

No week, month, or year is ever the same in the food garden. Use the alphabetical lists in Part Four (page 221) to make choices for each season, read up on favorite food plants, observe as they grow, and keep adjusting compost, mulch, manure, water, shade cloth, and companion plants until you get incredible results. Because you are gardening on such a small scale, in one year, you can become an expert on food-growing, a chef in your own kitchen, and a healthier, fitter human bean.

HOW *to* FIND TIME *to* GROW FOOD

ONE MAJOR HANG-UP people have about growing their own food is not having the time. They look from their backyards to magazine pictures of gardens covered from fence to fence with productive beds and throw up their hands.

Do not do this to yourself! Small is truly beautiful. No matter how overgrown your garden is, you can weed one 3-foot square, plant it, and keep it tidy. It may lead on to two squares or even a block of four—that is up to you. But be kind to yourself. Start with one Magic Square for the plot of your choosing.

At present, your problem is that you don't have time. You are overworked and a little stressed. You don't get much opportunity to relax, and when you do, you'd rather . . . whatever. You worry weekly about the bills or the amount of fast food consumed. You may be depressed and unable to appreciate the good things in life. You are always busy— yet bored, not stimulated—and you don't get enough exercise but hate jogging, the gym, hitting a ball—all those purposeless remedial activities.

If any one of these conditions depicts your life, change it instantly by digging up one 3-foot square. It won't take much time or work, as it is only 36 × 36 inches, one stride by one stride. But it will relax and delight you, make you feel a long-forgotten feeling, and put you in touch with your wild side without leaving home! In a short time, it will provide you with fresh food. Your depressive moods will evaporate when you tend your Magic Square, and you'll discover other micro worlds than the world you thought you lived in. Boredom will subside and you will do a daily three-minutes bending-and-stretching routine without being aware of it. Hand watering the square will become your meditation.

Where to find these minutes? Time is a gift from nature's own lovely chaos. So many books on growing vegetables show photographs of neat, weed-free rows of carrots and beans with not a shriveled leaf in sight, bed after bed in similar order. These are ready-made free dinners for hordes of insects that can identify whole rows of their favorite food from the sky. Control your urban yearning for straight rows! Grow vegetable varieties in minute little plots within your square, interspersed with companion plants, self-seeding herbs, and marigolds—the hordes will fly over and the weeds will find no space.

You will argue this won't be enough to feed a family, and you'll be forced to dig up more squares once your loved ones are hooked on garden produce. But in Part Four (page 221), you'll find tips to grow vegetables other than shop produce, so that you get by with a few broccoli, kale, come-again lettuces, and Asian greens for months of picking. Grow carrots closely and pull as needed, making space for the remainder to grow. Plant chard in a dense drift and pick it tender for several seasons. One square of sweet corn can yield fifty cobs, or twenty fresh fava bean portions and another twenty for the freezer compartment. Potatoes, beets, rutabagas, tomatoes, beans, cucumbers, and antioxidant greens are all high yielders in small spaces.

Less time spent on shopping for vegetables provides time to tie up the beans and plug in a few seeds. Bend, reach, turn, stretch, and take deep breaths of fresh air, so you don't need to go to the gym, saving time and money and escaping conversations that go nowhere. Move beyond one square and you won't need to go jogging, either. Forego boring club meetings with the excuse that you have to get stuck into the food garden (don't say "veggie patch" lest someone tosses

"corny" jokes). A food garden will soon acquire status. Be subversive in controlled green silence. Food gardening is the most intelligent adult endeavor on earth and ought to be understood by anyone who eats.

More time can be found by working according to methods that suit you. Let method be your mentor. "Small is beautiful" also means not saying, "Oh, it's a mess, I must clean up the plot and weed that path." Instead pick over a quarter, plant seedlings, sow seeds, water them, and call it a day, satisfied. Another day, remove spent plants from a productive corner and manure and water that, ready for replanting.

Work in time increments. Ten minutes of mulching. Time yourself. Don't cry: "Oh Mother of Cabbages, I have no time for all that today!" Look at one aspect, like staking three tomato plants before dinner. On your weekend afternoon in the yard, the very worst you can do is cast eyes over a four-square food garden and wonder how in heaven you can do all you want to do by evening. The whole vision can be depressing. Deny the greater picture—go for the detail. Most plants and plots can wait another week, but there may be one thing that is urgent. Do that!

List small tasks, decide priorities, and do one of these only:

- weed and mulch one corner and feel good.

- string up flopping beans.

- prune broccoli and pumpkin vines to increase productivity.

- free up two tiny plots for sowing next week and manure now.

- spray the whole plot with liquid seaweed and feel virtuous.

These jobs take from five to fifty minutes, depending on how long you linger, so there's also time for a break with a drink in the shade to admire your work. Enjoy your garden. Don't despair of an overgrown plot after being away, big rains, or plain neglect. Think of how the wildlife enjoys it. Don't abandon it, but do a corner, a bit, or a border. In no time, things will be back on track. You will experience abundant satisfaction.

Just like abandoning straight rows for sweet chaos, so, too, can composting be simple. If you prefer to process kitchen scraps instantly, read about worm farming in Compost Compositions (page 34). Some plants lend themselves to self-mulching. Decaying leaves of artichokes, chard, cabbages, squashes, and pumpkins can be cut and folded at the base of plants to return their nutrients to the soil. The leaves soon decay or can be covered with straw.

Try achieving closed cycles in what you do in the garden to save time and money.

Consider livestock to help you in the garden. In urban areas, roosters may not be welcome, but hens may be allowed. Maintaining a feathered flock creates an almost closed cycle—you need to buy or construct a coop and run, buy straw for bedding, and distribute a handful of grain before sunset. The fowl mix their manure with soil, straw, and vegetable remains into ready-made compost. Pure chicken manure needs composting with other ingredients before going on garden beds, but I spade out composted black earth from the run several times a year to use straight on vegetable plots. Bedding straw goes as mulch on unused plots to break down further before I make ditches to fill with compost. Outer leaves of vegetables, fallen fruit, and other plant debris provide food for the flock to turn into eggs.

Read Permaculture (page 124) to save time in the long term and Easy Vegetables to Grow (page 126) to plan the best garden for your lifestyle. Plan for later if you can't do it now.

GARDENING *with* ATTITUDE

TO SOME, a backyard is a combination graveyard for deceased cars and stalled machinery and a playground to plant a barbecue and basketball pole. Or it may be your spacing-out secret place, or a display the neighbors judge you by. If you fall in between, why not put up a sign near the gate announcing "Work In Progress," to tell visitors what not to expect and stop yourself apologizing.

A work in progress allows freedom to refrain from interfering, an important activity that takes place in the mind and consumes no real time. It happens when you see a new green shoot not far from an old plant, or in an unexpected place, and contemplate what it might be. If you have an anti-weed attitude and pull it up, you will never know. Why not watch it for a few weeks until it declares itself? In this way, I gained good self-sown fruit trees, herbs, and vegetables. One memorable nectarine seedling bore delicious fruit.

You can be a food gardener, although still burdened with society's attitudes. Step back from these to notice and give gratitude for a giving garden. You know how much edible vegetable matter is wasted in retail outlets: outer leaves of cabbage and cauliflower, tops of celery, beets, and carrots, and only broccoli heads are being sold. Only big vegetables reach the supermarket, except in country towns where local growers sell surplus through the local shop. There is nothing wrong with small beans, carrots, and cabbages. There is food value in outer leaves and tops.

Your supermarket-shopper attitude may turn around 180 degrees. In shops, we expect perfect looks to make up for lack of taste. In the garden, a cabbage with holes in its socks is still a great-tasting cabbage. The holes prove it was organically raised. Shopping for vegetables and fruits makes people choosy, rejecting broccoli with yellowing tips, limp greens, and discolored fruit. But if you have backyard fruit trees, you do not throw away half your crop because some fruit has spots, bumps, or bird bites. You treasure homegrown fruit enough to sort the good from the not so good, and clean up damaged fruit for juicing, stewing, and freezing.

When growing your own, you proudly bring in a broccoli head, enough to feed the whole family, but remember not to rip out the plant, as it will continue producing shoots for months. These shoots, as nutritious as the head, are never seen in shops as they cost too much to harvest and have a short shelf life. Undersize late tomatoes are almost as good in the kitchen as big early ones. A tender leaf with a hole cooks up just as well as a sprayed shop leaf, and is better for you.

The most important attitude for the food gardener is to eat what is in season.

Cabbage is a wonder food. Those outer leaves the greengrocer lops off, leaving only the pale inner cabbage, can be utilized in your kitchen if grown organically and not filmed over with insecticide. You can eat broccoli leaves stir-fried with garlic and soy sauce, dark green and delicious. First cut out the fat ribs and then juice these with carrots or apples for an energy-boosting drink. You can also juice kale and cauliflower ribs. Steam the tops of organically grown beets, rutabagas, turnips, and mustard. Make green tomato chutney. Sauté baby carrots. Weave baskets with sweet corn leaves. Cut and dry herbs every few months for herbal tea. You can do so

much with the produce of your Magic Square that you could never buy in shops.

Trade in perfect looks for good taste and high nutrients—a recipe for a good marriage—and build up a relationship with your food plot that satisfies stomach and taste buds, but also your spirits.

As a child, I used to help my mother sort vegetables. They came from the greengrocer but, as all vegetables were organically grown, we floated each batch in a bowl of water to inspect the leaves one by one. Beans often carried caterpillars, and spinach came in bunches cut with seeding stalks that had to be removed. Cleaning and washing vegetables was normal then. Ironically, it went out when insecticides and herbicides came in, delivering clean-looking vegetables that carry invisible toxicity instead. Cultivate vegetable attitude. Pick over your own vegetables rather than chopping up something from the shop without even rinsing, as so many cooks do.

Vegetables and fruits are at their best when ripened in season. Eat them then and do not desire them too early or too late. Grow early, middle, and late varieties, but go without sometimes to experience the joy of a transient food coming into season. You waited half a year, now the moment has arrived. You know you are eating the best when you pick your first artichoke, strawberry, or baby squash.

TEN GREEN RULES

GOING ORGANIC makes gardening easier. There are a lot of things you don't have to do anymore, and going back to basics allows nature a chance to show what it is capable of. Nothing is wasted; all is used or recycled. The rules for organic farm certification are very strict, but by using common sense, the home gardener can achieve almost the same.

1 Think of a garden as a community where many different plants help each other and attract insects, which in turn attract birds to nest in thickets, contributing to a healthy balance without the need of toxic substances that harm birds, frogs, lizards, wildlife, and you.

2 Care for the soil. Don't leave it bare for long. Don't rototill. Keep digging to a minimum. Use a garden fork when loosening is required. Build soil with compost, mulch, manures, and green crops.

3 Compost manures or spread them under CM, keeping away from plant roots. Use LS, B&B, OF, and natural pest-control methods.

4 Never burn garden waste. "Cook" diseased waste in plastic bags in the sun. Don't bring healthy garden waste to the dump. Compost everything to make your own soil and mulch.

5 Set up a worm farm and frog pond after you have stopped using toxic sprays. Plan to enclose your orchard trees and put in a few hens to control codling moth and other pests.

6 Rotate crops in the food garden, plant fragrant and pungent herbs for pest control, and practice companion planting.

7 Raise your own seedlings from open pollinated seeds, not genetically modified seeds. Save seed from your best plants and swap with others. Leave some vegetables to go to flower to attract predator insects.

8 If you need to buy mulches, potting soil, and other garden products, buy organic products or buy from unsprayed environments.

9 Never use toxic sprays, not even the one you are told breaks down quickly—yeah, sure—and

disappears into groundwater until elements of it come up again to issue from someone's tap. Don't use snail pellets. They will kill frogs, lizards, ladybugs, lacewings, worms, small birds, and other assistant gardeners. Contact your local agency to dispose of your collection of toxic substances. They have facilities to do this without the substances leaking into the environment, which would happen if you just put them in the bin. If you must spray, make garlic or soapy water spray and keep well away from your pond and worm farm.

10 Utilize weeds for their nutrients in compost and green mulch. Control seed-setting weeds by cutting off flowers. Where weeds are rampant, mulch with wet newspaper, cardboard, telephone books, and pea straw. Then plant groundcovers and a tree, use that area as a pumpkin bed, or grow a crop of potatoes.

Think of your garden as your paradise, and paradise will emerge within a few years. Celebrate your garden's birthday!

PART 2

TIPS
and
TRICKS

Starting and Maintaining

HOW *to* SET UP *a* FOOD PLOT

MAKE A SKETCH of what you want your food garden to become. Not in one year, but eventually. Cut out illustrations from magazines and newspapers to make a collage of your future food garden and hang it on the wall. Importantly, mark locations for perennial vegetables that stay for years: asparagus, globe artichokes, rhubarb, and perennial spinach. These are quite ornamental in season, so plant some in the front garden or along a boundary or fence.

Next, make a list of things to grow in Styrofoam boxes: mint and sorrel (to prevent roots from spreading), salad greens, radishes, or garlic. Finally, plan where your rotational plots are going to be. You may only plant one plot this year, but the cabbage family and leafy greens, root crops, onions and garlic, peas and beans and sweet corn, and the Solanaceae family of potatoes, tomatoes, eggplant, bell peppers, and chilies all need to be rotated seasonally or annually. So mark six plots in the sun, a 3-foot square each, and don't panic. If they are not too weedy, you can cover five with layers of cardboard, manure, and thick mulch, so they'll be ready when you are.

Prepare your first winter plot. If the ground is hard and has sparse growth, dig it once to a depth of one and a half spades. Hard work. Hence, I keep urging new gardeners not to start with more than one or two plots in the first season.

If the plot has grown plants other than lawn, you can get away with testing how easily a trowel enters the soil.

Remove all weeds and plant remnants. If you can surround the plot with an edging, it will help to keep mulch in place. Don't use treated timber because toxic substances will leak into the soil and get into your skin or even the vegetables. The pH of your soil is important. On a scale of 0 to 10, it ought to be around 6.5 to 7 for vegetable production. If you suspect the soil is acid (lower), or if you live on alkaline limestone ground (higher), buy a cheap pH testing kit at the garden center and do the simple one-minute test. For acid soil, adjust by lightly sprinkling lime and raking it through, then wait three weeks before planting. Repeat this every season until the pH reading is at 6.5 to 7. To adjust an alkaline reading, sprinkle sulfur, following instructions on the packet. In both cases, make a note of the date and reading, test again in spring, note date and reading, and adjust soil until it has a pH of 6.5 to 7.

Enrich soil by digging in well-decayed animal manure. If you can't get this from a farm, garden centers have small bags of aged manure, and a helpful attendant may even lift it into your car trunk. Use this with a few handfuls of B&B.

After a few years of adding organic matter and manure each time a bed is empty, the results in levels and produce will be fantastic.

After the hard yakka and scientific testing, you are suddenly ready to commence planting. What shall it be? See Common Vegetables: How to Grow and Use Them (page 229). Buy seedlings or sow seeds directly or in containers with six toilet paper tubes each.

Organic matter is food to a garden. Mulch also becomes soil food. Anything organic that will decay can become compost. Buy a bag of compost to start with, but set up bins to compost all organic matter from kitchen and garden—see Compost Compositions (page 34). Enrich home compost with dolomite lime, lucerne pellets, B&B, charcoal, wood ashes (from untreated wood), shredded woody herbs, and a few yarrow leaves as activators. For small conical compost bins, buy a corkscrew-like implement for a few dollars to aerate the contents regularly.

Using ready compost, build up garden soils organically to hold moisture like a sponge, keeping plants alive even in very high temperatures. Plants in such soil, protected by shade cloth during the worst heat waves, will be able to set fruit and produce, whereas without soil improvement, plants may wither despite daily watering. If you can obtain coarse sand, mix it in with compost when you fill a bed to improve drainage.

You are sequestering carbon by composting so many organic materials. Worms move in and work it over, adding fertile castings. It gets better every year. It also sinks every year. If you are filling raised beds, you may despair whether the soil will ever reach the top, and if it does, stay there! After a few years of adding organic matter and manure each time a bed is empty, the results in levels and produce will be fantastic.

Improving the Soil

Drainage: Add gypsum and coarse sand to heavy soils.

Structure: Add plenty of organic matter, compost, and manures.

Moisture: Mulch to prevent evaporation.

Protection: From extremes of heat, wind, and lashing rain by means of shade cloth, wire or netted cages, racks and trellises.

Trace elements: May be needed by impoverished soils.

PHOSPHATE

An important component of fertile soil that used to come from Nauru is harvested from guano, or bird droppings. That source was used up, and the world will be out of phosphate in a decade or less.

But wait a minute, we all produce phosphate. The word is out: urine is a universally sound and sterile fertilizer for all soils, and a good source of phosphate. Or should we say: the word is out again, for the Yates garden guide of 1914 advised to activate compost with urine and during World War II the Victorian Department of Agriculture recommended a pint of urine diluted with a gallon of water as "a good liquid manure."[6] Although rustic people have peed on their compost heaps and around lemon trees for centuries, one scientist finally made this century's official statement in 2010 that urine was a reasonable replacement for mined phosphate. Unless you have acres to fertilize, you don't have to collect urine every day. Think of placing a lidded bucket in the toilet for males on weekends, when people have time to think about what they are doing—in this case, helping you to grow the food they eat. Or dole out a little daily, on the soil, not on the plants, diluted with water 10:1. You will see a difference in the depth of color of vegetables and the leaves of trees before long. In permaculture, this would be a pretty tight closed cycle: eat greens, return yellow pee to the soil, eat greens again.

If you can't get over the idea to do this yourself and would rather buy greens in the shops, take note: urine, said the scientist, is now being separated out from our other excretions and collected by farmers who put it straight on their crop lands.[7] The choice then is: use your own or eat vegetables fertilized with communal donations.

WEEDS

If you mulch your plot well with straw, weeds will be suppressed. Weed seeds blowing in will grow new weeds, but these are easily pulled. Make a virtue of weeding by adding these nutritious green plants to the compost, or lay them flat on the soil, or gradually fill a bin to grow potatoes in next year. In the latter case, alternate layers of weeds with sprinklings of soil and/or straw until the bin is full and no longer sinking. It makes such a nutritious medium to grow food in.

When I had large gardens, I made it a morning exercise to pull a bucket of weeds to feed the chickens, ducks, and geese in their run. It gave them pleasant work to do the sorting and made their eggs' yolks deep orange. Mixed with their droppings, the dried leftover weeds eventually returned to the garden.

Weeds are not a problem, but an asset. Each weed, depending on its root system, delves into the earth to bring up one nutrient or another that can feed your vegetables. Don't waste them. Badly infested weedy problem areas can be covered with layers of wet cardboard and newspapers, covered with layers of straw. Leave for a year, and the problem will be gone and a new plot of arable soil created.

The main mistake is to let weeds go to seed. Weeds are weeds because their survival tactic is to carry thousands of seeds. When you see weeds flowering, pull them up. Put pretty flowers in a jar in the kitchen. You'll come to love your weeds. (Also see What to Do about Weeds on page 83.)

SOIL SECRETS

THE 2000 CENSUS found that 80 percent of the United States population lives in cities, towns, and villages with millions of backyards. Backyards may have suffered less of the contamination caused by the agricultural revolution, although Bill Mollison, the founder of permaculture, believes the opposite. Gardeners do buy a lot of toxic sprays, but look in any shed, and they sit there mostly unused as many never bother to use them.

There are still soil secrets in suburbia. Microorganisms do have a life in backyards. Without microorganisms in the soil, plants cannot take up nutrients and good soil structure is not maintained. Compost and mulch add to soil structure, keep soil moist, protect from UV rays, and so help microorganisms to work. Seasonal small applications of calcium-containing lime help if the soil is acidic. Rather than turning soil over, put on layers of manure, compost, and mulch. Don't walk on garden plots.

Some plains' soils are very ancient, while the Hawaiian Islands have the youngest soils, which are still being formed and added to. Land-hungry Europeans are a relatively recent addition to North America's ecosystems. Forests were cut, rivers were tapped for the irrigation of export crops, and superphosphate was imported to whip tired land into productivity. Wind and water erosion became rife; salinization administered the death knell.

At this point in time, vast stretches of land have been subjected to various degrees of industrial pollution and may harbor accumulations of agricultural chemicals. Billions of tons of topsoil are eroding annually. Yet, most arable land grows crops for export. Some small farms grow excellent food for local markets and restaurants, but much of the food North Americans eat is produced hydroponically in tunnels or is imported from thousands of miles away. It's time to consider what's left.

What remains apart from the land is what was brought to the continent: domestic animals and millions of people. Both produce more manure than this continent saw for millennia. There are decreasing amounts of hay and straw from introduced crops. There are mountains of old newspapers instead of the forests we once enjoyed. There are still leaves for sweeping up and a lot of other vegetative remnants. What can be done with these if one doesn't have a composting toilet yet?

I wish I'd been paid ten dollars for every person who told me: "Oh, you can't grow anything in my soil/your soil/that soil, it's no good!" Wholesale condemnation of soil is just an excuse to get out of gardening. Soil can be made by "industry and art," as the Shakers said. The chapters on compost (page 34) and mulch (page 69) tell you how. The first year you have a vegetable plot, you may resort to buying bags of potting soil to start plants off, but in the second year, you'll have your own compost.

Before asphalt roads and refrigerated transport brought food to faraway places, the people of the frontier and indigenous peoples of the Southwest and Great Plains grew vegetables and fruits in what soils they had, adding wood-fire ashes and animal manure and watering with pure soapy washing water. Now, they, too, can choose from seven long-life vegetables and pay a dollar for an orange.

My forest garden's subsoil in the Adelaide Hills was tens of thousands of years old, studded with ancient rocks releasing prehistoric smells. We pick-axed planting holes to fill with potting soil, mulching the surface. We pruned native shrubs to bulk up compost and backfilled. Plants did not curl up stunted when roots filled the holes, but took off as if they'd hit the jackpot! This happened in the second or third year. The secret was good drainage due to all those rocks and minerals unlocked by moisture and mulch. We used manures and compost, but minimal fertilizers.

In our alluvial clay garden, we could grow anything as long as animal manures, compost, and mulches kept the top from drying out to a hardpan surface. We used gypsum and mulch on "concrete" plots. Had the clay been stickier, we would have had to double dig—once to work in organic material, but mostly it responded to top dressing. Holes for fruit trees received compost and gypsum. The only snag with clay soils is that they must be made to drain well. Compost mixed with gravel can improve drainage.

Our ridge garden seemed to have easy soil, but nothing grew beyond adolescence due to a pH of 4.3 which is very acidic (7 being neutral). This soil required lime, dolomite, and gypsum as there was hardpan clay underlying the sandy soil at a depth of 15 inches. After repeat applications of compost, manure, and mulch, vegetables grew to edible size. This soil, looking easy on the surface, turned out the hardest to raise vegetables on, although, by the third summer, we had small amounts of broccoli, cabbage, cucumbers, garlic, kale, lettuce, onions, pumpkin, chard, spinach, squash, tomatoes, zucchinis, and herbs.

~~~

Do test your soil for pH and chemical makeup.

~~~

Do pH test your soil—simple test kits are available from garden centers. Adjust acidic soil with lime. If your soil is too alkaline—above 7—adjust with a mulch of acidic material, dust with sulfur, or sprinkle with 1 cup of vinegar per bucket of water.

The Obamas' organic White House garden, widely publicized when begun in spring 2009, made news for a different reason a few months later, when it came to light that the soil had tested positive for lead. Despite initial alarm, the initial lead level of 93 parts per million (p.p.m.) was well below the EPA danger level of 400 p.p.m. The good news is that the very things done to adjust the soil's pH and improve its fertility—such as adding lime, green sand, and crab meal—also helped reduce the lead levels to 14 p.p.m. The example set by the White House garden is a good one in more ways than one. Not only should more people be growing their own food organically at home, but before doing so, it is important to do pollutant testing in addition to pH tests if you live in an area that has been inhabited by humans for any length of time. The story is equally valuable for demonstrating that the very organic and mineral soil supplements that are good for plants are just as good at helping to make soil healthier for all living things.

So, if you set out to make an urban or suburban garden and your soil tests positive for heavy metals or other pollutants, don't throw up your hands in despair. Take a leaf from the Obamas' book (or garden) and set about improving your soil today, test again, and commit yourself to its continued improvement over the years.

If your soil grows a bounty of different weeds, it is probably fertile and well drained. Weeds protect soil from baking in sunlight and many have deep roots that aerate the soil, while decaying weeds leave a beneficial layer of humus. Weed-supporting soil is often crumbly and friable; just keep weeds down with mulch where you plant vegetables.

If you are starting out new on rocky soil, you'll have good drainage. Plant trees whose roots can find their way deep down to where the nutrients are. Within two years, they will form a windbreak for your food garden and provide leaves for compost.

If your soil is totally bare, the question is: why does nothing grow here? Has the soil been chemically contaminated? Try to find out your plot's history. Have cars driven up and down here, or leaking lawnmowers? Stick a spade or fork into the soil. Can it be rehabilitated by forking, adding gypsum to break it up, a wetting agent to make it take up water, or digging in compost, and mulching? Most probably. One instructor with whom I taught a vegetable-growing course grew carrots in his driveway!

Soils range from pure clay to pure sand. Many gardens have something in between, a loam of sorts. Experiment with pots containing the same soil, adjusting the pH in one, adding gypsum to another, fertilizer to a third, all three in a fourth, then grow lettuces in all pots and see what does best.

Clay Soil Working Bee

You can easily prepare one or two square plots on a weekend morning. Have a soup-and-sandwich Saturday to free up time to bake a soil cake in the garden! During the week pick up:

- a bag of mushroom or other compost.

- a bag of organic potting soil.

- a bale or pack of straw.

- a bag of animal manure. (Available from garden centers. Horse manure from roadside paddocks where kids bag it up for pocket money is probably safer than from racing stables, as hobby horses are less full of antibiotics. Chop manure with a spade before spreading.)

- a small bag of gypsum for clay soil.

- a tiny bag of lime for acidic soil.

- organic fertilizer pellets or liquid seaweed fertilizer.

Many of these are available in small packages you can sit on the backseat, cradle in your arms, or put in your shopping cart.

That was hard work and quite an outlay of money, but you'll get it back with interest. Some supplies will last years. If unable to lift bales and bags, ask the garden center people to deliver, or lift them into the trunk of your car—then ask a neighbor to help you unload. Open a bag of manure inside the trunk and spade the contents into buckets. Wear garden gloves and do the same with the potting soil, gypsum, and fertilizer. Borrow a wheelbarrow and sweep up a heap of fallen leaves or grass clippings. Collect seeds and/or seedlings.

From here on, it is as easy as making a layered no-cooking cake!

First, aerate the soil by pushing a garden fork in many places and wiggling it. Pull out any clumps of weeds and rake in gypsum, following directions on the packet. Add lime if acidic. Rake in chopped manure to compost in place.

Lucerne, pea straw, or wheat straw are good in descending order, as are the prices. Baled straw usually peels off in "biscuits." Cover your plot entirely with straw biscuits. If tightly packed, tease them out and fluff them up. Most gardeners settle for pea straw—it turns into beautiful soil.

Water well to settle the "cake."

Leave for three weeks if you limed. Draw a planting plan, start off seedlings, and remove weeds around the plot while waiting. Read other relevant chapters.

Then, open pockets in the straw and fill with potting soil and water. This is easiest on the junctions where biscuits meet, but for small plants, make more pockets by pulling straw apart. Plant seedlings, sprinkle organic fertilizer, spray with diluted seaweed, and water in well. When planting seeds, sprinkle fertilizer after plants emerge.

All done! Water daily. No weeds. Soon, you'll eat!

Sandy Soil Workout

If you have pure sand that runs through your fingers, it may not retain water and could be magnesium deficient, causing yellowing of leaves. Add magnesium by mixing a spoon of Epsom salts in a bucket of water. To make the soil hold water, make a thickly layered plot on top of the sandy soil. Hold layers in with rows of half-buried, water-filled plastic bottles, planks, or railroad sleepers. If you can obtain a bucket of clay, make a clay slurry (one spade to a bucket of water, stir well, and pour onto raked sandy soil). Do this several times to increase water retention. Put down layers of wet newspaper over animal manure to attract earthworms, and layers of straw in which you will make pockets for potting soil to plant in. Keep mulching as the season progresses and add all the organic matter you can find: leaves, seaweed, broadleaved weeds (without seeds), seedless grass clippings, small twigs.

Both the pure clay gardener and the pure sand gardener have to start a compost heap quick-smart, for these soils need more organic matter than others. Prune and chop anything growing in your garden that will benefit from a haircut: daisies, low acacia branches, ornamental shrubs. Mix with kitchen scraps, leaves, lawn clippings, and manure.

On a nice loam, you still need compost to maintain fertility. So after planting your first square, read Compost Compositions (page 34). Start a compost heap now to be ready the following season. Get into the rhythm of the seasons, those realms they write music about.

COMPOST COMPOSITIONS

SOIL ENRICHED by organic matter is the foundation of a healthy food garden that produces vegetables and fruits of high nutritional content. Compost gives plants the opportunity to graze about with their roots for what they need, just like chickens are healthier when able to scratch around an orchard for grass, worms, and herbs than when they are fed a scientific formula.

Shaker Compost

The Shaker community in America, where the renowned Shaker furniture was produced, was almost totally self-sufficient. Shaker compost—now there's a concept worth exploring—was made from vegetable refuse and herb stalks with guano, gypsum, seaweed, fish waste, pond mud, and ground-up bones. Shaker gardeners added this compost with animal manure to their shallow, rocky soil. Herb plots received as much as vegetables and fruit trees. Their recipe—moderated by leaving out salt and adding extras—goes somewhat like this:

◆ One part mineral substances: wood ash, lime, sand or clay, gypsum or dolomite.

◆ Five parts organic matter: weeds, straw, leaves, roots, stalks, thin bark, sawdust (from untreated wood).

◆ Six parts animal manures (animal manures should be composted where possible before use to prevent *E. coli* and other bacteria proliferating).

◆ For a 3-foot-square plot, you can stir this up in a bucket! Decide whether your soil needs sand, clay, or neither. Don't overdo the sawdust, and balance it with a handful of lime.

◆ Having acres of food gardens, the Shakers collected organic matter all year, piling it in layers to compost. When matured, they spread the compost at the rate of forty oxcarts per acre, and became the best food gardeners in 19th-century America.

Making Compost

Compost is new earth made from old organic matter, including kitchen scraps, lawn clippings, ornamental garden prunings, leaves, twigs, and anything organic that is locally available. It can really end up looking like that beautiful black stuff you see on TV. But

Making compost at dawn.

even before it looks glamorous, it will be useful.

There are a number of ways to make compost. Choose the one that gives you the least pain and most pleasure. Remember everything that is or was alive, and is subject to decay, will convert to compost. But don't add meat scraps and bones into your garden compost as they attract vermin, although you can pulverize the bones. Depending on matter and method, you should have compost in a few weeks, months, or years.

HOT OR COLD

Not everyone agrees. Hot composting destroys pathogens. Cool composting is now said to be better as the "cooking" process uses up lots of nitrogen and carbon. No doubt the last word is still to be spoken.

USING BINS

The gentlest composting is done in bins. Keep two composting bins behind the shed and as you fill up the second, the first will be composting. Or if yours is a small operation, use two plastic laundry baskets lined with wet newspaper and covered with doormats held down by a brick (this may not be critter-proof!). Or, buy a tumbling bin on legs and turn it twice a day. You will need a covered storage bin for scraps while the bin is filled to capacity yet still composting. In the bins, the material should be mainly kitchen scraps, lawn clippings, soft weeds, leaves, vegetable matter, and soft prunings.

Put hard prunings in a heap at the back of the yard and don't look for a year—they will compost eventually. Gardeners working on a larger scale, or people with lots of ornamental garden prunings, will profit by building a composting area of pea straw bales. Throw it all in, as shredded as possible. When it's time to turn or take the compost out, simply remove one bale. Bales attract earthworms, which live underneath until the compost has cooled enough for them to work it, lacing the stuff with their castings.

Build a small compost heap using a round circle of chicken wire, 3 feet in diameter, pinned down with stakes. Line it with layers of wet newspaper and throw in organic matter. Sprinkle occasional handfuls of lime, straw, and manure into the mix and water regularly. When the bin is full (it sinks constantly, so this may test your patience!), cover it with a piece of old carpet and set up another wire bin. When that is full, the first bin will have useable compost.

TURNING COMPOST

There are those who do and those who don't, but turning speeds up the process. Build two adjoining square bins from corrugated iron or planks, no less than a cubic yard each, for it is mass that produces enough heat to make hot composting work and break down plant pathogens and weed seeds. In a wet climate, build bins with slats for air circulation.

If you have space, build three, four, or five bins in a row by extending the back wall. The extra bins allow you to turn compost a second time from Bin 2 into Bin 3, to obtain that friable black and gold of TV pictures. Bin 4 can be a long-term composter for tough stuff such as wood thicker than your thumb, thorny rose prunings, and shredded paper. A year later, it will be compost without any turning at all. Bin 5 is for bad weeds, things you never want to see in the garden again. Leave them composting for a small eternity, or "cook" them in plastic bags.

USING A RIDING LAWNMOWER TO MAKE COMPOST

Collect and spread where you will mow:

◆ prunings from the ornamental garden.

- weeds, except bad ones likely to regrow from pieces.

- leaves.

- very thin bark.

- a bag of animal manure.

- a small bag of lime (you only need handfuls).

- other organic matter, like spoiled hay.

- fallen branches no thicker than your finger.

If you like, add onion material, citrus peel, nut husks, rhubarb and elderberry leaves, tea leaves, and coffee grounds. Spread shredded paper and a layer of wet newspaper in the bottom of a bin.

Use two shredded yarrow leaves as a compost starter. There are commercial compost starters if you don't grow yarrow, or a cheap starter is urine, diluted with water and sprayed between layers—magic stuff. Or mow the lawn first—the clippings can also be used. Finally, make sure the mower's blades are sharp. Wear goggles, earplugs, and steel-toed boots!

Spread out the collected material and mix with a garden fork. If it's too wet, let it dry off. Spread out part of the material and mow across it several times until it is roughly shredded. It doesn't matter if there are small sticks in the mix, as they

will break down, if not in the heap then later it will compost in place.

To build a heap, spade in an 8-inch layer of shredded matter, a handful of lime, a shovel of manure, hay, or straw, and add a compost starter. A dry heap won't compost fast, so water as you build. When the heap is finished, water the top long and hard, then cover with carpet (or other porous material), and wet that also. The heap should start "cooking" within hours.

To check whether the heap is brewing, lift up the carpet on day three, poke a hole in the top, and watch steam rising! Cover up and water twice a week. When the heat subsides, worms will move in and accelerate the process. After one month, turn the heap with a garden fork. From Bin 2 or 3 it can be returned to garden plots. Your compost could be ready one month after turning, depending on your climate and what went in. If a handful looks like soil—albeit full of twigs and on the rough side—fill a wheelbarrow and spread it between the vegetables, worms and all. It will compost further on the plot. If you want finer compost, turn it into Bin 3.

IN-BED COMPOST

Should you have gone beyond a one-square food garden, you'll have spent vegetable plants by summer's end. After feeding your feathered flock and worm farm with greens, tops, and fallen fruit, and after the backyard bins are full, you may still have heaps of decaying organic matter to clear away. Then do it in bed, as follows.

In autumn, clear one plot to be a composting bed and spread manure. On this, throw excess chard, zucchini leaves, pumpkin vines, vegetables gone to seed, and anything else that is reasonably soft. Shred big cabbage trunks first. When the bed is covered with 12 inches of organic matter, sprinkle with two shredded yarrow leaves and cover with 4 inches of compost, straw, or layers of wet newspaper held down with stones. When watering food plots, also water this bed.

Depending on the weather, the composting bed will be ready to grow cabbages or cauliflowers by late winter. Remove skeleton stalks to composting area. Some partly-decayed matter will continue to compost over time. You can fork the bed over or plant straight into the compost cover. If you used newspapers, peel these off carefully, guiding worms back to the soil, and place decaying newspaper in your compost bin or worm farm.

Commercial composters use a lot of cardboard and shredded office paper, but in backyard compost, I find these a nuisance. You have to shred it fine and disperse it so it doesn't form lumps, and even then, paper often shows up in the final compost as just what it is. Use it underneath compost instead.

Some seeds survive the composting process and, once back on the plot, will surprise you with vigorous seedlings. If they are vegetables, leave these where they are, they will turn out the best!

Scott Nearing, inspiration for the *Good Life* series of books written with partner Helen Nearing, built eight compost bins to grade material according to hardness. The hardest bin would not be used for several years, but eventually even thick branches decomposed.

TREE COMPOST

Harvest fallen debris from your trees—leaves and twigs will compost, branches can become fire wood, edgings, or brush fencing or be put in long-term compost. Nothing need go to waste; nothing should be burned.

WORMS AND WORM FARMS

Worm farms can range from a size you can put on the balcony to vast structures housing zillions of the critters—city councils with foresight feed the district's organic rubbish into enormous worm troughs and sell the compost back to the public.

The balcony-size farm is a clever set of plastic trays that fit on top of each other and hold a worm population, kitchen scraps, and weeds. The bottom tray with tap drains off the worm juice. The sets are rodent-proof. This is the ideal composting system if you live in an apartment or condominium and should produce enough castings and worm juice to keep several boxes with food plants in optimum health. Larger sizes are available for gardens.

Worm farms come with instruction booklets listing the addresses of where to buy composting worms (epigeic, smooth, several varieties), which apparently do like living in small apartments and will procreate in plastic trays. There is some controversy about whether composting worms will ever thrive in garden soil as earthworms do. They will, but only in the top layers where they compost leaves and sticks and become bird food. The earthworms that turn over deep soils are anecic worms, which have a red band around their bodies. Cardboard boxes with a thousand worms that will breed in the box are recommended for worm farms. If your worms don't thrive despite regular feeding, seek advice from the supplier.

Worm juice is liquid fertilizer, a fine boost to young vegetables. Tap it regularly and dilute with water 1:10 before spraying on plants. The worms' main product is castings, which is pure compost. When this matures, pick out any tardy worms and surprise your seedlings and vegetables.

Old bathtubs are popular as worm farms, with a wooden cover and old car-

Two compost bins are sufficient to recycle all vegetable and fruit remains. If worms are active, a bin can mature for six months, with compost spread each spring and autumn.

pet to keep the worms cool. Collect the juice by placing a tray under the plughole, plunging your hand in the mass and pulling the plug.

Always place worm farms in the shade and cover with wet carpet, felt, or towels. In winter, a small farm may do better under cover, but if you put it in the shed, don't forget to bring food. The worms will let you go on holiday for up to a month if you leave them a big feed. Give them cores, stems, and peelings, cut fine like you would for kids, as well as old manure, tea leaves, tea bags, coffee grounds, eggshells, fallen fruit, shredded wet cardboard, and newspaper, old vegetables, and mixed weeds. On special occasions, for instance when a worm has a significant birthday, throw a few lettuce leaves their way. They love rotten apples.

SEEDS *and* SEEDLINGS

T HE GIVING GARDEN has to be a sustainable garden, because above all, it is the seed base for the future. The seeds nature drops, the ones the birds drop in, and the seeds we gather, dry, and store, ensure that plant-friendly micro-climates continue as long as we are here to gather, maintain, and sow, and to refrain from interfering too much.

Seeds

The inventors of the commercial seed packet were the American Shaker gardeners, adding value to their products. Growing vegetables from seed is extremely economical, especially with open-pollinated seed, as the resulting plants produce seed true to type to save and plant again. These well-tried heirloom and heritage varieties, kept going by farmers and gardeners since the beginning of time, produce seed reliably.

Why is this so desirable? Just as you appreciate the taste and quality of home-grown vegetables, so you will appreciate the taste and quality of heirloom vegetables. Some may not produce as prolifically as hybrids whereas others may outperform those. Grow a variety of vegetables, rather than overproducing a few.

An heirloom is something precious passed down through the generations. In my understanding, an heirloom vegetable is from before the time of widespread commercial genetic engineering, like seed my grandfather grew because his grandfather told him it was dependable.

The word "heritage" could imply that something has inherited qualities or characteristics. That may apply to my great-great-grandfather's cabbage seeds, but with a bit of word wrenching it could also be claimed for a modern seed emerging from a GE laboratory, as ultimately its ancestor is also ancient seed. After all, everything has qualities and characteristics that come from somewhere, no matter what they have been turned into.

There was a time when large seed companies feared small seed companies offering open-pollinated, organically grown seed of common as well as unusual heirloom and heritage vegetables, herbs, flowers, and trees. There are several such small seed companies now, as well as the Seed Savers Exchange, that offer this type of seed. If you like buying from catalogs, take the time to ponder hundreds of varieties and send away for a few (check Useful Addresses on page 317 or organic gardening magazines carrying advertisements from sellers of seeds, roots, and bulbs).

Commercial seeds in shops are increasingly based on fewer varieties, may be genetically modified, and are often impregnated with toxic substances to ensure shelf life. Most are hybrids, bred by companies for improved size, production, and pest resistance. Hybrids may grow fast but do not usually produce viable seed, or if they do, it may not breed true to type (i.e., the hybrid type it grew from), or its offspring may deteriorate after a few seasons. Lack of quality control can occur under the biggest labels. A representative of a large seed company once tried to convince me that their packet of undersized and broken fava bean seeds would still grow good beans! Not for my money. Some commercial seeds don't germinate at all, which could be the fault of retail outlets. Never buy seed from a counter in the sun, for it will be cooked.

Seed Savers Exchange (SSE)

The Seed Savers Exchange is an amazing non-profit volunteer foundation that, since 1975, has collected in a seed bank as many varieties of open-pollinated vegetable, herb, and fruit seeds as its members can find, including heirlooms from immigrant gardeners. Its newsletter offers seeds of unheard of vegetables. Annually, SSE prints a catalog of seeds offered by members from which subscribers can buy old heirloom varieties. Members grow these seeds on and some donate supplies back to the seed bank. The SSE label "Give Peas A Chance" claims that whereas people once planted sixty-five varieties of peas, now they choose from less than ten. Their "Let Lettuce Be" sticker encourages gardeners to let lettuce go to seed, let seed fall, rake it in, and watch new lettuces come up. The Seed Savers Exchange founders have also published *Seed to Seed*, the essential seed saver's handbook.

In America, the Seed Savers Exchange has collected 18,000 vegetable varieties grown across the country. Such networks are of crucial importance in preserving global food resources. A tragic story of seed-saving dedication comes from St. Petersburg in Russia. During the Second World War, German forces besieged the city (then Leningrad), and the population was starving. The Soviet Union's seed bank was located in the city, protecting a store of containers preserving the seed of many varieties of grains, oats, peas, beans, and other food plants. These could have provided food for many people. But the seed bank personnel were so dedicated to their task that not a grain or bean was missing by the end of the war, even though some of the guardians died of starvation themselves. They believed the seed bank was so important to the future of all Russians that they laid down their lives to protect it. Director Nikola Ivanovich Vavilov, who founded that seed bank to eliminate hunger from the world, died of starvation in one of Stalin's prisons, suspected of espionage. He probably corresponded with seed savers abroad. The Vavilov Institute in St. Petersburg still maintains a seed bank despite dire economic conditions.

Shopping for Roots and Seeds

While out shopping for other supplies, keep an eye peeled for roots in Asian groceries. Unless your knowledge of Asian horticulture is academic, buy good-looking roots, cook half to see whether you like them, then plant the rest. Some rot, some die, but some may grow.

Potato onions can still be found in farmers' markets. Pounce on them, propagate, and share them with friends to grow on, as they are quite rare. Look for slim bunching onions, Egyptian onions that produce tiny pickling bulbs

at the top instead of underground, and other old onion varieties. Make space for these hardy varieties so you'll always have onion material for the pot, be it tops or bottoms.

Buy lemongrass with a bit of root left and plant in a warm spot. Look for other vegetables to grow on. Just as potato pieces with an "eye" will grow a plant producing potatoes, so will sweet potato if grown in a warm place. Experiment.

Spices are bought more economically in Asian and Middle Eastern groceries. Lay in a store of "whole" spices, which keep their aromas better: aniseed, cardamom, coriander, caraway, cumin, fennel, fenugreek, mustard. Keep the jars in a dark cupboard to keep seeds viable for growing. You can enhance all you bake or cook with spices. You are now ready to sow some spice companions such as dill, cumin, and cilantro. Pick the green leaves of spice plants to create a gourmet feast.

Asian Vegetable Seeds

Asian vegetable seeds can be found in most Asian supermarkets. Some packets have English text, but for others, you'd better brush up your Mandarin and Japanese. Plant some seeds in spring and again in autumn to find out which season they prefer. Experiment using the pictures on the packets. Gourds, squash, and beans are mostly summer vegetables, but many leafy greens like cooler seasons.

Asian vegetables still have good resistance against many North American pests and diseases, with the exception of the greenish-white Chinese cabbage, which gets attacked by snails, slugs, cabbage moth, and aphids to the point where you don't want to deal with it in the kitchen. Most Asian vegetables presently available are the products of forty centuries of companion-growing horticulture, mostly in China, and the Chinese were too hungry and too practical to waste time on vegetables that could not survive prevailing conditions.

Planting Good Seeds at the Right Depth and Time

The right depth is generally held to be the thickness of the seed, but sow beans two to three times their own thickness. Rake very fine seed through the top of the soil. A very loose straw cover provides protection. Use a fine nozzle or mist to water seeds.

There are systems to guide gardeners to plant seeds on beneficial days.

Planting by the Moon is an ancient method based on the notion that when the moon is waxing, it draws new seedlings toward its light, and when it's wan-

ing, root growth takes place. Fruiting and leafy plants are sown in the last quarter, beans and peas three days before full moon, and root crops in the middle of the first quarter. That's a rough guide, but you can buy moon-planting charts, and some magazines print monthly directions.

Biodynamic Planting Calendar: If you like order in your life, then the biodynamic planting calendar is for you. Biodynamics was Rudolf Steiner's answer to feng shui. This is where every possible function of plants and trees guided by the moon and stars is worked out annually by a very knowledgeable person, so the calendar tells you every morning just what you can and can't do in the garden. This presumes you are available for horticultural work at any time, so it works best for full-time farmers.

If through necessity you are a weekend gardener, you can probably manage to keep to the rough moon-planting scheme. If your gardening has to be done whenever life allows you a few moments, plant and harvest to your heart's content when you can. Nature always strives for the light, always prefers growth, and ever renews itself, so you will have marvelous successes just the same, even if a little slower. You can blame the few fiascos on the weather. Even biodynamic and moon gardeners find excuses.

Soak hard-coated seeds such as beans in water with a few drops of LS before sowing. As seeds germinate, apply LS every few days. Seedlings can go into the ground when the first root tip comes out of the bottom of a toilet paper tube, or a seedling is about 3 inches high with at least four leaves.

Where to Raise Seeds

Seeds raised outdoors, protected from wind and sun and raised up from the ground, will be hardy. But as a lot of summer crops need five to six months of warm weather to mature, an earlier start may necessitate starting seedlings indoors. This avoids rodent damage, too. Seeds do not need much light to germinate, so you can start containers off in shed or cellar, moving them to windows when two leaves have appeared.

Bottom Heat: Containers set on a small electrically warmed bottom-heat mat will have improved germination rates. For a one-square plot, it may not be worth the outlay.

A Cold Frame warmed by the sun gives seedlings an early start (see The Seasons on page 116).

An Old-fashioned Hot Frame is fun to make. Start late winter and find a glass window or door to place on top.

Alternate rows of lettuce and beets with carrots seeded under the straw.

In a sunny, sheltered place, mark out a frame with four bales of straw, or make a frame with planks or bricks to fit under the glass cover. Dig out the floor area to a depth of 10 to 12 inches and fill with animal manure, straw, and grass clippings. Water in well and spread the soil on top.

Place the glass across the frame. Give it a week to heat up, keeping it moist. Then half submerge pots with seedlings or seeds into the soil. Ventilate as you do for the cold frame.

Weaning: When seedlings have at least four leaves, wean them from the protected environment through "hardening off." Place seedlings outside on nice days and back in the frame at night until they appear robust enough to go into the ground when the weather is fine.

Problems

A number of things can upset your plans. "Damping off," causing seedlings to rot, occurs in containers when the soil is too wet or air doesn't circulate. After a particularly hard winter, the wildlife may be so hungry that whatever you sow they dig up and devour! Resort to timing and hardware until it becomes routine. Once you master seed raising, you will only buy shop containers as an exception. Water seedlings with weak LS solution twice a week.

Preventing Transplant Shock: The roots of many seedlings get transplant shock when taken out of a container and put in a hole in the ground. This may set them back weeks. No growth occurs; sometimes death follows. The way to avoid this is to grow seedlings in biode-gradable toilet paper tubes (see opposite page) so that most of the roots remain protected when the tube is planted in open ground. Transplant shock also occurs when directly sown seedlings are thinned out. Pulling them up by the roots exposes neighboring seedlings and these may die. Better to let them grow to toddler size before pulling the bigger ones.

Row Covers: By covering a row of early seedlings while the soil is still cold, you help them get into gear in their cozy tunnel. Make your own covers by bending reinforcing or chicken wire in a V- or U-shape and covering with transparent plastic punched with breathing holes, shade cloth, or hospital gowns—see Hardware in the Food Garden (page 105).

Hardy Vegetables can be raised in the open. You can't raise pumpkins in winter, as they expire on cold nights, as do tomatoes, beans, melons, and cucumbers. But the cabbage cousins are hardy customers. Cabbage, cauliflower, *Brassica juncea* and other mustards, broccoli, brussels sprouts, bok choy, kale, tatsoi, and Chinese cabbage can all be sown in open ground in autumn and mild winters, growing on into spring. If your winter is not mild, sow Asian greens in open ground in late winter and start broccoli, cabbages, and cauliflowers off in the cold frame at the same time.

A small Percy's portable plastic roof also helps germination—see Hardware in the Food Garden (page 105).

A Seed-Raising Table is useful when temperatures rise and the cold frame starts toasting seedlings. I found a waist-high small workshop bench measuring 1 × 2 feet. Around the edges, I placed water-filled plastic bottles in a metal filing system frame I just happened to have. Seed containers sit inside this instant mini-hothouse open to the air, but an old fridge grid with shade cloth attached to it lies across the top to keep birds out. This table holds six containers containing thirty-six seedlings. By always keeping the space occupied, it provides plenty of well-formed seedlings grown to the stage where they can hold their own in the big world. These need no "hardening off."

Continuous Sowings: Raise single containers of six beans from October to January for a continuous supply. Also raise back-up pumpkin and squash seedlings, as in some years the weather destroys early ones in the ground. In late summer, start raising autumn vegetables.

Toilet Paper Tubes: Raise seedlings in toilet paper tubes to avoid root disturbance when planting out. This is not

Brassica and bean seedlings raised in toilet paper tubes in a sunroom. The bowl contains six small baskets with six rolls each, enough to fill one Magic Square. The beans are ready to be planted out.

necessary for vegetables that are best sown directly into the ground, like root vegetables and sprawling greens such as chard, spinach, Asian greens, mustard, arugula, and the like. But toilet paper tubes can prevent mishaps with beans, broccoli, brussels sprouts, cabbages, cauliflower, corn, cucumbers, melons, peas, pumpkins, and tomatoes. If wildlife digs up your directly planted sweet corn seeds, re-seed in toilet paper tubes and place in seed-raising mini-hothouse as in A Seed-Raising Table, above.

Collect toilet paper tubes in a cloth bag hung in the bathroom. Start saving today. Six rolls fit into a margarine container and four in a seedling container, so you need forty to sixty rolls to sow ten varieties of four to six plants each. Punch drainage holes in margarine containers. Fill rolls with potting soil and tamp the container a few times to compact soil, then fill tubes to the top. Push in one seed per roll, add a nametag, and put in the cold frame, hot frame, or on the seed-raising table, depending on the time of year.

The advantage of tubes is that they double or triple the height of a container, allowing strong root growth. Often the roots hang out of the tube when seedlings are big enough to go into the ground. At this stage, the plants don't seem to suffer the brief exposure of root ends during transplanting. Dig a deep, narrow hole and half-fill it with water. Plant the tube, push it down a little, and tuck in firmly with soil. These plants grow much better than seedlings that have to be torn apart from a container or have bunched roots from lack of space. The cardboard tube disintegrates to become part of the soil.

EASY-CARE FRUIT TREES

FRUIT TREES are as sensitive to climate as vegetables but have to cope with more wind, rain, and scorching sun, while providing shelter for lower plants. They may dry out at the wrong time when fruit is developing, have all their fruit blown off when half ripe, or attract possums and fruit bats, bugs, and diseases. So for the beginning food gardener, fruit trees should be of the hardy, easy-care type.

Easy-care fruit trees that leave you time to be an intensive food gardener as well are those still close to the wild. In my garden, the very first fruit in spring is the loquat. If you have heard that loquats are all pips and not worth bothering about, you haven't tasted loquats from a tree that receives manure in autumn and a pruning after harvest. After winter rains, the fruit is plump and sweet and can be harvested for two months as bunches ripen gradually.

By then we are into early stone fruits: apricots, nectarines, peaches, plums. Mulberries and bush berries follow. Near summer's end, pears and apples ripen. The home fruit harvest ends with grapes and quinces in autumn. Because quinces keep so well, their fragrance perfumes the kitchen until January. My small espaliered orchard together with some old inherited fruit trees provided fruit three-quarters of the year, some of which was preserved. Lemon trees carry fruit virtually all year, while other citrus species fruit for extended periods to ripen in winter, as do persimmons.

Do keep in mind that even if a fruit tree is bred for optimum production, some revert to the natural system of carrying only a few fruit the year after a bumper crop. Don't expect big crops every year from each tree. Plant a mix of early and late fruit, feed them all spring and autumn, and you will be richly rewarded. Stone-fruit trees often bear from their second year, others may take a little longer. Quinces and loquats are quick to bear, and berry bushes fruit in their first year.

The Shakers, renowned for their food-growing success, planted fruit trees in very large holes filled with rubble for drainage, old broken-down manure, and compost. They tamped down the earth and put fences around the trees. They had magnificent fruit harvests.

Espalier

Espalier is a system of training young fruit trees on wires. Run wires north-south if possible, to gain light and fruit on both sides. It is not advisable to espalier on fences as the fruit may get too hot and not get ventilated. Set up poles at either end, with strainers, and run four or five horizontal wires at 12-inch intervals. Don't place wires higher than you can comfortably reach. Plant trees 2 to 3 yards apart in a 10- to 15-yard row. If you have less space, erect four posts with wires in a rectangle of 6 to 12 feet and plant six fruit trees around it. Plant the rectangle full of companion herbs (see Part Four on page 279) to help the fruit trees. This arrangement is easy to net.

As each tree grows up, let the leader (the main stem) grow, bending branches to left and right on the first and second wires, and attach with pruning tape or pantyhose strips, which expand with growth (wire ties and string will cut into branches as they thicken). Prune off superfluous branches. In the next growing season, let two branches reach the third wire and so forth until all wires are occupied and the leader has also been espaliered. In summer, the tree

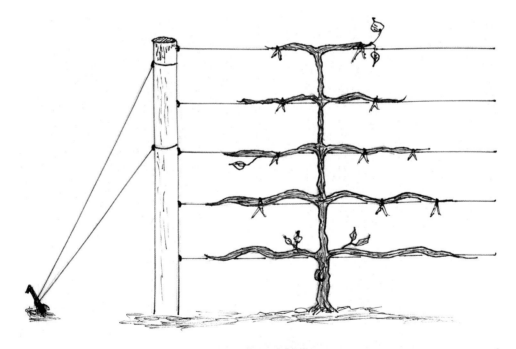

An espalier.

looks like a curtain of leaves and fruit. Prune summer and winter to retain this shape. Espaliered trees fruit more heavily because they are restricted from putting effort into lots of branches.

Netting

Netting fruit trees is necessary if you want to eat the fruit yourself. Use appropriate wildlife-safe netting. The birds may get some fruit before you have netted and peck fruit pressing against the netting. Espaliered trees are easy to protect from birds. Throw a long length of netting over the wires, pull down and away on either side, and pin to the ground with bricks to prevent birds crawling underneath.

For freestanding trees, you need one big square net per tree. Tie the net underneath the tree, for birds will try anything to get in. Knitted nets can be used for years with a little repair. Nets do double duty by protecting first the early-fruiting trees, then the late-ripening ones. Once you get serious about netting, you will work out your own system. The price of posts, wires, trees, and netting, may be what you pay for shop fruit, but your fruit is sweet, organic, and fresh, and in following years, you will buy nothing but a bag of manure.

Never water fruit trees with overhead sprinklers; instead lay out drip irrigation with a timer. Mulch trees to reduce evaporation and protect roots. During dry summers, water once a week for a set time. If you should be so lucky that it rains for an hour once a week where you live, the trees will do with that.

The spraying of fruit trees against pests and disease is generally unnecessary in a small mixed orchard situated in an organic mixed garden with vegetables, herbs, flowers, shrubberies, and hedges. This environment helps maintain fruit trees in good health, attracting birds to control insects and disease-bearing grubs.

Old fruit trees that do not look well need a good pruning and thinning out in winter. Remove grass around the trunk for more than a 3-foot circumference and under-plant with feverfew, tansy, and yarrow. Spread a load of manure and mulch under the tree's drip line (the perimeter of the branches), and see what happens in spring.

Now turn to the List of Easy-Care Fruit Trees and Berries in Part Four (page 295) for more detailed descriptions.

COMPANION PLANTING
and INTERCROPPING

JUST AS with humans, some plants retard each other's development while others flourish in each other's company. Companion planting and intercropping is a science born from millennia of observation by food growers. The oldest known example is from Mexico where, some eight millennia ago, the Aztecs grew corn, beans, and pumpkin or squash together.

Climbing peas under-planted with French and red chard, bordered by mignonette and oakleaf lettuces. Siberian kale near the bee bath.

The main reasons for intercropping and companion planting are to group together those plants that chemically enhance each other's growth, stimulate fruit-set, protect each other from predators, prefer similar conditions, and provide or seek shade. Plant shallow-rooted lettuce between deep-rooted carrots and beets that find nutrients further down and provide shade when planted south of lettuce. Tomatoes stay healthy with chemicals exuded by mustard plants.

Companion plants are listed in the List of Common Vegetables (page 230), but should you plan to expand your food gardening, buy a book on companion planting. Many of the companions listed I observed in my own food gardens. It was a surprise to see a tomato plant intertwine spontaneously with an onion plant to their mutual benefit, or lettuces gallop along with beans. Just observe your square to see what works and what

Onions benefit by cohabitating with pansies.

doesn't. Get familiar with different vegetable groups in Part Four (page 221), as their growth habits and requirements are often similar.

Intercropping is what the Aztec Plot (page 182) achieves. It is a regulated type of companion planting, the beans enriching the soil for the corn in exchange for a climbing stake or perhaps chemical protection, while pumpkin leaves shade the soil. Slow growers planted with quick ones save space, like carrots with lettuce. Radishes sown with seeds of carrots, turnips, beets, and rutabagas loosen the soil for germination and provide growing space for the others when pulled.

Carrots, onions, and lettuce are intercropped, growing roots at different depths. Radishes and green onions are compatible, while climbers like peas, beans, and cucumbers benefit from having low-growing lettuce or bok choy nearby to shade their roots. Sow small turnips, rutabagas, and radishes between cabbages and cauliflowers, but don't forget them. Carrots with spinach, spinach with kohlrabi, lettuce, and beets.

The seeds of any vegetables to be transplanted can be mixed and sown together. Any combination of plants that you see doing well can then be intercropped on a larger scale. Feed the soil beforehand and sow plants as close together as their adult size allows—for radishes, green onions, and carrots, 1 inch; onions, 2 to 3 inches; beets, 3 to 5 inches—on the understanding that you regularly pull the biggest plants to make space for others.

Some plants decidedly retard each other's well-being, or one grows at the expense of the other. Garden writers differ on what benefits and what impedes. Sometimes, I wonder whether it was an onion that made my beans crumple or whether the soil was deficient.

When at a loss, I put mustard seeds near a plant needing rescuing. Mustard comes up in a week and exudes a gas that keeps pests away. But when the mustard reaches a height of 3 feet, it robs nutrients from the plant it is protecting. Cut it down and spread the leaves and stalks between the vegetables. Such is mustard's fate. When space allows, let mustard grow to full height—the flowers attract a beneficial insect bonanza.

And if you find all this too confusing, just plant what you want, mix it up thoroughly, and observe what happens. Do this for ten years, and then write the definitive book on companion planting in your region!

WATER *and* WATERING

N THE management of water, the home grower has the same problems as the American farmer. Water is not always in abundance. Whether you depend on tanks, a dam, well, or city water, restrictions apply to all if the rains fail.

David Holmgren of Permaculture fame has provided figures showing that every dollar's worth of conventionally grown fruits and vegetables has needed 27 gallons of water to mature. Every equivalent dollar's worth of home-grown food uses only 5 gallons.[8]

For healthy development, vegetables need water regularly. Water restrictions are an advantage because vegetables grow best when hand watered at the roots, rather than with sprinklers. On hot days, when you may have to water seedlings more than once, fill a watering can in the morning to see tender plants through days of 90 to 100 degrees and hot winds. Use shade boxes and cloth—see Hardware in the Food Garden (page 105).

Hand Watering

While hand watering, note what every plant needs. More mulch here, plant food there, a cloche or a stake. Onions are dying off when tomatoes and carrots need extra water. Hosing lets you discover a big cucumber under the leaves. Douse indi-vidual plants after a dust storm to assist leaves in taking up moisture and nutrients from the air. This daily attention to the food plot, whether it is one square or ten, creates a bond between grower and plants that leads to wonderful results.

Consider doing away with sprinklers altogether. Instead, collect crippled umbrellas, beach umbrellas, and shade cloth. Put these around during hot weather to reduce water needs. The old days of letting a sprinkler dump water on a vast area for hours are gone forever. Sprinklers water indiscriminately, and sometimes plants miss out, dying before you notice.

Start small, think hose and watering can. It puts you in control and you get a daily thrill from the plants' efforts.

You know that too much irrigation can cause salinization by raising the water table. Therefore, deliver water where needed, and no more than needed. Crushed rock increases the water-holding capacity of the soil. Mulch vegetables with compost and/or straw, even those in part shade, and try skipping a watering occasionally.

Although an established garden benefits from reticulated watering systems under mulch, I will have nothing but a hose in the food garden where planting patterns change week to week. I like the interlude in my days, sauntering along, watering, and selecting the next meal.

Nozzles

You need control at the tap: wide open, half open, or drizzling. You also need control at the nozzle: fine spray, wide spray, or a narrow jet to hit one spot or hose off aphids. Select a nozzle that will do a fine mist, as well as a squirt. It's a myth that spraying plants on hot days causes leaf burn. Rain doesn't burn plants, does it? Leaf burn results from lack of water at the roots.

Position

It is no longer good advice to say that all vegetables need full sun. Six hours is enough for most. Plant tomatoes and lettuces in part shade, and root crops, beans, and corn in the sun. With increasing temperatures and periods in the 90- to 100-degree range, plus ultraviolet radiation, many plants benefit from filtered light, as do people.

To save water and raise stress-free vegetables, position your food plot:

- where the full blast of the afternoon sun is tempered by a tree.

- where dappled shade is available part of the day.

- where a house or shed will shade it part of the day.

- where other structures (water tank, hedge, fence) give protection.

Shade

Provide shade by temporary means and observe shade patterns before installing anything permanent, remembering that during winter, plants need more light.

If you are planning to keep your food plot small, rig up a semi-permanent structure to support a shade cloth or deciduous vine to protect in summer, letting light through in winter. But don't plant a grapevine, as the birds will paint your vegetables white! Passion vines or climbing vegetables can benefit ground dwellers.

A.M. or P.M.

Debates whether to water early mornings or evenings pass you by if you are a working person. You are unlikely to do it in the heat of day. In summer, water before breakfast, if possible, as evening moisture attracts snails and slugs.

If your plot is densely planted and mulched, there should be little evaporation after morning waterings. In dense plantings, any evaporation is likely to benefit the plants. Seedlings and young plants need daily watering in hot weather and twice daily when the mercury rises above 95 degrees or during hot winds. If these conditions are predictable, avoid having seedlings at those times.

How Long to Water

Impossible to answer. It depends on microclimate, soil, mulch, compost, and the plants. Water must get to the roots, so stick your finger in beside plants to test how deep it goes. Wait a few days to see how plants cope before watering again. Generally spaced-out deep watering is better than daily shallow watering, but many vegetables have shallow roots and grow fast in summer, so water daily then if possible. It takes five minutes to hose a 25-square-yard food plot.

Water Storage

If you are on a water main and don't have a rainwater tank, consider installing one or several now. They come in a variety of materials, sizes, shapes, and colors to fit every situation, and rainwater is a saving grace for vegetables if your water is brackish, too chlorinated, or contains unwanted growths from the reservoir. By using rainwater on seedlings and young vegetables, more survive than if they have to battle salt, chlorine, or competitive organisms.

Tanks fill up quickly from the average house roof after a few downpours, and even dew raises a tank's level. Install gutters on your shed to harvest more water. Consider installing gutter guards for cleaner water. Some agencies will even buy surplus rainwater. Contact a water technology shop to work out the logistics for your situation. Ask about water filters, or install a filter pot in the kitchen that prevents bacteria getting to you.

If your garden water supply comes from a well, you would do well to have it tested for salt and safety, as runoff from other properties may affect water quality, and therefore the vegetables you eat.

If the water comes from a dam, you may face periods of brackishness as the water level drops mid-summer, just when you douse vegetables daily.

I have learned which vegetables can survive on brackish water, although none do terribly well. These include:

- globe artichoke

- cabbage family, including hardier Asian greens

- onions, garlic, chives, leeks

- chard, perennial spinach

- asparagus, lettuce, chicory, endive, salsify, scorzonera

- most herbs, especially Artemisia species

- gray plants such as succulents and lavender

Other Water-Saving and Delivery Systems

Drip irrigation under mulch saves water, but is inconvenient in small plots.

Composting toilets need no flushing and will gain in popularity as water bills increase. They provide compost and will become almost maintenance free as technology improves.

Envirocycle systems benefit the surrounding garden where the household water ends up, freeing up water for the food garden if you rely on tanks.

Waterwise planting: Vegetables in densely planted, well-composted, and mulched plots need less water per plant than those standing solitary in bare soil in rows wide apart. Dense plantings don't wilt easily on hot days as the plants shade each other's roots, and the compost and mulch hold moisture.

Raised beds and trenches: The method of planting vegetables in raised or hilled-up rows came from England, where it rains a lot, soil seldom dries out, and roots rot. If you expect months of rain, make hilled-up rows.

A wooden pyramid of terraces creates more space for small plants.

But faced with having to grow food in rocky sub-clay in a dry climate, remember the Israeli desert kibbutz where pumpkin seedlings were planted in trenches, the very opposite of a hill. Hack a trench in "concrete" clay, fill it with manure, and compost and plant pumpkins. They will produce beyond expectation.

Is your soil water-retaining, does it drain excessively, or does it not hold water at all? How long between rains? Is your wet season long enough to rot roots?

When living in a hills village where I had to call the landlord to pump water for the tank, I grew vegetables on flat soil, each in its own earth saucer. I watered with cup and bucket each evening, and they did all right. On one square, that takes one minute. Earth saucers work especially in impervious soil.

Let your unique water situation determine whether to hill up, dig a trench, or grow on the flat.

When the rains stop, the tank gets low, and tender things begin to wilt, have a "bird wash" instead of a shower on days you don't mix with crowds. Life is a trade-off. During water shortages, you either smell good or you eat well. Those that do both are running taps on both ends.

BIG YIELDERS *and* GROSS FEEDERS

SOME PEOPLE revel in growing a great variety of vegetables and herbs, and I labor under that collector's instinct myself. I grew sixty varieties of vegetables in a round garden with a diameter of perhaps 10 yards and have quite forgotten what they all were. Two herb gardens grew 165 different herbs, leading quite naturally to a monthly stall at the market to sell the overflow.

Big Yielders

Eggplant, bell peppers, chilies, potatoes, and tomatoes are all members of the Solanaceae family. One chili plant can deliver 100 chilies; eggplant and bell pepper plants can produce a dozen or more; potatoes grow ten spuds from every seed potato; and tomatoes go on and on and on. They do this in good soil with compost. But hold back on nitrogen (especially chicken manure), or you get more leaves than fruit. They all love mulch and liquid seaweed showers. A Solanaceae plot must not be used for others of the same family for four to five years to prevent disease from taking hold. You could try growing them together in a plot of their own, then shifting them to another communal plot the next year. Or, grow chilies, bell peppers, and eggplants in large pots, discard soil in another part of the garden, and start next season with fresh soil. That leaves only potatoes and tomatoes to rotate in open ground. Keep a garden record book! And don't overwater this family.

Practical people look at the size of their household and decide to go for sensible quantities of staple foods and a few good yielders. They will eat well.

Carrots grow close together in deep sandy soil. Carefully pull the biggest to make space for the littlest. Cucumbers and zucchini are such good yielders that, in a small household, you may decide to grow them in alternate years. One plant of each is enough for small families. Plant more if you plan to pickle. These two are not choosey, but compost, manure, and liquid seaweed foster great fruits. Don't overwater; it produces monsters of watery consistency.

Eggplants produce big yields. Pumpkins are hardening off to the left in the background.

Strawberries are big yielders because they "flush" three times—in spring, summer, and autumn—before falling dormant. They are also gross feeders. Apart from well-prepared soil (dig in horse manure and compost), give them an organic fertilizer. If you make liquid manure or compost tea, they'll love you. Worm juice and liquid seaweed does them no end of good. Do all of the above, and you'll have the tastiest strawberries ever. But do pro-

tect them totally, if you have wildlife, birdlife, and crawlies in your garden, by growing them in boxes wrapped with netting or stretched over hoops, tight fitting. Shade cloth is excellent to exclude small intruders. Although commercial strawberries are grown in full sun, in the wild, they hug shady hedgerows. I've also seen commercially grown strawberries in hilled-up rows covered with black agricultural cloth and a thick layer of wood shavings between the rows to deter the usual intruders. There may be some spraying going on around the edges, but for a small bed, you could avoid that with an impenetrable "fence" of dug-in shade cloth.

Gross Feeders

The big eaters are the brassica family: broccoli, cabbage, cauliflower, brussels sprouts, all kale, and a great many Asian greens. I read somewhere that brussels sprouts grow best in unimproved soil, but have not tried this. It makes sense, because these stems full of sprouts are really setting seed, which plants do when under stress from weather, soil, or both. All brassica produce fantastic leaves, including those that produce edible heads: broccoli, brussels sprouts, cabbage, and cauliflower. In fact, the leaves are equally edible, steamed with onion, garlic, a lime leaf, and a few herbs.

Two large green cabbages squeeze into the corner of a square, edged with water bottles, taking up less than one eighth of the space.

Prepare the soil by working in plenty of manure. Chicken and pigeon manure is fine for these plants. Add plenty of compost—homemade or bought. Add an organic fertilizer or B&B. As seedlings grow, keep up weekly liquid seaweed applications, every two weeks when maturing. Maintain mulch and extra liquid manure, compost tea, or worm juice to keep them growing and producing good heads and/or seed. All brassicas are capable of feeding you again and again, so choose half a dozen from season to season, but always include a kale, as it's a superfood.

PLANT FOOD *and* SOIL FOOD

F YOU live on a valley bottom, surrounded by hillsides that for centuries have deposited topsoil and organic matter on your patch, the soil may contain all that your plants need for years to come. Gardens on flat ground may have lost nutrients to huge trees, or may have become deficient due to old age. Certain shrubs survive in impoverished soils, but vegetables don't. The better you feed your soil, the better fed your vegetables are, and the better fed you are.

Synthetic Fertilizers sold as compounds of NPK (nitrogen, phosphorus, and potassium) also contain salts harmful to soil microbes, depleting the soil, which then needs more fertilizer. Chris Alenson found leafy green vegetables grown with synthetic fertilizers are in danger of having a high nitrate intake. His paper notes that vitamin C reduces in these green leaves as nitrogen increases.[9]

NPK are only three elements of about fifteen needed for balanced plant health. For reasons of continuous fertility, runoff into waterways, and the high cost of fertilizers, organic growing—using compost and manure—is more sustainable.

Mineral Soil improvers like gypsum break up clay, dolomite adds calcium, granite adds minerals, and volcanic rock dust has it all.

The food requirements of vegetables differ. It is a generally held view that root crops need little food, but that depends on how much nutrition was left by previous crops. At the other end of the scale are the gross feeders. What are gross feeders? Cabbage, cauliflower, broccoli, and brussels sprouts. Fork in CMC several weeks before planting, spray seedlings with LS, give them side dressings of B&B a week later, top up CM regularly, and apply one or the other of these nutrients every two weeks. Stop applying B&B when plants are well established.

Animal Manure: For health reasons, it is important to compost manure before using it on food crops. Chop it up and mix with other composting materials (see Compost Compositions on page 34) or, if you can obtain old dried pats of cow, horse, donkey, camel, or elephant manure, use a shredder or lawnmower to turn it into fine manure dust. Only put manure on a bed you prepare several months before planting, and always cover it with mulch, straw, or compost to assist earthworms in breaking it down.

The major plant foods used when growing organic vegetables are animal manures and compost, as these contain the variety of nutrients plants need to access as they grow. If you can't use animal manure, remember Scott and Helen Nearing, North America's gurus of the self-sufficiency movement. They didn't believe in exploiting animals, so their food production was fed entirely on compost made from everything they weeded, pruned, and swept from their own land. Fortunately, they had tons of deciduous sugar maple leaves. They fed themselves and countless visitors for decades.

On a scale of manures, chicken and pigeon contain the most nitrogen, while pig poo is powerful and provides phosphorus. Sheep manure is an all-rounder. Horse and cow manure contribute potassium—cow is more acidic, so add some lime, while horse manure builds soil. In Australia, you can often buy roadside bags, or ask a farmer whether you may fill a bag or trailer in his paddock. Donkey manure takes time to break down; chop or mow it and dig it in during autumn to soften. When the circus comes to town, people rush the elephant keeper with requests. No doubt big poo is a major soil builder, but, being fresh, it needs composting.

Blood and bone (B&B): This widely used by-product of the meat industry has been observed to keep rabbits at bay when incorporated in seed-bomb trials. A seed bomb is a clay ball packed with selected tree seeds, which is thrown onto bare land at the start of the rainy season to germinate. If rabbits are put off by B&B inside seed balls, they are also likely to object to the stuff lying around their favorite vegetables. This may explain why some gardeners claim there are rabbits in the next paddock, yet they don't touch their vegetables. If you are plagued by bunnies, try it around seedlings.

Clay has essential locked up nutrients. A bucket of clay, broken up carefully and mixed with gypsum, can be forked through sandy soil.

Dolomite/dolomite lime corrects acidic soils. Use when a plot is cleared for new crops. Provides lime, calcium, and magnesium.

Epsom salts provide magnesium sulphate for prematurely yellow leaves. Apply 1 teaspoon per watering can.

Green manures: Plant barley, buckwheat, fava beans, fenugreek, lupins, red clover, mustard, oats, peas, or other legumes, and dig in before they flower. If you have too many old vegetable seeds, plant some to grow vegetables and rake the excess through a bare plot. When the plants are four to eight weeks old, fork them in, cover with CM, and water. This makes soil structure and attracts earthworms. The patch will be ready for sowing a few weeks later.

Green crops can be sown in the heat of summer, when you can't plant seedlings, or during winter. Sow a green crop after harvesting a patch, even one quarter of your only square. For the one-square gardener, mustard is quick to grow and the seed widely available. Eat some, dig most in, and let some produce seed.

Gypsum hardpan: Sticky clay or compacted soils can be "opened up" by forking in gypsum, starting in autumn and repeating in spring.

Hay bales: In a garden magazine, I spotted a most delightful photo of two tomato plants growing in a tiny hay bale still in its plastic wrap.[10] Make drainage holes in the bale and make holes for plants by taking out some hay and replacing it with soil. Soak plants in weak LS solution before planting. Water the bale thoroughly through the holes before planting. This is an elegant solution for small patios. Experiment with other vegetables in hay bales.

Humus is the soil nature makes unaided. Leave a heap of leaves, twigs, and small branches alone for a year, then lift them up and scoop up the humus underneath.

Iron chelate: Apply when plants have yellow leaves, are stunted, or bear rather small fruit.

Lime supplies calcium to soils. Apply at rainy times to prevent it blowing away. As lime takes away nitrogen from manure in compost when it breaks down, apply three weeks before planting. Alternatively, add B&B three weeks after liming. Plants that don't like lime are amaranth, eggplant, blueberries, celery, and potatoes.

Liquid manures: Make these from potent herbs, like stinging nettle or comfrey. Chop up plants, steep in plenty of water in a bin, and cover. After ten to fourteen days, stir and apply the liquid around vegetables and seedlings, diluted with water 1:10. Brew up a smellier and even more potent manure by adding a variety of other soft-leaved weeds, such as milk thistle, dock, and dandelion, herbs and plants like borage, fennel, nasturtium, cosmos, and leaves of arum lilies, and succulents. It is best to use rainwater as mains water may contain chlorine, which will attack the bacteria that breaks down the organic matter. If you have no rainwater tank, catch buckets of rainwater for a liquid manure experiment (then install a rainwater tank!). Scoop off a pint of liquid from the bucket per week, pour into an almost full watering can, and sprinkle around vegetables. Add more plants and water to the bin and repeat weekly.

Liquid seaweed (LS): If you won't have a smelly bin around, the commercial liquid manure of highest value is LS, used so greatly diluted that a container lasts a long time. Seeds, cuttings, and uprooted plants can be soaked in a weak LS solution before planting to encourage root development. Spray any seedlings and young and maturing plants with LS, especially when they meet adverse conditions in soil or weather.

Seaweed is good for all stages of vegetable growth, but it is still necessary to prepare plots with manure, compost, and mulch to create soil. Use LS as the icing on the cake—or the greening on the broccoli. Spray the whole plant, as LS is taken in through the foliage as well. LS improves soil structure and can be used to prevent plant diseases and treat soil where predators lurk, like codling moths under apple, fig, pear, and quince trees. Fresh seaweed put on the garden will contain sea salt.

Lupins are a green crop for poor sandy soils, adding calcium and fixing nitrogen.

Mineral rock dust: Another mineral food for new plots, or to dig in with green crops.

Nitrogen is contained in the NPK synthetic fertilizers that organic gardeners avoid. Nitrogen produces huge leaf growth and has been overused in agriculture, in parks, on golf courses, and in backyards.

In the '80s, the amount of industrially fixed nitrogen applied to global crops was evidently more than all industrial fertilizer spread in the whole of humanity's history prior to 1980. Moreover, a doubling of transferred nitrogen from the atmosphere takes place due to the way humans treat Planet Earth. When soil saturated with nitrogen goes into the waterways, it takes along calcium, magnesium, and potassium, making soils acidic, killing fish in lakes, and causing toxic blooms.[11] Yet nitrogen is a plant food. It occurs in high amounts in poultry manure and B&B, both of which should be used sparingly. If your zucchini leaves are the size of dinner plates and your chard is 3 feet tall, you have used too much.

Organic fertilizers: To maintain the gross feeders of the cabbage family, you may need to sprinkle organic fertilizer pellets once a month for three to four months. There are slow-release fertilizers also.

Potash: Essential for plant growth and development. A small bag goes a long way and results are swift for ailing plants.

Urine: Human urine is a sterile commodity and was once widely used in first aid to treat wounds when water was putrid. It is still used for the fulling of cloth and dying of yarn in cottage industries. Urine contains the growth hormone auxin and comes free. A lidded bucket in the bathroom allows those household members who are purpose-built to aim well into it. Take the bucket to the garden tap and fill it with water. Spread liquid across yet-to-be-planted garden beds and around fruit trees, especially citrus. No smell lingers, and since the stuff is sterile, no dangers to health occur. So cheap.

Wood ash: Add sparingly to acid soil, or spread widely as it contains sodium that affects soil micro-organisms. Don't disperse it hot from the fireplace. Beets love it. Pear and cherry slugs hate it when applied to the leaves they are devouring. Keep a supply handy in the shed.

Grouping Plants According to Needs

Sometimes, it may be possible to plant lime lovers together and lime haters somewhere else, or those that need much nitrogen here and those that prefer poorer soil over there. If you want to grow a variety of vegetables every year, plan your food garden in four plots, however small, and rotate crops seasonally so that root crops follow gross feeders and organic matter lovers take up the soil left by lime lovers, with additions of organic matter. A permanently no-lime corner may support a blueberry bush under-planted with potatoes, eggplant, and the glorious red amaranth, an untried combination. It may not always work, but keep lime haters away from limed plots for two years. A planting notebook comes in handy here. Consult Part Four for more on growing needs (page 221).

Truly gross feeders are the brassica family, which need manure, compost, and organic fertilizers.

Moderately gross feeders: While they establish themselves, feed eggplants, bell peppers, cucumbers, lettuce, potatoes, pumpkin, chard, spinach, strawberries, sweet corn, tomatoes, and zucchinis as you would brassicas.

Extra nitrogen should be worked in well before planting and applied again in small amounts throughout the growing stages for amaranth, eggplant, garlic, chard, and sweet corn.

Low nitrogen suits all root crops, beans, lamb's lettuce, and peas and can either

Savoy: a "gross feeder"

be leftover nitrogen from last season's crop, or a sparse application.

Lime is required to be worked in three weeks before planting for beans, Florence fennel, garlic, onions, peas, and strawberries. Also use for parsnips, tomatoes, and turnips in acid soil.

No lime for amaranth, eggplants, blueberries, celery, or potatoes.

Organic matter comprises old compost, old manure, lawn clippings, and leaf mulch and benefits beets, broccoli, cabbage, cauliflower, cucumbers, Florence fennel, gherkin, and zucchini.

The MESSAGE of MULCH

WITH TEMPERATURES increasing due to global climate change, and long dry summers with more frequent storms, our vegetables have come a long way since their ancestors grew in sheltered valleys in Asia and Europe, where the best agricultural land was once found. In the 21st century, North America's agricultural land is suffering from wind and water erosion, acidity, salinization, chemical pollution, and the deadening effects of frequent droughts.

Even though our backyards may not have inherited pollution from agricultural practices, they are still subject to climate changes. Once soil repeatedly dries out, microbiotic life and earthworms disappear, and water is not taken up when applied. Therefore, we mulch.

However, once the heat has gone and rains bring cooler conditions, there is no need for thick mulches. Wet straw can become a hotbed for slugs. So let summer mulch rot away, or fork it in and let the soil air a little, unless your region experiences continuous drought

Laying out a no-dig garden on top of lawn. Despite carpet strips and wooden edging, grass roots did invade and sheet-metal strips had to be fitted later to a depth sufficient to keep them out.

with erosive winds. If weeds come up, pull them for compost or liquid manure. Never let them set seed—keep track of weeds. Mulch again in late winter.

Mulches do not have to cost much. Newspaper, cardboard, old clothes, and stones cost nothing. Stones trap moisture when placed around plants, be they lettuce, cabbage, or tree seedlings, but they also attract slugs and snails.

If your soil is rocky, acidic, or unworkable, you may choose to start your 3-foot-square garden from scratch like a no-dig garden, a method developed by gardener Esther Dean.[12] Mark a 3-foot square, or build a box with sleepers or planks. Lay down twelve to twenty layers of soaked newspaper with cardboard and old T-shirts as underfelt to prevent persistent weeds breaking through. Make a doorstop sandwich (with thick "slices" of bread) by layering old animal manure, compost, and Lucerne hay. After watering well, make holes in the straw, fill with soil or compost, and plant vegetables. The garden will gradually sink, so keep topping off with CM, hay, or straw. In the first season, plants may not grow fantastically, but the sandwich improves with time.

The most fertile mulches for vegetables are compost, pea straw, or Lucerne hay. The latter is expensive, but gives a new garden a good start. If your climate is severely hot and dry, think in terms of "putting the vegetables to bed." As soon as plants are above ground, lay sheets of soaked newspaper between them, add wet bags, shirts, or shorts, and top with CM, compost, hay, or straw. After the first watering, watch how long the plants can go without. There is always one plant that is first to look distressed. Keep mulch slightly away from stems and trunks to prevent collar rot.

Mulches

Black plastic is used for commercial strawberry growing and to suppress weedy lawns. But it cooks the soil and should not stay there long. Weed suppression is its main benefit, and newspaper, cardboard, and telephone books can do that and decay in a timely manner, so that you can mulch and plant on top.

Bracken fern: I wish I still had our forest to pick bunches of bracken. Bracken contains nitrogen, phosphorus, and potassium. Apart from spreading shredded bracken on beds to decay, use ferns as parasols for seedlings.

Cardboard is good for a path between new beds or between straw-filled, no-dig garden plots. If used to suppress lawn or weeds, cover with chipped branches for good looks. Line slatted or wire compost bins with cardboard, pizza boxes, or paper party plates, or use as underfelt in no-dig plots. Only use uncoated cardboard between vegetables.

Clothes can be slow to disintegrate. For that reason, they are best used around the edges of plots for weed suppression or as underfelt for no-dig plots. Half-rotted clothes mulch can still mulch fruit trees.

Grape residue: If you live near a winery, try grape residue from the winemaking process on your plots. Investigate what other free—and safe—residues your neighborhood produces.

Gravel is a marvelous mulch if applied 2 to 3 inches thick. It is mainly used in ornamental gardens around succulents, cacti, and sword-leaved plants, but should you have a supply, try it as a mulch on sturdy vegetables of the cabbage family. Most woody herbs prefer gravelly soil for drainage; just mix gravel with garden soil.

Hay: Legendary tales are told about the effects on a garden of one bale of spoiled hay. Be wary of weed seeds in meadow hay. Great plant food, now sold in handy packs.

Herb stalks: Should you have a flourishing herb plot, do as the Shakers did. They stripped herbs for tea, cooking, and medicine, then spread the stalks as mulch under fruit trees, some acting as a

pest repellent. Stalks are best over newly applied compost because they take time to break down as they shade the soil.

Lawn clippings are a quickly decaying mulch, best mixed with coarser materials, such as leaves and broken twigs. Otherwise, apply dried.

Leaves should never be burned, as this causes air pollution and asthma and robs the soil of valuable mulch. First, sweep a layer of leaves under the tree canopy as food, then compost the rest with other organic matter. To make leaf mold for mulch or potting soil, put leaves in a wire cylinder until broken down. Leaves cleared from the gutter in spring are suitably decayed. Sprinkle lime to counteract acidity, and B&B to encourage breakdown.

Mulch blocks are available commercially. Add water to a block to get a wheelbarrow of water-holding mulch to spread around plants.

Newspaper sheets make a weed-suppressing mulch in layers of ten to twelve, but cover this with leaves or straw or you get impervious papier-mâché. Don't use between small vegetables, which prefer an airier mulch, but use underneath and around the perimeter of plots and under fruit trees.

Oak-leaf mulch or bark repels slugs.

Olive-leaf residue can be used as a mulch should you live near an olive oil press. Ask whether you may have some to experiment with.

Pine needles are a great mulch around strawberries. Remember, the pine tree needs at least a 4-inch layer itself.

Rock, crushed or as rock dust, contains minerals.

Sawdust must be from untreated wood from your own workshop or your own trees. Use only on paths, in the ornamental garden, and sparingly in the compost, balanced out with lime because many woods are acidic.

Shrub foliage: Prune a few branches. Mow or shred them to make a mulch, or separate leaves from twigs and spread crosswise in layers between plants.

Stones: If you are blessed with a million stones on your land, use them. By planting each plant in an earth saucer surrounded with stones and filling the saucer with CMC, you trap moisture and attract good beetles. To keep slugs and snails away, spread coffee grounds around the stones.

Straw: Keep straw away from seedlings and young plants as there can be some harmful fumes during the breaking-down process.

Sugar cane mulch: This evidently excellent mulch may not be available everywhere, but if it is where you are, look out for the organic variety. Available in small bags.

Twigs: If you are strapped for mulching materials but have wattles (acacia) or shrubs, prune twigs and spread crosswise in layers between plants. This provides an airy mulch that, in time, breaks down into compost.

Weed Mats: Buy only the biodegradable type that lets water through and acts as a mild mulch. For a single 3-foot-square vegetable plot, buy 18 inches of the double width. Depending on the spaces needed between vegetables, cut weed mat into strips of 8, 12, or 15 inches. Place strips in a grid across the plot and plant vegetables in the interstices. Once young plants are well above ground, remove strips or cover with CM and water well. Re-use weed mats.

Woodchips: Some electricity utilities and city councils offer free woodchips after pruning roadside trees. Use for paths in the food garden. Pine wood is beloved by strawberries.

At the end of summer, when there is little food about for wildlife, your mulched plots may be dug up at night by unseen creatures—lizards, possums, rats, and early birds—because only there in the moist mulch can they find something to eat. Hence, when planting winter vegetables in autumn, wait to mulch until the days are getting cooler or protect plantings with racks and cages. Mulch again when plants are established and there is plenty of other food for the wildlife.

PRUNING, PINCHING, *and* THINNING

'M HAVING you on, am I? Too right I'm not! Pruning growing vegetables of excess foliage and stems promotes better growth of those parts you want to harvest. Pinching out tips does the same.

Pruning

Beans run out of steam mid-season. Prune off dying sections.

Broccoli produces shoots for months after the head has been harvested. Prune as you pick shoots for the pot, but also prune woody sections and lower leaves to keep this hard-working plant in condition. In our household, broccoli and cabbage leaves are eaten together with kale leaves as a "green slurry" stir-fry with ginger, onion, and garlic. The taste far surpasses the name. If you don't eat the leaves, strip the ribs for juicing, and feed the leaves to chickens, worms, or the compost.

Cabbage and cauliflower: Near where I live, the growers regularly pull lower leaves off by hand, laying them on the soil as mulch.

Fruit trees: Pruning is discussed in Easy-Care Fruit Trees and Berries (page 293).

Pumpkins have non-flowering vines that use food and water; cut them.

Spinach and chard go to seed as they please. If a strong plant has the bolting stem cut out, you can harvest the leaves longer. Or cut off all but the main stem if you want to save seed. Even when slightly bitter, the leaves taste good in a mixed stir-fry.

Zucchini plants produce a jungle of giant leaves to protect their fruit. But enough is enough. Regularly prune lower leaves, making sure the fruit remains protected.

Pinching

This is done more frequently than pruning.

Pumpkin vines need their tips pinched out or they will go on forever, producing longer runners with more infant pumpkins that won't have enough "oomph" or time to even get half grown before cold nights finish them off. Calculate when new pumpkins will no longer mature, and cut off the tip above the last viable pumpkin. Do this on all runners. These tender tips of leaves, including tiny pumpkins, can be steamed lightly and served in coconut cream, a favorite meal in Papua New Guinea. I pinch mine in mid-summer, unless spring is cold and summer is late.

Tomatoes bearing heavily can also have their tips pinched, as can eggplants bearing more than half a dozen fruit. Some do it to cucumbers, but I let them ramble, not minding that the fruit gets smaller as the season advances. Pinch wherever you want strong growth.

Thinning

Whereas I apologize to plants about to be pruned—"This will stop you feeling so exhausted, sweetie"—and it hurts me to pinch out young tips, I draw the line at the thinning of seedlings. My respect for the life force in every seed that has managed to break the surface of the earth is such that, if seedlings must be thinned out, I will transplant them immediately somewhere else. It is a gross waste of seed to sow pumpkins, cucumbers, and corn in threes, then thin out two, only keeping the strongest one. That may be commercially preferable, but the home grower raising vegetables in toilet paper tubes plants each germinated seedling. We don't need giant sizes, preferring flavor and quality.

Carrots, onions, and beets have to be sown thinly, but excess little ones can also have their time in the sun. In Part Four read under Carrots (page 240) and other vegetables how to harvest thickly sown vegetables or vigorously germinating ones. Respect for the life that goes on in your food plot could well be registered by the plants and discussed at night! "Food should be produced kindly," writes food scientist Colin Tudge.[13] Although he is referring to animals raised for meat, the same goes for fruit and vegetables. Love is not wasted on them.

CROP ROTATION *and* GREEN CROPS

CROP ROTATION restores the nutritional balance in the soil and prevents plant diseases from developing, but it cannot restore all nutrients taken from the soil by previous crops. Therefore, soil needs additional nutrients through green crops, compost, manure, and organic fertilizers.

The word has been out a while now that mono-cropping—the growing of one variety on the same soil year after year—leads to root diseases, fatal for root crops, as well as those on big feet like the large brassicas. Mono-cropping is putting all your eggs in one basket and is frequently practiced with vegetables that increase prolifically, delivering the greatest harvest for the least amount of cost and labor. Mono-cropping is performed by poor people who need to feed many mouths for next to nothing.

Such was the case in Ireland where potatoes were the staple food until, in 1845, the Great Potato Famine struck. Cold wet weather gave rise to a fungal disease, and the potatoes rotted. One million people died of starvation and two million migrated, leaving five million to try to survive off the blighted land. In the hills where I live, the growers of an entire valley were prohibited from cultivating onions for five years because of a disease caused by continuous mono-cropping.

In Bali, the hills have been terraced to grow rice for a thousand years. But with a recent surge in population to 3.5 million, in a climate where rice can grow all year, continuous mono-cropping was reducing soil fertility and causing problems requiring chemical spraying. Now, Balinese farmers practice crop rotation with peanuts, corn, sweet potatoes, tapioca, and vegetables after two rice harvests. Their fields are small, and those surrounded by shelter belts of mixed trees and weeds have the best-looking crops.

From a train window, traveling from Hong Kong to Guangzhou, I watched spellbound as we rolled past thousands of market gardens doomed to become concrete jungles during the 21st century. Chinese farmers in Guangdong Province practice the most intensive vegetable culture I've ever seen. They have many mouths to feed, but they can grow food all year in a subtropical climate with an annual rainfall of 76 inches.

Every bit of arable ground between villages is taken up by straight beds, two arm's-lengths wide, and divided by narrow paths where people hunch to weed, hoe, or harvest, filling huge reed baskets. Every second or third bed has bamboo lattice running through the center with peas, beans, cucumbers, eggplants, and squash vines shading rows of leafy vegetables underneath. Each bed grows at least half a dozen vegetables, including onions, celery, and broccoli.

Later, I learned that apart from lots of manure and compost made from street sweepings, the only other fertilizer used was nitrogen in the form of ammonia or urea. This went on all the beds, whether they would grow brassicas or root crops, mainly to save time. About five combinations of vegetables inhabited the beds in turn, so crop rotation was assured. Only aquatic vegetables like *kangkong*, lotus, water bamboo, and water spinach were grown as mono-crops in watery regions.[14]

Even rotating half a dozen crops is not always enough to keep blights, root disease, and insect infestations at bay. A mixed farming approach is needed, taking into account mini-climate, indigenous pests, and predators.

The home grower can use mixed farming on a small scale and succeed.

Else Jansen's attractive kitchen garden is situated on a slope between a bank and future orchard. It has four mulched plots for crop rotation and citrus trees in tubs.

Make each bed a mix of three to four vegetables with companion herbs and flowering plants. Read about rotating crops in Part Three (page 145) and Part Four (page 221). If you are not following the succession of plots in Part Three, here are some other scenarios for you to try. Sometimes, you will plant mixed vegetables, other times a mono-crop like onions and garlic. But a mono-crop on a 3-foot square causes no problems if followed by mixed species.

Alternative Scenarios for Crop Rotation

SCENARIO 1
You might first plant your square in early autumn as a Curry Plot with carrots, cauliflower, daikon, rutabagas, red onions, kale, and herbs.

SCENARIO 2
As you dig up carrots and rutabagas, sprinkle B&B and sow arugula toward a Salad Plot to fit in with onions that sit in the ground till mid-summer. The kale keeps standing a long time. Cultivate around it, sowing red radishes, and when the weather warms up, plant one prolific, staked tomato plant and a rambling cucumber. Rake mixed lettuce seeds in between and there's your Salad Plot.

SCENARIO 3
When the Salad Plot comes to an end and the onions are drying in the shed, add manure and compost. Plant cauliflowers, broccoli, tatsoi, and bok choy around the edges and fava beans in the center. There's your Stir-Fry Plot.

SCENARIO 4
It's spring once more. Eat or freeze any green food left growing. Rake in CMC for pumpkins, squash, zucchini, and melons, or bell peppers, eggplants, and tomatoes.

SCENARIO 5
Add lime in late summer, three weeks before planting onions and garlic. Mulch between rows. Have a quiet winter.

SCENARIO 6
Since it may be a while before the onions and garlic dry off enough to be pulled, now is the time to expand. Dig up another 3-foot square of lawn and plant spring vegetables.

SCENARIO 7
The onions and garlic are harvested; it is mid-summer and hot. Plant a quick green crop like mustard and dig it in before it sets seed.

SCENARIO 8
Time for a nitrogen fix: plant winter peas along the edges of the square with

at least four Asian greens taking up the center for a different Stir-Fry Plot.

SCENARIO 9

Give that square plenty of manure, compost, and B&B for an Antioxidants Plot.

The 1, 2, 3, 4 Method

Should you find that intricate pattern of mixed vegetables over four years too much to keep track of, consider laying out four strips, each of 18 × 36 inches, or half the size of the square plot. Mark them 1, 2, 3, and 4 with numbers on stakes and keep a notebook. Whether you start in spring/summer or autumn/winter, plant as follows:

PLOT 1

Leafy vegetables (chard, bok choy, cabbage).

PLOT 2

Any root crop.

PLOT 3

Any leguminous crop, beans in spring/summer, peas or fava beans in autumn/winter.

PLOT 4

Fruiting crops (cucumbers, pumpkins, melons, zucchinis, and in theory also eggplants, bell peppers, and tomatoes).

Next season, shift these categories up one so that Plot 1 becomes a fruiting crop, Plot 2 a leafy crop, Plot 3 a root crop, and Plot 4 a leguminous crop. Apply manure and other requirements for each crop—see Part Four (page 221).

The 1, 2, 3 Method

This simple method still assures reasonable crop rotation on the same plot if you are not trying to grow food for all your needs.

SEASON 1

In autumn, plant any of the gross feeders from the cabbage family or leafy crops. In spring, plant eggplants, bell peppers, cucurbits, pumpkins, sweet corn, tomatoes.

SEASON 2

Plant root crops that can live off the residue of the heavy manuring applied for Season 1. Beets, carrots, onions, rutabagas, and turnips are all good.

SEASON 3

Plant peas or beans, depending on the season, or a green crop to dig in.

As a rule of thumb, remember that rotation starts with gross feeders when you lay it on with CMC, CM, OF, and/or B&B, plus a sprinkling of lime. For root crops (except potatoes), also add a sprinkling of lime and top dress with some CMC if soil is poor. Lime again for peas and beans, but hold back on OF and B&B.

Then manure all other crops, and lime where soil is acidic. Problem is, potatoes like manure but not lime. When digging in green crops, add a few handfuls of dolomite, gypsum, or rock dust.

In a notebook, draw a plan of your plots on a double page, write the year and season in one corner, and note where vegetables were planted. It's an easy record to help you plan following seasons. Rotation for a minimum of three or four seasons, and as many as six seasons, avoids troubles.

Now that your first plot is underway, plan to develop another square each year until you have four square plots. This streamlines crop rotation. Simply shift the Salad Plot from Square 1 to Square 2 and so on, until it returns to Square 1 in the fifth season. The other three squares follow a different sequence, or carry a mono- or green crop.

Let the peas and beans family only touch corners with the onion and garlic plot. In winter, this four-square bed might be one square of cabbages—planted as a border or cross—a diagonal half square of chard, a half square of carrots, another of leeks, and a whole square of mixed cauliflower and broccoli, all intermixed with rutabagas, parsley, arugula, marigolds, and borage, and plastic butterflies hovering across the cabbages (see page 239).

Going into your second winter, there will be a profusion you had not planned. Self-seeded arugula may have to be pruned. Kale seedlings are likely. Give some away, with the recipe for green soup (page 197)!

While you eat out a plot as the season advances, start planting suitable vegetables in vacant spaces, so that by mid-spring, you still have some winter crops, interspersed with lettuces, peas, and beets.

Of course, such intensive growing depletes the soil and thus, whenever space becomes available, tip in a bucket of CM before replanting. This almost automatic crop rotation never grows the same crop in the same soil in consecutive years. Together with companion planting, you can see how complex it threatens to become, but that is where green-cropping comes in to give you a break.

Digging crops in is green-cropping

By growing food in rotating beds, a section occasionally becomes vacant to plant a cover or green crop. In autumn going into winter, try barley, buckwheat, oats, peas, or wheat. In summer, try buckwheat, millet, or sorghum. Dig in before they set seed. Buckwheat leaves are a fine vegetable, but some swear by wheatgrass.

Green-crop a dense leafy crop for the sole purpose of fertilizing the soil. Not only does the soil get a rest from producing crops that must grow to maturity as green crops are dug in before flowering, but plants returned to the earth at optimum vigor make the best green manure. Allowing a month to let the crop decay, this plot would have a healthy rest for three months before returning to full production. Seeds of common green crops are obtainable in small to medium quantities.

Common Green Crops

Buckwheat: Any season. Available from health shops or groceries.

Fenugreek: Autumn and spring (see List of Common Herbs on page 279). Enjoy spicy leaves while young, then dig in.

Lupin: Before flowering starts, cover plants entirely with a layer of newspaper and 2 inches of soil or compost.

Millet: Sow in a warm season. From groceries.

Mung beans: Spring and summer. The same beans as used for sprouting. Need warmth to germinate.

Mustard: Any season. Benefits soils harboring nematodes. Available in large bags in Asian and Mediterranean groceries. Sow yellow or black mustard, a handful per square. Grow your own seed.

Oats: Put a handful in a mix of green crops.

Red clover: Widely used by farmers, very nutritious when dug in. Available at farm supply stores.

Soybean: Spring and summer. The world's most nutritious bean. From health shops and farm supply stores.

Wheat: If organic wheatgrass and wheat juice is so good for people, it must be good for the soil. Mix with other seeds, like mustard and oats.

Nitrogen-Fixing Crops

Peas and fava beans in winter, other beans in summer. These are not dug in, but harvested. Cut plants at soil level, leaving nitrogen-fixing nodules in the ground. Jackie French advises to use wattle foliage (*Acacia* spp.) and fava bean plants after harvest as a mulch between other crops. Cover the Fava Bean Plot with its own stalks after cutting down the plants, until the leaves become one with the soil. Then carry the stalks to the compost heap.

Problem-Solving

WHAT *to* DO *about* WEEDS

T IS USEFUL to know that weeds have tremendous benefits as plants and are only weeds because we did not plant them where they are. I shudder at the sight of yellow dock carrying a seed head for a thousand potential deep-rooted dockies, yet know that deep dock roots bring nutrients to upper soil layers.

Our friends bought a property in a country area where everyone appeared to be members of a land care or tree-planting group, so they were expecting to join a community that took care of the environment. This was true only insofar as the neighbors were changing a farming district into a region looking prettier by the year, with flowering natives marking boundaries and daffodils popping up in green grass during winter.

But spring was the neighborhood's cue to spray weed killers. We saw large brown areas between the greener ones, poisoned and ready for weed-free planting. Our friends found that, although the previous owners had maintained an annual poison program on the property, it still sprouted an abundant crop of multifarious weeds. They decided to abstain from the September ritual, save the money, and get some exercise by controlling weeds by mowing. By not using poisons, they prevented toxic residues running into their dam, creek, and water table.

Weeds are weeds because they are vigorous plants that survive without human interference. The first rhododendron, carefully collected in the wild, became a weed in England! Each weed has unique properties. Some are toxic; others are beneficial herbs. Due to the war against weeds waged by humans for centuries, only the toughest survive. In nature, trees stand in fields of weedy herbs or herby weeds beneficial to their health. If you care to imitate nature, let some weeds and grasses grow in your orchard and just keep a circle 3 feet in diameter around young trees for manure, mulch, and watering. You can still mow the orchard, or have it grazed and fertilized by geese and ducks—see Easy-Care Fruit Trees and Berries (page 293).

But What to Do with Weeds That Overwhelm the Garden in Spring?

Start on sunny days in late winter and don't leave weeding till mid-spring, by which time your chosen plants demand space. Pull one bucket of weeds every day as exercise. A feathered flock living in a run will thrive on these morsels. Chickens, ducks, and geese each have their favorite weeds, and some they all squabble over, turning them into eggs and manure. Poison those weeds, and you get nothing, while creeks and the water table collect toxic residues. Regard weeds as plant food to toss in the compost or liquid manure (see Plant Food and Soil Food, page 63) or spread on a vacant plot to dig in. To solve the problem in a few years, always pull weeds before they set seed.

For extensive areas, apply hot water or steam weeds with appropriate equipment. Alternatively, cover temporarily with black plastic or weed mat, making slits to insert plants, and mulch with straw. Buy UV stabilized, permeable, and biodegradable weed mat so the soil underneath doesn't dry out (consult advertisements in organic gardening magazines).

My friend Gay covered a weed-infested area with telephone books opened in the center, placed in overlapping fashion. Collect them from friends and neighbors. Give the weeds two to three years to die down. Cover phone books with straw and potted plants to make it look pretty. This worked for me on suckering bamboo.

Different weeds pull up minerals from different soil levels: calcium, copper, iron, magnesium, manganese, nitrogen, phosphorus, potassium, silica, sulfur, and more. Should you be so lucky to have nettles, you may be happy to know that your soil is rich. Nettles love growing near compost heaps and are an excellent fertilizer in a similar way as seaweed. Pick nettles before they set seed, steep in a bin of water, and leave to rot. Scoop off some "nettle tea," dilute, and use on your vegetables. Dry young nettles to make a velvet herb tea for human consumption. Leave a few stalks going to seed.

That said, weeds going to seed spells trouble. Pull or mow weeds early and don't let them seed. Don't let bulb-setting weeds flower, as they set new bulbs at this time. Dig them up and compost. Each area has its own notorious weeds. Some are edible. Talk to locals and find out how the worst weeds propagate themselves—by seed, bulb, root division, or all three? Then eradicate each weed just before it sets seed or forms new bulbs. Most weeds can be composted, but never put dock root in the compost! This sort of knowledge takes the panic out of spring and the weed issue. Suspect seed heads and roots should go into plastic bags, knotted at the top. Growing and managing weeds is part of healthy gardening, and your compost heap makes short work of most of them.

All this good news about weeds should be enough to make you quite relaxed on the subject. In dormant times, spot what is coming up and saunter out for your daily bucket. Pull selectively, according to what needs to be stopped in its tracks rather than weeding a whole area, which is what you do just before the new planting season.

Enjoy your weeds, get to know them. Learn that the pointy, striated leaf of plantain (*Plantago lanceolata*) is nick-named "gardener's Band-Aid" because it stems bleeding should you cut yourself. Simply rinse, crush a leaf, and apply.

PESTS *and* PREDATORS

The first line of thought is: Leave well alone. Most pests are temporary phenomena.

The second line of thought is: Every critter has a role in the great web of life. Pull one out, and a connection is broken; pull out another and several connections break, until the web collapses. This is what the chemical revolution has partly achieved. Its other achievement is that it made certain weeds and pest species resistant to simpler pest management.

Let your garden accommodate all insects, butterflies, bees, birds, lizards, rodents, and possums. You may be fonder of some than others, and if there are rodents, it is because no one can stop them. Protect vegetables likely to be attacked by wildlife (see Hardware in the Food Garden on page 105). Usually, there is but a brief time slot when certain crops become attractive to certain creatures, so why wipe out a whole species because they have your vegetable on the menu twice a year? My early artichokes were chewed by rodents or possums. By placing shade cloches over the globes, I harvested several months longer. The chewed plants grew more stems that produced late artichokes as well. Prolific bearers such as tomatoes and zucchinis may get bugs, slugs, or mildew, but you can still pick a fair crop.

The third line of thought is: Since eradicating so-called pests has not been successful, and they are still with us despite the billions of tons of chemicals bombed on them (rather like humans do to humans, no?), shouldn't we perhaps accommodate them? Why not make them comfortable by planting their favorite habitat away from the vegetables or fruit we want to protect. The favorite dwellings of earwigs in hot seasons are roses and artichokes—tightly folded, cool apartments where they spend the daylight hours. Planting these may keep them away from your cabbages. Before eating artichokes, soak out earwigs; they never penetrate beyond the outer layers.

Identify the pests in your garden, then seek remedies that work with nature rather than against it. If you have a problem with grubs and caterpillars, you may have to deep dig the vegetable plot where some lay their eggs and let blackbirds or chickens clean it out. Plant flowering native shrubs to attract small birds for future pest control. Read a book like Jackie French's *Natural Control of Garden Pests*, and allow your views to do an about-face. Let the critters have some of what you grow. Learn to take tiny losses.

Snails are the logo of the Slow Food Movement. They love agapanthus clumps. It's too hot and rough a crawl from the agapanthus bank to the vegetable garden, so they leave the vegetables alone. What works in my garden and climate may not work in yours, but try not to overreact to a bit of damage. It is early days yet for the idea of accommodating other species instead of annihilating them, and the last word has not yet been spoken on the subject. Try out biological methods and observe what works in your garden. Apply coffee grounds, wood ash, sawdust, or lime around plants susceptible to slug and snail attack.

The fourth line of thought is: Pests attack the weakest plants, leaving others alone, at least in a multi-mix organic garden. This is nature's way of preventing weak plants from having progeny by setting seed. The other thing nature arranged is that even one old broccoli plant full of aphids will attract hordes of predators to take care of pest control. Isn't that wonderfully organized?

Unfortunately, humans mess up this well-laid, survival-of-the-fittest plan by spraying at the first, second, and third sign of a pest, thus keeping weak plants alive at the expense of the well-being of the whole species and killing good bugs in the process.

My first impulse when spotting a seed-setting broccoli sporting a gray mess of aphids reminiscent of asbestos is to pull the whole plant out and throw it on the compost heap where birds and nature's processes do what they must do. I don't like unsightly plants in my food plot. But I have learned to look and see before I pull. Predators will invade the garden to clean up aphids, attracted by flowering vegetables going to seed, of which I leave several standing. If you pull the affected plant, aphids may attack the next weakest specimen. You must trust the organic process to have its way. Leave the aphids and their host. Should the whole garden become infested, you undoubtedly have an impoverished soil that can only produce poor plants. Read again the chapters on compost and soil and this time do it: add compost and manure, grow green crops, start all over again!

Add OF and LS for plant health. Use LS on weaker plants worth reviving—it's medicine! Rotate crops, plant companion plants, and grow green crops. Strong plants cope better with the vagaries of pests, weather, and climate change. These jobs are done in no time by intelligent gardeners on their tiny plots. Whereas a hundred years ago, the cry was "We must tame nature!", now it is "We must repair and restore nature." If we do that, nature will take care of its own. That includes us.

If we repair and restore nature, nature will take care of its own—and that includes us.

One way of assisting natural processes to attract beneficial insects is to plant herbs and flowers in the surrounding garden. Plant feverfew rather than using pyrethrum spray. See List of Common Herbs on page 279. You avoid killing beneficial creatures while keeping unwanted ones at bay. Practice companion planting.

According to research at Utah State University, you can attract ladybugs by sprinkling some of your garden area with sugar water. Melt ½ cup of sugar in warm water and top off with 1 quart cold water. Apply with a watering can. Do 1 to 2 gallons at once. Increases of 200 to 1,300 percent were noted in the ladybug population within a few days, which is a lot even if you only had one ladybug to start with. Ladybugs feed on aphids, mites, and cabbage moth eggs, among others. Sugar water also attracts lacewings and beetles.

Alternatively, buy some *Hippodamia variegatae*. Not a variety of hippos, but a species of ladybug that come through the post as eggs on tape. (See advertisements in organic gardening magazines.)

What? No Sprays?

In our litigation-happy times, it is not wise to give advice that encourages other people to use any substance whatsoever. What is an allowable chemical and what is not remains a contentious issue in government departments that seek to protect us all from harm. Not all substances used by gardeners have yet been classified. At the time of writing, garlic and milk, used by organic gardeners as sprays, are unclassified in some states, although we use them freely in our cooking. You can see where this is going, can't you? I am not keen to advocate sprays or applications no matter how innocent the substances appear to be, lest you are allergic. I rarely use any myself, preferring to let nature do the healing.

IMPORTANT: When spraying, no matter whether a homemade brew or a commercial product, wear gloves, mask, goggles, long sleeves, and trousers. If there is a label, read it, and follow the directions for use.

VISITORS *from the* BIOSPHERE

THEY COME from everywhere, and most of them fly in or arrive on foot in our space that is the food garden. In whatever space they once made a living, they now set up among our vegetables and fruit trees. Then it only takes weeks for some species to give birth and their offspring is indigenous to our little space. To tell the truth, some were indigenous before birth, because the eggs that contained them simply lay in the soil waiting for the right conditions, which are, of course, the application of water, mulch, and edible plants.

"Aha! A gardener has arrived, so now we can get born—or airborne." And bingo, we have an ecosystem on our garden gloves, with the first arrivals being the plant eaters and the last those that eat the plant eaters. If only it were the other way around, the first year of a new garden wouldn't be so nerve wracking.

If they are so inclined, home gardeners can spend more than the weekly food bill on chemicals for their flower, fruit, and vegetable gardens. But even organizations

like the Food and Agriculture Organization (FAO) and the World Bank, who both supported the chemical "green" revolution in the past to make the world free from hunger, have changed their collective minds and declared that organic farming methods are the only way to go forward in global food production. And that goes for home gardeners as well.

Biological controls are always preferable.

There is a predator or plant-derived deterrent for every pest in nature. Scientists and gardeners are finding them, and we shall, in future, all garden with this in mind. The first thought food gardeners have about insects is that they don't want them because they eat the vegetables and fruit we are growing for ourselves. This attitude has brought about a century of spraying with chemicals capable of killing everything that crawls or flies. Together with harmful insects, all the beneficial insects go to the grave as well. And so the predators are killed with the pests they could have controlled.

This practice has opened ecological niches for new hordes to enter and wreak damage, for nature never leaves a niche unfilled. Worse, pest insects have developed resistance, so some sprays don't affect them. It happened with weeds, now chemical-resistant weeds abound. One town had sprayed its roadside for many years with glyphosate only to end up with resistant rye grass and two other resistant grasses. They now have to revert to mowing and slashing at the right times to control these indestructible weeds. GM crops are sprayed with such chemicals, and problems of glyphosate-resistant weeds are occurring in the United States where 80 percent of corn and soya crops are GM, as well as cotton. So, having taken this road in the past, American growers of GM crops now have to try to grow crops without chemicals.

Experiment. If one insect does not like a smell, then plant a plant with that smell near the plant you need to protect. On the other hand, if some like a certain smell (such as fish oil), then put some away from the plants to be protected. If snails prefer to live in agapanthus leaves, then don't plant aggies along the vegetable plot, but plant as a catch crop as far away as possible.

Practice companion planting in the food garden and surround it with aromatic plants to attract beneficial insects. You can buy fruit fly thingammabobs to hang in fruit trees that may attract these destructive flies. Finding out how to protect our food plants from attack is work we can do with our feet up, reading a companion plants book, or looking up a website.

Gardening Organically

Joy and Ken, friends who have rescued and raised wildlife, were given a fledgling bird that had blown from its nest. Joy doubted it would survive, blind and featherless as it was. But it did and was given its own cage until it was ready to be released. Ken fed it broccoli from the garden, which the little bird gobbled up daily. When the broccoli ran out, Ken bought some, but the bird retreated to a corner of the cage and wouldn't touch the shop product. When organic broccoli was obtained, the bird ate it again with gusto. This story alone is enough to make me an organic gardener.

Originally, I thought of giving my next book the title *Eating Holes* after my apparently notorious remark on the television program *Gardening Australia* about insect damage to leafy greens: "You can eat holes, you know. They cook up quite well."

When I met Irene, who lives in her town's original watertank on less than a tenth of an acre and opens her garden to the public twice annually, she said: "I thought of you the other day because my bok choy is being eaten by something. But I said to my friends, 'Lolo says you can eat holes.' So I eat holes, and all my friends do, too."

Holes are evidence of insect visits, sometimes of egg-laying on the underside of leaves. You probably don't want to eat cabbage butterfly eggs, but you can tear a small hole in the leaf to take them out. For over three decades, I have gardened as organically as possible in five gardens, and biodynamically for a number of years, using no chemical sprays, and applying B&B and other natural fertilizers from as organic a supplier as I can find. Life is a compromise, whatever you do. Gradually, the insect population in a new garden reduces, overcome by the resistance some plants develop through being fed well, especially with seaweed solutions. Only a long wet period increases the slug and snail brigades. The main point is: we eat almost daily from the garden despite the freeloaders.

Holes do not worry me one bit. What concerns me is that my vegetables are looking vigorous and deep green.

One gentle remedy against insect attacks is a collection of mobile herbs in pots, which I place where needed: mint and celery herb either end of the kale patch; mint and chives where slugs are in evidence. Slugs also stay away from garlic—most critters do. Scented geraniums apparently make an anti-slug hedge. Strewing fennel ferns between vegetables also keeps slugs away; for bad cases, lay elderberry branches around. For this, you must first grow your elderberry tree for a steady supply, but they grow pretty fast.

A most unusual warning appeared in the news about a Sydney man who ate a slug for a dare. As a result, he came down with a rare form of meningitis called rat lungworm disease, caused by a parasitic worm carried by slugs and snails. The disease can be fatal. If it does not become fatal, only the immune system can deal with it. Ugh![15]

WARNING: For the above reason, always wash fruits and vegetables thoroughly, and wash your hands after handling slugs and snails, or pick them up with a paper scoop. But don't the French eat snails? Yes, but they cook them. Good hygiene avoids problems.

Collect snails from their hiding places between stones and pots. If you know your garden, you also get to know where snails spend the night. Collect them by the handful and migrate them to a far part of the ornamental garden where they can do little harm. If they have been breeding and suddenly there are minute little baby snails everywhere, make sure to wash your vegetables very well, drain them, and leave in a colander or bowl for half an hour. Any little snails will by then race around the edge of the container and can be migrated as well. Check for snails between the leaves of large vegetables.

Earwigs like fish oil in water. Slugs hate sawdust and like beer. Slaters like damp newspaper. Rabbits apparently regard a line of B&B as a fence not to be crossed. It is also said that they can be deterred by a border of onions or other alliums.

Homemade sprays can deter insects that come in for a short time when a crop is young or fruiting. A homemade garlic spray is about the easiest to make. Boil a knob, sieve the liquid, and use it as soon as possible. Sprinkling with liquid seaweed deters those insects that come in for the kill when a plant is weak, such as aphids, because seaweed strengthens the plant's immune system.

Unavoidably, at busy times of the growing season, all or part of your food garden may take on the appearance of a mini-junkyard with its little squares and rectangles filled with upturned yogurt containers, plastic bottles, PVC rings, netted cages, and portable shade cloches. Hardware is truly harmless to you and to the insects it deters. See Hardware in the Food Garden on page 105. Protecting plants with hardware is a marvelous recycling game, making you inspect all packaging to see whether it might do some good in the garden. Delight in it, because it is all temporary, usually for the duration of the baby to teenage period of the plants. Once they are strong, they can stand what wind and weather sends their way.

A healthy food garden should not be devoid of winged creatures. Have insects and bees buzzing about on their quest to make a living from your flowers. Plant for them. Perennial wild arugula (the one with the narrow serrated leaves used as decoration in restaurants) will flower for months to the delight of local wild bees, who will also come in to pollinate your fruit trees and pumpkin and squash vines. Let a few healthy vegetable plants set seed, as the flowers attract beneficial insects. Learn to live with visitors from the biosphere, even if you cannot accommodate them all.

An A–Z *of* PESTS *and* PROBLEMS

List of Common Pests, Problems, and Remedies

APHIDS

If you decide to spray soapy water under the leaves, remember that soap kills frogs and probably salamanders as well. Study the List of Common Herbs (page 279) that can be planted for long-term prevention. Feed the soil to return plants to health. Plant a southernwood in a large pot to shift between vegetables prone to aphids.

BIRDS

Netting may seem drastic but is very possible if you only have one or two squares to protect. Don't use monofilament netting that snares and kills animals, but buy netting that does not endanger birds and wildlife, like long-lasting, double-knitted netting with holes allowing bee access. Thrown over fruit trees, it has to be clipped tightly underneath or the birds will come in off the ground floor. Netting saves most of the crop for you.

To discourage birds from pulling up seedlings, nipping beans in the bud, or shredding the lettuce for you, push in short stakes and crisscross sewing thread above the plants. String aluminum yogurt covers on wire, or clip on folded bread bags with the ends cut into fringes. Make pinwheels on sticks or push thin branches on either side of seedlings and bend together. Evidently, jars and bottles painted red and stuck on sticks do the job. It may look like a carnival, but if it works? Wire cages are my first protection—see Hardware in the Food Garden (page 105).

CABBAGE WHITE BUTTERFLY

Introduced to this continent by mistake through Montreal, Canada, in 1860, these pretty butterflies have spread like bunnies throughout North America. They feed on brassicas, nasturtiums, and some ornamental flowers. You may find the urn-shaped eggs and greenish larvae and pupae, ornamented with one thin stripe, on the leaves of host plants. Plant brassicas in small squares with stakes on the corners. Cut simple butterfly shapes from white plastic lids and containers and tie these onto thin string at intervals of 4 to 6 inches. Or, use Styrofoam packing fill that has a sort of butterfly shape. String butterfly garlands from stake to stake and diagonally across—they spell out "occupied territory." Or, try a molasses spray (see page 98). Plant large pots with thyme and sage, or southernwood with chamomile and place between cabbages.

CODLING MOTH

If you see brown caterpillars on your apple, fig, pear, or quince tree, pick them off because, after feeding on your fruit, they cocoon themselves to turn into larvae that pop up again as moths, which lay eggs and give rise to the next caterpillar population. Interception is the name of this game, as once infected, it may take years to free a tree of this pest.

In deep winter, buy several yards of thin unbleached cotton or similar material and sew a supply of small drawstring bags. In late winter, fix corrugated cardboard around the trunk before the tree starts flowering. Caterpillars shack up in the corrugations. Clean it out twice a week after dawn and dispose of the contents.

When the petals start to fall, make an exception and spray with Garlic Spray, (see page 98). Next, cover fruit that has just set, but has not been bitten by a caterpillar—while the flower petals are still dropping—with the cotton bags and tie the strings above the fruit. Through spring and summer, inspect the fruit and pick off by hand whatever should not be there. Clean out old leaves in the crooks of branches and periodically brush trunk and branches with a steel brush to rid them of loose bark where caterpillars full of apple pulp might want to spin a cocoon. Clear the ground underneath the tree of all fallen fruit, bits of wood, bark, and leaves, and dispose of them thoroughly. Don't put down mulch, as it makes hiding places, but do empty pots of earwigs as these clean up codling moths—see Earwigs on page 97.

Unless you have chickens, under-plant apple, pear, and quince trees with the sort of plants that attract hosts of small wasps, flies, beetles, and spiders which dine on codling moth, such as alyssum, buckwheat, carrot, daikon radish, parsnip in flower, dill, red clover, mustard, Queen Anne's lace, and yarrow. Mix the seed of a number of these to attract the greatest range of beneficial insects.

Chickens will dispense with codling moth if allowed to scratch under mature fruit trees. Protect them from dogs and foxes by enclosing even a small orchard with a fox-proof fence, or with an apron of wire netting buried outwards around the run and an outward curving overhang at the top of the wire to prevent a desperado vixen digging under or climbing up. Or, invest in a "chicken tractor," a tiny mobile

Flowers between vegetables attract beneficial insects that keep pests down and confuse predators looking for a particular crop to settle on.

run to wheel around where you want a couple of chickens to work for a day. Protect that, too, from dogs and foxes. It sounds like a lot of work, especially if you have three or more trees to treat. But you will get results and, once you have these measures in place, it becomes part of a seasonal routine. Write the dates in your notebook for next year.

Commercial products such as a horticultural glue fixed around the trunk to prevent caterpillars climbing up may help, or use petroleum jelly. Sticky traps and pads to render the male infertile are advertised in organic gardening magazines. Other baits that can be hung in jars from the tree are apple juice with a spoon of olive oil, or dissolved molasses with the same—but they could trap beneficial insects also. If you decide to use organic sprays, apply before fruit sets. Spray all hiding places in the trunk, branches, and ground around the trunk, and spread elderberry prunings. Pheromones issue a safe scent that disrupts the mating procedure, said to work on areas of a hectare and larger.

CURLY LEAF

The bane of stone-fruit growers. The old remedy was spraying with a cup of copper sulphate and a teaspoon of agricultural lime dissolved in 15 liters (4 gallons) of water. This has to be done when buds are just appearing on the branches, or it will be too late.

Bordeaux spray, although organic, contains arsenic and is therefore not recommended. You could try a stinging-nettle infusion or LS before buds open and again a few weeks later. Spray under the tree as well. A more hands-on treatment involves picking off diseased leaves into a plastic bag—easier with espaliered trees than huge canopies. Burn the end points of each affected branch with a cigarette lighter—at last one good use for those!—as the disease starts in the tip leaves. Do this daily for a week. Give tree and surrounding soil a dousing with LS for the remaining leaves to take up. Hang a bag of diseased leaves inside another bag in the sun before disposal. Under-plant the tree with tansy, feverfew, and yarrow to form a dense mat. Hanging mallow weeds in affected branches seems to work. Pigeon manure is said to help. Also, place eucalyptus branches under the tree in spring.

EARWIGS

If you can't plant a "catch" crop like roses away from the food plot, put out pots on their sides, stuffed with moist newspaper. Empty the pots away from the veg-etable garden; migrate the little darlings to under the apple, fig, pear, and quince trees to take care of codling moths.

FRUIT FLY

Food growers in warmer states, especially California and Florida, are at risk for this serious disease, which can ruin fruit crops for miles around. It has to be reported to each state's department of agriculture, which put a ban on any fruit moving out of the affected area. Seek out local advice if you live in an area prone to fruit flies. Check advertisements for fruit fly traps in organic gardening magazines. If your crop is small, tie bags of paper or cloth around clusters of fruit. If you expect fruit flies, sew up a supply of light cotton drawstring bags during winter. Put them on as soon as tiny fruits appear and check regularly. Dispose of affected fruit not collected by local authorities by "cooking" it in black plastic bags in the sun for a month, and find out what combative measures are being taken in your area.

FUNGI

There are many, but when you see the first sign, spray with milk and water mixed 1:10 and repeat before going for heavier antifungal sprays. If the weather is about to change, it may not be necessary.

GARLIC SPRAY

A homemade spray for use with persistent pests or diseases. Make several days before needed. This recipe is from the renowned Henry Doubleday Research Association of England, reprinted in *The Organic Gardener's Companion*. Chop half a head of garlic, mix in 2 teaspoons of liquid paraffin, and soak for forty-eight hours. Add 1 quart of water and 1 teaspoon of an oil-based soap as a disperser. Mix, filter, and store in a plastic container. Dilute with water 100:1, or for persistent cases, 100:2.

GRASSHOPPERS

Grasshoppers are more likely to swarm in drought-stricken areas. The best controls are biological. Plant shrubs to attract birds, flowers to attract insects, and any of the beneficial herbs named throughout this book. Make hiding places for lizards, create a frog habitat, and keep chickens. Protect your best vegetables with hospital gowns or other covers that prevent ready access to the hoppers. Unfortunately, they lay their eggs in the soil. Try garlic spray (see above). Should they appear the next season, protect crops early in the hope they dine out elsewhere.

Molasses spray: Dissolve a tablespoon of molasses in ½ gallon of warm water. This discourages flying and chewing insects, and maybe even grasshoppers. Being sweet, maybe it attracts ladybugs? There's still much to discover.

NEMATODES

These eelworms suck the fleshy roots of potatoes, cabbages, cauliflowers, radishes, and carrots, making them look pockmarked. Read up on marigold and mustard in List of Common Herbs (page 279). It may take a few years to clean the soil, but damage gradually dwindles. Nematodes don't like fresh chicken manure, but neither do plants, so apply to soil several months before planting.

PEAR SLUGS

Pear sawfly larvae suck the green out of pear, plum, and cherry leaves, leaving leaf skeletons. Douse with water, then with dry sand or wood ash. For long-term prevention, spread oak-leaf mulch.

POSSUMS

Plant floribunda roses in the surrounding garden, and the possums will go for the buds. Or install a blinking nightlight—see Hardware in the Food Garden (page 106). Be wary of ultrasonic devices to keep animals away. These could create an inaudible, interlocking web of ultrasonic beams from many backyards that may also scare off birds—check out thoroughly before using.

POWDERY MILDEW

Vegetable families host specific powdery mildews that do not cross-infect other plant families. If leaves of pumpkin, cucumber, and zucchini are affected, that doesn't mean the grapes will get it, too. Mildew thrives in damp conditions where ventilation is restricted. Growing cucumbers and pumpkins on a trellis may prevent it. Sprays of milk and water mixed 1:10 or whey and baking soda have been effective. Where fungal diseases and molds persist, prune affected leaves, and compost in a hot heap or covered bin. Mildew weakens its host, so if productive plants have a bad case, collect a handful of fir needles, boil, and dilute to 2 gallons. Splash this on affected plants every two weeks.

RABBITS

Sprinkle B&B where they have been nibbling.

RODENTS (INCLUDING SQUIRRELS)

If you do not currently have rodents prowling your garden, they may come when you start growing vegetables. They love germinating peas and beans, fava beans, sweet corn, melons, and ornamental bulbs. Protect germinating seeds with cages, dish racks, or similar obstructions, or use rings of PVC pipe with screening. Really keen rodents may still uproot these. Raise seedlings inside, because once seeds have sprouted a plant with four to six leaves, the attraction appears to vanish.

SNAILS AND SLUGS

They are beautiful creatures. Nice children look on in wonder when snails carry their elegant spiral houses slowly through the grass. They eat certain plants, including weeds, so we don't want to eradicate them. Organic growers used to make their vegetables unpalatable to snails and other diners by making a spray from wormwood, garlic, or white cedar. There is a withholding time of two weeks after spraying, so this method is not attractive if you want to pick greens daily.

The alternative is to collect snails or place a flowerpot with moist newspaper upside down on a stake overnight. Migrate the snails to another "country" early mornings before they wake up. Oak-leaf mulch or coffee grounds repel slugs and snails and add nitrogen to the soil. After a wet spell with intervals of sunshine—great slug weather—I picked a lovely cabbage surrounded with coffee grounds. Only one slug lived in the outer leaves.

STRAWBERRY PROTECTION

Strawberries test the gardener's ingenuity. Everybody loves them. We've had bandicoots coming to feast, as well as

Strawberries produce from spring to autumn but need netting or shade cloth as protection from birds and lizards.

snakes, birds, rodents, millipedes, and lizards. Most objectionable are millipedes that tunnel into big strawberries and disperse their body odor through the entire fruit. Snakes can strangle themselves in netting to get at strawberries. The best protection I've used was black shade cloth, as strawberries ripen as much with warmth as full sun. Spread shade cloth, propped up to raise it above the plants, then weigh down the edges with stones.

WEEDS

For infestations that can't be fixed with exclusion, hot water, or mulches, an organic pine oil product is available.

WHITEFLY

These sap-suckers attack beans and tomatoes, leaving plants yellow and stunted. Ladybugs, lacewings, and other flying pest controllers clean up whitefly infestations. Try a sugar solution to attract these good insects to your garden (¾ cup of sugar per bowl of hot water; add enough cold water to cool it before sprinkling around plants), and provide a habitat for them of flowering herbs in pots and perennial flowers in borders. My friend Maureen sowed lots of marigolds along her tomatoes and whiteflies disappeared!

General Prevention

For plant health, feed and mulch regularly, know what your water contains, do rain dances in dry seasons, and take responsibility for what you do in your garden. Even so, when making a garden pest-free with all the tricks you know, you and your garden are subject to forces greater than us all. Sometimes, you can do naught but cut your losses. Learn to

Repelling instead of destroying improves biodiversity.

live with things you cannot fight. You can always sprout mung beans should the vegetable plot fail. But it will never fail entirely. Study organic gardening magazines, as organic growers come up continually with novel ideas and harmless repellents.

By practicing the good gardening methods previously discussed, you find that the war-like terminology other gardeners use will disappear from your vocabulary. No more fighting plant diseases, combating, blitzing, bombing, and zapping unwelcome insects. No more killing sprees. Instead, practice preventive health care in the garden. Protect and plant wisely so that nature can do its best practice. Then, your garden will bring you peace, as well as the best food possible.

LIVESTOCK, BIRDS *and* BEES, *and* FROGS

Livestock

Chickens lay eggs, produce manure, and are sociable. In suburbia, you can comfortably keep two or three chickens, roosters usually being prohibited for their melodious but premature announcements of daybreak. Chickens foraging around fruit trees keep these disease free, but in the food plot, they cause havoc.

Consider enclosing a fruit-growing area of six to ten trees with wildlife-safe netting on high poles, fencing it off and using it as a fowl yard. The feathered flock fertilizes trees, gobbles up ground-dwelling pests, and provides eggs. Feed mixed grains at dusk as they will peck a confined area pretty bare. Kitchen scraps, fallen fruit, and spent vegetables complement their diet. Twice a week,

A few well-fed and densely planted garden beds also attract birds, insects, and other small wildlife.

add a bucket of succulent weeds and a bowl of bran mash. Some gardeners prefer ducks on their gentle flip-flops, foraging for slugs and snails between the greens. Ducks don't dig.

No matter what animals you choose to inhabit your garden, make sure their quarters are dry in the wet, shady in the heat, and dog- and fox-proof. If you let them range freely during the day, make sure they can find shelter when predators fly over. As for terrestrial predators, secure your fences, and shut your flock in before dusk.

Birds and Bees

Water makes a garden come to life. Birdbaths and ponds create a more moist atmosphere and microclimate. Although birds scratch up the food garden, they do so in their capacity as pest controllers. Place birdbaths throughout your garden. Earthenware bowls on a tree trunk look good. Place bowls well above ground where birds in flight can see them and the neighbor's cat and your dog can't. Birdbaths entice helpful birds to become permanent residents.

In the food garden, fill a bee bath on a barrel or stand. Place a rock in it so bees don't drown when drinking, and keep a stick nearby to fish out hapless bees. Attracting bees ensures pollination. In hot weather, the bee bath is their pit stop.

Frogs

At the back of the food garden, hidden among daisies, lavender, sage, and wild fruit trees grown from pips, is my frog pond. Just a deep plastic bowl dug into the ground, it has an 8-inch rim above ground so scratching creatures don't fill it with mulch. It contains plants such as papyrus and water iris. In the center at water level, there is a brick stack with two pieces of broken brick covered by a flat stone, making a hidey-hole for frogs when predator birds appear. A wire rack covers all. Frogs can't stay underwater for long when danger lurks, and coming to the surface to breathe could spell death.

To disguise a frog pond, cover it with coarse chicken mesh or two bent poly

A frog with lily pads and rocks soon becomes at home.

pipes crossing over each other, stuck on four stakes, and covered with mesh. Alternatively, tie a tripod of stakes or bamboo surrounded with plastic mesh, supporting climbing peas or beans.

Why accommodate frogs? They eat their weight in mosquitoes daily and are an endangered species, no matter which frog we talk about. They are the first to die when the spray unit comes past. Could it be that in countries without frogs, or where people eat frogs, lethal malaria and dengue fever are rife? In parts of the world where frogs are in decline due to spraying and loss of habitat, dengue fever is on the rise. Provide for frogs, and learn to love their croaking concerts at courting time. When you hear a croak distinctly different from the usual ones, something may be going in the right direction.

HARDWARE *in the* FOOD GARDEN

THOSE LOVELY PICTURES of vegetable gardens featuring colorful rows in beds of heaped black soil may be reality somewhere, but not in my climate and not always in gardens run on clean and green principles. Such ordered beauty is sometimes preceded by spraying the life out of soil and surroundings to keep weeds and pests at bay. In reality, the opposite, an imitation of nature's chaos, spells plant health.

If you live in an agricultural district where spraying takes place, you may not have many insect problems and you can garden organically by default. Yet, if spraying has been taking place over many years, you may have more problems as insects become immune to the chemicals applied. Find out what happens in your environment.

For a clean and green gardener, protection of vegetables and exclusion of pests, without spraying, is the aim so that the micro-environment can find its own balance. Temporary protection of crops takes many forms, all highly visible and all spoilers of poster versions of self-sufficiency.

Much recyclable hardware aids the gardener's work. Start by collecting

A late-winter garden with hardware.

cast-offs and recyclables, and visiting junkyards.

List of Common Hardware

BALING TWINE
Briad together three or four strands of differently colored twine from straw bales for a strong rope to stop sweet corn and fava beans from breaking in the wind.

BAMBOO
Bamboo makes tepees, trellises, and temporary fences.

BATHTUBS
Bathtubs can be converted to become worm farms.

BLINKING NIGHT-LIGHT
We heard that a local sheep farmer had placed a number of amber blinking lights, formerly used to mark a hole in the road, around his sheep paddock. Since then, none of his sheep were attacked by foxes.

As we were having trouble with possums running across our roof at night and causing havoc in the food garden, we thought we would try it. The light runs on a large battery (many of which come with solar-panels made especially for garden lighting), comes on at dusk, and stops at dawn. We placed it on a plank in the food garden. No more possums. We planted 500 trees in our adjoining paddock, and it is my conservative opinion that the possums ought to make themselves comfortable there and leave my vegetables alone.

Since the light blinks on both sides, place it so that it does not blink into your neighbor's bedroom window or the chicken coop as that may deprive the flock of sleep and affect egg production. Our chickens seem to cope well with the winks being 10 yards away.

BRICKS
Bricks can be used for propping up top-heavy plants, holding down a line of twine pulling a heavy plant upright again, placing under pumpkins to prevent rot, under a hot frame, or under mint pots to prevent "rooting down."

CAGES
You attract a lot of birds if you plant densely, plant shrubs suitable for nesting, or plant native trees and nectar-producing flowers. Birds pay rent by keeping your garden fairly pest free. Our river-flat garden was full of nests in fantastic places. Birds don't eat vegetables but can pull up seedlings as they scratch soil for worms and insects. You can't have an organic garden without birds, but you can't always have vegetables with them!

The simple answer is cages. Not for the birds, but for the vegetables! Anything from an upside-down dish rack to a carpentry job of wooden frame covered with chicken wire can be a cage. My cages are 18 × 36 × 18 inches of painted wood or steel rod with chicken wire attached.

Each covers almost half a square, and two cages fit on a square with space between them where I can plant something without much chance birds will go there. When planting seed or seedlings, arrange them inside an imprint of the cage edges. When the first plant pokes through the top of the cage, you can remove it as they can stand on their own at this point.

A protective cage kept company by fava beans.

CARPET

Carpet is the best cover for a compost heap. Clean with strong detergent, hot water, and a broom to remove residual chemicals. Ask a carpet dealer for odd pieces. Underfelt—without plastic coating—makes good mulch and is easy to cut. Lay along plots or around fruit trees to suppress weeds, or use to line wire cylinders (see page 113).

CHAIRS

This is a tip from Chris Watters, who taught in the Strathalbyn square-yard vegetable-growing course. An old cane chair placed upside down makes a great frame for a sprawling cucumber or cherry tomato. So do old kitchen chairs. As for a cane lounge—wow!

CLOCHES

Cloches are as old as farming itself, and they look better than cages. A cloche protects an individual plant from heat, cold, or birds. In England, they make them from bamboo. Use cheap baskets with enough gaps for bees to get through, but not mice. Bottomless baskets past their use-by date can be given a cheesecloth bottom to start an upside-down life as a cloche. As long as air circulates and bees can go in and out, most wicker ware can be used to make a cloche.

Fashion cloches for early seedlings from plastic food containers, bottoms cut out and replaced by clear plastic with breathing holes, fastened with rubber bands. Push into soil over bean seedlings for warmth and protection. In spring, when insect populations explode, you can't have enough tiny cheap protectors like these.

COLANDERS

A plastic colander is great for spreading lime, B&B, or gypsum if you are preparing more than one square. Or, use a flowerpot with just the right array of bottom holes.

EGG CARTONS

Egg cartons (pressed paper) provide twelve biodegradable seed-growing pods for tiny plants of lettuce, chilies, lamb's lettuce, and tender herbs. Pierce draining holes in each pod. Set the carton on a tray of compost and fill with soil. Plant seedlings in their paper pod, after cutting each off the carton. There is no root disturbance and the pod disintegrates.

FLOWERPOTS

During hot weather, earwigs like damp, crumpled newspaper in upside-down flowerpots on sticks. Place pots under apple trees so earwigs can help control codling moth.

HOSPITAL GOWNS

In a hospital clinic, you may be handed a gown made from a kind of paper, white or blue. The gown is thrown away after one use only, but if you ask, hospital personnel are happy for you to take it home. Many people wear these paper gowns when painting the house or a canvas.

The material can be used in the spring garden to make row covers over bent wire. Use it whole or cut it into wide strips, weighing down the edges with stones. As long as seeds germinate underground, the gown can lay flat on the earth. When seedlings come up, push the fabric up with short sticks, like a Bedouin tent. Once seedlings have four to six leaves, they are of less interest to wildlife and you can take the gown off.

Paper gowns facilitate germination by keeping the soil a few degrees warmer. Sew the material around a wire cylinder to keep a small citrus tree or tropical herb warm. The blue ones look good amidst the greenery, and rain does not dissolve them instantly. One gown protected my infant citrus tree through the wettest winter on record.

KNEELING PAD

Wrap a firm foam rubber pillow in plastic, then an old sack. Or stuff leaky hot-water bottles with sand—they hang nicely in the shed on their ringed lips.

MILK CARTONS

The waterproof insides have obvious gardening possibilities, especially for the balcony gardener. Wash empty milk cartons in soapy water and cut two bottom corners for drainage. Stack a box ful of milk cartons, fill them with potting soil enriched with a sprinkling of B&B, and put one or two seeds in each carton. Grow lettuces, beans, carrots, chives, garlic, radishes, or anything small.

Stacking them together avoids drying out too quickly, and the extra height of the milk carton allows roots to go deep. Raise native shrubs and trees in milk cartons, too.

Another use for milk cartons is to make plant tags. Cut each side through the middle and again diagonally. Each side yields four tags, sixteen in total. Write on them with a ballpoint pen, and they should last a season.

NETTING AND NETS

Wildlife-safe fruit tree netting is also useful on vegetables if you have lots of munchers. Our little black dog likes to crawl under the net protecting the apple tree to eat one apple a day. From inside the net, she stares at her bigger mate, who isn't so smart. But she can't always get out when she wants to and sometimes has to be rescued!

Net bags from store-bought oranges and nuts are useful to pop over three sticks to protect a small plant, or to wrap around ripening fruit. You can also make netting hoods with elastic to pop over large pots and seed boxes.

PANTYHOSE

Onions, garlic, and butternuts can be stored by hanging them in pantyhose in a dark shed. Alternatively, use orange bags.

PERCY'S PORTABLE ROOF

Hills gardener Percy McElwaine built the roof to protect young plants in spring when the nights were still cold. He found that wherever he placed the roof, young plants grew faster compared with those left unprotected. Pumpkins and spring vegetables benefited especially. He transfers the roof on his back by stooping under it, but two people can shift it with ease. Made of corrugated plastic sheeting on a metal cross frame, it is something gardeners in cooler districts may find useful. Make a few in smaller sizes.

Percy McElwaine extends summer or brings spring forward with his homemade portable plastic roof.

PLASTIC BOTTLES

Fill plastic bottles with water and dig them in as edging around vegetable plots. Scratching birds don't like reflective obstructions, although mice will still go in. In late autumn or early spring, the water absorbs the warmth of the sun and, at night, the bottles give off this warmth, keeping plot temperatures more even. In a region prone to night frosts, this can help plants survive. See Seeds and Seedlings (page 47) for a seed-raising table turned into a mini-hothouse with plastic bottles.

A dozen water-filled bottles placed around a plant in strife or danger will save it. In autumn, my lemongrass gets a bottle fence to "overwinter" it. Bottles placed on their sides make a safe area for small plants. You will find other uses.

When a bottle after some years of service starts to deteriorate, dispose of it immediately. You don't want plastic breaking down in your soil. It is said that plastic breaks down invisibly, giving off gases we could do without. If you feel strongly about this, collect glass bottles and keep all plastic out of your garden.

PLASTIC LIDS

Ice-cream tub lids are useful to put under growing pumpkins and squashes

Plastic juice bottles filled with water regulate temperatures on winter days and summer nights and function as edgings.

to prevent rotting where they touch the ground. Use margarine lids under baby squash, cucumbers, or low-hanging tomatoes. Zucchinis grow too fast to rot.

PLASTIC TUBS

Cut the bottom out of yogurt tubs. Push into soil over a just-planted pea or bean in its toilet paper tube, to protect it from birds' beaks or cold nights. Seeds sown directly inside tubs have less chance of being scratched up. Have a dozen on hand in spring and autumn when things pop up.

POLES

The traditional bean-pole structure is two rows of poles or long stakes leaning toward each other and crossing over a 1-yard width of soil. Place one pole in the crossover at the top and fasten with string.

POLY PIPE

One of the best inventions by do-it-yourself gardeners is the poly-pipe arch. Choose poly pipe of a diameter that fits over a dropper or non-rotting stake—ask your hardware store. Set stakes 3 feet apart across your square plot. Or buy enough poly pipe and four stakes to make two diagonally crossing arches, tied in the center. Either grow a quick growing vine or clip shade cloth over the top. Peas, beans, cucumbers, small squashes, and melons can be trained up the stakes. Or connect stakes with wire netting for vines to climb up themselves. Make poly-pipe arches to create height in your food garden. Place three in a row or in an L-shape.

POLY TUNNELS

If you don't have a greenhouse, set up a few makeshift green tunnels of bent poly pipe, plastic-coated wire, or trellis held down with bricks or stones. Short pieces of corrugated PVC sheeting bent into tunnel shapes and held in place by stakes take little time to set up. As you have to crouch down to stick your hands in, keep these tunnels short. You can close them at night with plastic and open up in the morning for ventilation, but even tunnels open on either end will help plants grow. They function as temporary cold frames for seedlings or late-summer plants when cold weather arrives.

POT SCRUBBERS

Push into PVC rings to protect germinating beans.

PVC RINGS

Large vegetables like cabbages and cauliflowers need more space than a cage provides. Plant them in individual rings of PVC water pipe with a diameter of 4 inches, cut about 3 inches high. Or, make collars from tin foil or milk-carton strips, or simply staple cardboard into rings. Push the rings into the soil around seedlings; they won't be bothered by any but the most brazen bird.

RACKS FROM OLD FRIDGES OR OVENS

These are useful protectors. Place them across a few bricks to give head room to seedlings or over a Styrofoam box. No birds will crawl under such contraptions, although rodents may.

SCREENING

Push into PVC rings to protect germinating beans from rodents.

SHADE CLOCHES

In hot weather, protect seedlings or tender vegetables such as beans from the worst rays. Use a 10-inch strip of open square wire with long spikes at the ends, with shade cloche fastened to it with clothes pins or sewn on with fishing line or strong thread. Bend in a U-shape. These little shade houses can be placed over groups of bush beans or seedlings. A slightly larger affair can be made of bent poly pipe. Put short stakes into the ground to stick the poly pipe on for a moveable installation. Or pin shade cloth over cages.

STAKES

Stakes are needed for climbing tomatoes, beans, and peas, although peas are happy to wind tendrils up a bunch of twigs stuck in the ground. Goldenrod twigs can support peas. Basic stakes are straight tree branches. Collect these, as wood products are expensive. If you know of a stand of bamboo, you are in clover. Thin out carefully and trim to size. Bamboo is the hardiest and cheapest wood in the world and grows sustainably. Your garden may grow ready-made stakes: sunflower stalks and buddleia branches.

STYROFOAM BOXES

Use for a balcony or condo garden, and in small gardens. Use boxes to grow chives, shallots, onions, lettuce, parsley, sorrel, and varieties of garlic. Their portability is an advantage. Two form a nice backdrop for your Magic Square without new ground having to be dug up. Six will enclose the square on three sides.

Styrofoam boxes are perfect for small crops like radishes and garlic.

TIES

Carry soft ties, such as pantyhose or cotton underwear cut into strips, in your pockets when gardening. You always see something in the food garden that flops when it shouldn't. Beans and peas need initial ties to the stake before they get the idea. If you grow heavier plants on stake or trellis (like cucumbers, butternuts, or tomatoes), tie them progressively as they grow. Wire and plastic ties will cut into stems as they thicken.

TEPEE

Much the same as bean poles, but placed in a circle and tied at the top. Useful for beans, cucumbers, small melons, or peas.

TOOLS

So what's wrong with a digging stick? Seriously, a square plot can be dug over with a borrowed garden fork and thereafter with a hand trowel and fork. Should you extend, a small hoe is useful twice a year. An old table knife stuck in a brick with a hole is handy to whip out weeds or seedlings. So is a hammer to pound in stakes. Your best tools in a small food plot are your fingers, which don't hurt the worms.

TRELLIS

Make one from wood, wire, or branches, held by upright posts or attached to a fence or shed. Or use posts with strings attached for climbing vegetables. Use strong wire when espaliering fruit trees.

TUBS

Tubs filled with manure, soil, and compost provide depth to grow carrots and daikon radish. For potatoes, see Part Four (page 259).

UMBRELLAS

Tie them to stakes or saw off the curved handles and stick them in the soil to protect vegetables during heatwaves. Put up the garden umbrella to shade a bean bed when temperatures hover around 100 degrees and the beans are being cooked on the stalk.

WIRE BASKETS

Use as cages over a seed patch or young seedlings.

WIRE CYLINDER

You need at least 2 yards of chicken wire or green plastic wire. Make cylinders about 3 feet high for composting (see Compost Compositions on page 34), and 18 inches for growing carrots, daikon radishes, or potatoes (see Part Four, page 221). Stake cylinders with three stakes or tent pegs. Line with wads of wet newspaper or underfelt up to the height you want to fill. Layer the bottom with wet newspaper, followed by pea straw, CMC, and straw mulch. Cylinders dry out quicker than ground soil, so don't forget watering.

WIRE TOWER

Form a 6-foot-high tower by bending a yard of open square mesh into a cylinder. The green plastic-coated type is best. Some wire has graded spaces, from narrow to wide. Wide spaces at the bottom of the cylinder allow hands in to cultivate. Secure the wire tower with one stake.

In spring, plant one squash inside the circle to ramble sideways, and six climbing beans around it. Or try romaine lettuce inside to shade two cucumber plants. Or pumpkin vines. After harvest, sow nasturtiums. In late winter, put in tall snow peas. Some garden centers sell wire towers for tomatoes.

Thinking Outside
the Magic Square

The SESONS

THINK SEASONALLY. Instead of assuming summer to be an ideal time for gardening because you like to be out in the sun, regard summer as a time to do little else but maintenance, feeding, mulching, and judicious watering. Prune away dead matter and remove spent plants, but remain aware that the main aim is to help your garden survive summer. It is not a time to plant unless you are given plants with big roots, for these are better off in the ground with a deep watering then waiting in a pot. Cuttings can be taken in summer to grow in a shadehouse, roses and lavender in summer, daisies and geraniums any time—all make excellent hedges around the food garden. Apart from puttering to keep you connected, read garden books, start a garden notebook, and make plans. Learn the habits of one or two vegetables and herbs in Part Four (page 221) for next season.

The gardening year really starts in early autumn. Plant shrubs and perennials to attract pest predators. Clear away spent plants, prune existing perennials and shrubs, and mark out a composting area. Set up compost bins (see Compost Compositions on page 34). Autumn is a good time to start a worm farm. Study the autumn list of vegetables in Part Four (page 225) and select what you want to eat in a few months' time. If all the plants in your square are spent, spread CMC and replant immediately.

Establish a Brassica Plot, an Onion and Garlic Plot, or a Stir-Fry Plot (see The Magic Square Plots on page 145). If an old plant is still forming seed, stake and work around it. Should you have more than one square, fork over plot after plot, apply CMC, and then plant. Position racks or cages to protect seedlings, and keep watering if no rain falls, even if there's dew. Within five or six weeks, you will eat the first pickings. Prepare a sheltered area (inside or outside, depending on the severity of your winters) to raise next summer's seedlings. My shadehouse (3 × 6 feet, with salvaged racks) is also the plant hospital, where dead sticks return to life, slow seeds germinate, and sick plants recover.

If you live in milder climes, such as the southern or northwestern states, the entire winter can be the busiest time for the gardener. In between rain showers, you are out in the fresh air preparing for spring, adding lime to acidic soil, planting shrubs, and pruning fruit trees and berries. After cleaning up, the compost is made and the previous batch turned. In mild winters, continue planting trees and shrubs so they can make use of good conditions.

Make an instant cold frame by bending a piece of reinforcing wire into a U-shape, folding plastic around it in such a way that you can open and close a front flap with a peg. Push the wire edges into the ground, place two bricks or pavers inside to capture the heat, and place seed containers on top of these. Don't forget to ventilate and water! Or, find a crate to cover with removable glass, or plastic sheeting on a stick to roll up on sunny days. Place it on black plastic to hold the heat. Use a cold frame to raise spring seedlings of vegetables needing a long growing season. For a hot frame, see Seeds and Seedlings (page 45).

Spring is the season of exuberance. Everything happens at once. That's why you did the preparatory work in autumn and winter. The weather goes from hot to cold and back again. Things want to grow but can't, or should but won't, yet trees and shrubs burst with buds and new leaves in thirty-seven shades of green. Crab apples and flowering plums are clouds of pink and white blossoms, and the orchard reveals daily miracles. Ani-

mals and insects wake from their winter sleep. In my garden, we are aware of snakes. They wake up on the first warm day and may decide to go for their first slither in the sun. I practically always wear boots in the garden, especially in hot weather. Snakes are part of our ecology, but we don't want to surprise them or be surprised by them, as snakes don't attack unless cornered or stepped upon.

Bugs and slugs may have crept into the cold frame. Remove all the containers once a week on a mild day and clean the inside of debris. Replace containers and water with LS to strengthen growth. Open the frame when the weather is warm, but always close up before dusk.

Press seeds of your favorite vegetables in containers of potting soil or seedling mix to keep the cold frame full. In its balmy atmosphere, many seeds can emerge within a week. Keep them growing with LS until they have four to six leaves. Don't plant out until danger of frost is over, but do plant potted plants you didn't get around to in winter. The rest of spring is taken up with weeding and mulching.

Start a Salad Plot now (page 147). Contemplate planting herbs. Take a look around the garden and see where you need to plug up a space or thicken a hedge. If you can't buy plants, this is another good time to take cuttings from perennials, while the sap is rising. Soak cuttings or "heels" in water with honey or a willow branch, to help root formation, then stick deep into a pot of soil in shade. If you have a superb white daisy bush, stick twenty to thirty cuttings in a Styrofoam box, feed with LS, and do a mass planting next autumn. If you love buddleia, the butterfly bush, take shoots and tips for a small buddleia forest. Mass plant your garden with beautiful hedges at no cost.

For years, I drove past a particular hillside vegetable garden. It always lay fallow in winter, was dug over in early spring, and not planted until late spring. But this unknown gardener knew what she was doing, for by the first day of summer, the vegetables in that garden stood as tall as mine. Gnash! They probably bought all those plants. . . .

There's the choice. By starting late, you avoid hordes of spring-born insect pests. Summer heat is advancing; nights are no longer cold. As long as you feed and water late seedlings, they may catch up on those raised early, but some may not get a long enough season.

These choices of when to grow major crops depend on your own rhythms, working patterns, and climate, or on whether you simply cannot wait after that first springy day struck you radiant in mid-March. If you have become an unstop-pable food gardener, you plant in spring as well as autumn and do progressive plantings through summer on cool days, or plant in the evenings to allow new plants to brace themselves for dawn. This way, you will have all the vegetables you need throughout the year. But it does require the patchwork method, planting in between maturing vegetables and seed-producing plants. Somehow, that takes care of crop rotation as well.

Summer comes around again, you have done those small jobs throughout the year, and the garden looks vastly different compared with last year. Should you live in a brushfire-prone area, remove dry grasses, clean gutters, and collect dead wood. Don't burn anything; there is enough air pollution and asthma already. Store wood for winter or pack a few bags for a relative. Dance on a heap of small twigs to make mulch, or compost them. Big pieces of wood shaped with an adze make natural borders for garden beds. Prune away dead wood on trees as high as you can reach, so that ground fires have no purchase on the trunks. Now, enjoy the results of your labor, and sit near a tree with a garden book amidst growth, colors, and birdsong.

A list of summer, winter, and all-season vegetables and herbs precedes their detailed descriptions in Part Four (see page 221).

CLIMATE, WEATHER, *and* MICROCLIMATE

SCIENTISTS ARE constantly readjusting predictions for the effects of human pollution on the world's climates. As gardeners, we must grapple with global warming, global dimming, evaporation rates, less or more rain, and ultraviolet rays. Where you live, it may become cooler and dimmer due to increased pollution fall-out. You may experience less or more rain, storms, droughts, or periodic floods. "May you live in interesting times," so goes the Chinese curse.

Relentless temperature increases of ocean waters have resulted in parts of the Great Southern Ocean being impassable for shipping due to floating ice. Surface melt of Greenland's ice sheet is even greater. The result is the steady rising of seawater levels everywhere. We already have a water crisis and a fauna- and flora-extinction crisis (that may rise to 50 percent of species) and can expect biodiversity collapse in some regions' near futures.[16]

More than half the world's ecosystems are about to collapse. Then, there is the underreported fact that the global female population has declined to 10 percent less than the male population through the termination of girl-baby pregnancies, female infanticide, and starvation of girl children in some countries. Females are food growers and nurturers.

So much for the bad news. There is a little good news named "microclimate."

As food gardeners, we rely on our understanding of regional and local climates. Your macroclimate may still be temperate or subtropical, with or without El Niño, but your microclimate is something else. After adding the peculiarities of your location—elevation, desert, river, forest, or seaside—the interesting phenomenon is that any number of gardens in the same macroclimate region may have different microclimates, and therefore different growing climates, depending on their surrounding gardens, built structures, trees, and aspects.

A garden in a suburb near sea level with all its built structures and trees may be easier to grow food in or more complex, depending on the ratio of trees to concrete. Gardens bordered by a park or reserve will have a different microclimate from the next street.

The beauty of a microclimate is that you can control some of it, whereas all you can do about your general location is plant trees with the neighbors and protest against logging. Anything you do to slow down global warming, climate change, and the effects of El Niño weather patterns is worth doing for future generations, but won't have much bearing on your food garden now.

You can influence your microclimate by manipulating details. When transplanting chilies into pots, create a favorable climate by doing it under a broad-brimmed hat to shade the little devils. Garden umbrellas save bean crops on scorching days. A length of shade cloth can be pulled as protection over a crop about to suffer sunstroke. In a cold snap, pack straw around root crops, fava beans, cabbages, and citrus trees. To protect against wind, erect a fence, screen, trellis, or fast-growing hedge of elderberry, artichokes, or fire-retardant agapanthus.

A body of water, however small, adds moisture to the atmosphere. At least fill up the birdbaths. A minute's hosing of the food plot makes a difference. Naturally, microclimate is first determined by the lay of the land, structures that block or tunnel sun and wind, and whether there are trees and shrubs to provide shelter and shade.

Observe your microclimate before laying out the food plot. If you locate the plot south of a row of newly planted trees, their roots will absorb water and soil nutrients, while dense shade can reduce your crops and prevent insects visiting for fertilization and pest control. On a sunny day, feel the heat bouncing off walls and fences, heat that could be a bonus to plants a yard away, but a killer to anything hard up against it. On windy days, test where the wind tunnels are in your garden, and don't plant your plot in their paths. But, remember that all plants need moving air, so utilize gentle breezes. Observe how much full sun, morning sun, or afternoon sun the area receives, remembering the sun is lowest in the sky in mid-winter, right overhead in mid-summer, and between these extremes in spring and autumn when you put in young vegetables.

Plan to create a more beneficial microclimate. Plant flowering shrubs for windbreaks and bird havens; they don't have to grow high to benefit vegetables. A shadehouse, bush house, or plastic tunnel not only houses delicate plants and seedlings but also provides four new possibilities. Grow heat-loving plants on the south side, lettuce on the north side, honeysuckle and pot herbs around an eastern entrance, and a hedge of strong plants on any side where ferocious winds hit: elderberry, crab apple, large daisies, wild plums, or goldenrod.

Any strong plant will do, but those with other uses are best.

Be aware that whatever you place in the garden—be it a tepee, birdbath, or table and chairs—changes the path of the wind, casts shade, and attracts perching birds. Your major success in creating a microclimate, beneficial to all types of fruit and vegetables, will come from how you plant your boundaries against the worst of weathers.

Just as you reshape your microclimate, so Planet Earth constantly reshapes the macroclimate. Coastal climates are moderated by warm ocean streams. Mountain ranges stop rain or provide snow melt. Volcanic activity destroys vegetation before creating new fertility. Wind and water constantly wear down the highest mountains and redistribute minerals across the valleys or carry them afar via creeks and rivers. Deserts march up or retreat. The whole amazing global fertility show is constantly shedding and adjusting to maintain some golden mean, which may well be what lies between those once prolific tropical rainforests either side of the equator and the two poles. Vast weather patterns do not stop at borders,

In a circular bed made with plastic water bottles, a tepee of wooden slats provides shade and shelter from the wind for climbing beans and other vegetables.

a change of season or hemisphere, until they have worked off their energy. When the Northern Hemisphere has a severe winter, it may be preceded or followed by a wet one in the Southern Hemisphere. If one hemisphere has a drought, the other is often sure to follow.

Climate is one thing, weather is another.

We used to think of climate as constant and weather as erratic. A weather pattern can afflict half the globe in one season. We see global droughts, floods and regional phenomena like El Niño and La Niña, and know we will be in for unusual weather events, although we may live far from the source. Continental weather of storms and rain patterns affects neighboring continents or islands. Eventually, when certain weather patterns become regular features, they turn into climate, that supposedly predictable phenomenon that rules our lives. Yet over time, climates can change considerably.

When summers turn cold or dry, food gardeners need to be stubborn. Fruit may not set, pumpkins hardly flower, tomato plants huddle. Even if you assiduously add manure, compost, water, and mulch, nothing grows well. Wildlife becomes desperate. Birds scratch mulches, lizards eat unripe tomatoes, possums dig for roots, and some unidentified creature removes hundreds of newly sown onion seeds, earning a tummy ache as well as bad breath! Rabbits may nibble suburban lawns. A mouse plague is likely. In such years, the harvest is miserable and even zucchinis fail to keep you supplied. Chard becomes the Great Standby, with kale, picked young.

You get one debacle or another, or two ganging up, but usually not all at once. But as times are unpredictable, it is wise to grow a variety of foods. One cold summer, we had good cabbages, quinces, and pears. The next spring came after a sunny, dry winter with frosts. When good spring rains arrived, the remaining cabbages, broccoli, and cauliflowers cried: "What's this? Rain? Never heard of it!" They took up the moisture all right, but soon one in every ten plants had a head full of aphids. Those were the weakest plants, out-competed for water and food by their relatives. Whereas I claim elsewhere that even the smallest brassica can suddenly decide to become a real cabbage, when it is aphid time, it's the runts that are attacked.

So you cannot wholly rely on charts telling you what you can grow in your climate. These are rough guidelines only. By becoming a food gardener now, you can make adjustments and invent methods that create a microclimate in which to survive the future. Macroclimate, microclimate, seasonal weather patterns, and your adjustments braid something unique together. This is where food gardening becomes as exciting as competitive sport—it's about having the edge on the odds.

Never garden in a mood of wanting to control everything. Observe nature's ways. Don't be quick to interfere when things grow in unexpected ways—there may be reasons. Patient gardeners discover out-of-season surprises, such as ripe pumpkins in winter. Fruit tree seedlings may spring up from the compost. Wait a year or so, and perhaps they'll become disease-resistant plants that bear unexpectedly good fruit true to type. Let nature take over a little—become her assistant. Feed and mulch where soil looks exhausted, and hand water to stay in touch with what grows where.

PERMACULTURE

PERMACULTURE IS a system devised by Bill Mollison and David Holmgren, and was first launched in Tasmania in 1980. Permaculture is aptly named as it strives to create agricultural and horticultural systems that become self-perpetuating. Human ingenuity blossoms in permaculture set-ups, and no two are alike, although there are now many properties and gardens in North America being run on permaculture principles. Permaculture embraces not only the food garden, orchard, and livestock but also birds, insects, surrounding gardens, land management, integrated functions of houses and outbuildings, and the use of people's time and energy.

There are permaculture books, courses, consultants, and open days. Permaculture is being exported to countries that need more sustainable agricultural methods to encourage food gardeners to stay clear of artificial fertilizers that ruin their soils and GM seed companies that deprive them of control over their own seed production. Bill Mollison has been tirelessly spreading permaculture principles in Africa and Asia, while those who have learned from him and David Holmgren have fanned out through the Pacific and Southeast Asia as far as Afghanistan.

Permaculture is about closed cycles in which each component aids the others. It means that if you grow something to provide mulch and food for animals, who then give manure to put around fruit trees and vegetables, and the cycle is sustainable, you have a closed cycle. For most home gardeners, this means kitchen scraps going to chickens that lay eggs and produce manure for vegetables and fruits that produce more scraps. In dwellings, it is about trapping heat in winter and excluding it in summer by using the orientation of windows, attached greenhouses, and slate floors to retain warmth, the angles of roof overhangs, solar and wind technology, and water management systems.

Another tiny closed cycle is created by excluding chemical sprays and instead running chickens in a fenced orchard to control pests where they scratch for insects, eat fallen fruit, and lay bonus eggs. If you have more land than one garden, grow the little amount of wheat the flock needs and exchange it for manure mixed with soil and straw from their run. Use this on vegetable plots or in compost to grow fruits, herbs, and vegetables of which the chickens get the peelings.

The closed cycle principle goes as far as the universe stretches, but you can attempt closed cycles in an ordinary backyard. Compost bins, worm farms, food production, pond life, energy, graywater disposal—all these fit on a suburban block and further your self-reliance.

If you have acres, you might be interested in land contours, wind and weather, and how to preserve and improve your piece of the planet and make the best use of it. Borrow a permaculture book from the library for a feast of ideas useful to your future. Put your thinking cap on as to how permaculture designs can apply to your patch of earth or your patio or balcony, and sketch your ideas on the back of an envelope.

POSTSCRIPT: In 2016, the first-ever Graduate Certificate in Permaculture Design course will be launched by Central Queensland University through a distance education program, but including fieldwork in two locations.

EASY VEGETABLES *to* GROW

PEOPLE IN full-time jobs have barely time on mild evenings and weekends to enjoy their gardens and food plots. People working at home can take their lunch breaks in the garden. Saving time by not commuting, they could spend ten to twenty minutes daily doing small jobs and picking the night's meal. Refreshed, they work better in the afternoon. Retirees and those mostly at home for other reasons, will soon find the food plot becomes their first destination each morning for a good intake of fresh air and a noseful of fragrances. These three groups have different needs their food plots must meet.

Here are suggestions for crops suitable in a small food plot, to be adjusted by your taste, time, and passion.

GROUP ONE: FULL-TIME WORKERS, VERY PART-TIME FOOD GARDENERS

Grow open-headed lettuces, perennial sorrel and spinach, Swiss chard, Siberian kale (Red Russian), and broccoli. These can produce for six months, any season, but sorrel mainly in spring and summer. In summer, grow well-mulched potatoes, pumpkins, green beans, one zucchini or one cucumber or one mini-squash (tiny but prolific), one tomato, and open-headed lettuces. Plant one rhubarb crown. Plant parsley and let it seed itself. Plant your three favorite culinary herbs in a box. In autumn, plant two boxes with garlic. This is a low-maintenance, long-lasting growing pattern that will provide countless quick, flavorful, fresh meals. Remember to water regularly and douse with liquid seaweed twice a month. Easy!

GROUP TWO: PEOPLE WORKING FROM HOME, VISITING THE FOOD PLOT FOR BREAKS

In autumn, plant broad beans, snow peas, broccoli, kale, and salad greens. In spring, plant cucumbers, eggplants, bell peppers, broccoli, mulched potatoes, one each of mini-squash, zucchini, tomato, rhubarb, and a few pumpkin vines. Plant parsley. Plant half a dozen culinary herbs: oregano, thyme, and a rosemary bush; and for herbal tea: lemon balm, sage, and tarragon. Or the other way around! Sow marigolds (*Calendula officinalis*) between vegetables. Dry some flowers and store the orange petals for a festive touch in rice pilaf, pasta, crumbles, cakes, and biscuits.

GROUP THREE: RETIRED OR HOUSE-BOUND PEOPLE, LEISURE GARDENERS

Plant French beans and peas in spring and broad beans and snow peas in autumn. Plant enough dark green vegetables for a daily feed, as these boost your immune system and keep your eyes, blood, and brain healthy: Swiss chard, kale, giant mustard, broccoli (stir-fry the leaves), spinach, cabbage, beets (sauté the leaves). Sow carrots, rutabagas, onions (eat green straps), and garlic. A Florence fennel can be grown for the bulb and for fragrant fern to pick as an herb. Sow parsley in the soil and your favorite three herbs in a box. Also keep a pot of mint on a saucer, for pep-up mint sauce and tea.

Easy vegetables are those growing in winter, as rain is the best water supply for plants. Days are often sunny and nights cool. All vegetables hate heat waves, often going to seed, but many love growing in winter—check seed packets. Many insects are dormant until spring. Snails and slugs overwinter, but are easily collected. Seedlings are sown or planted in autumn while the soil is still warm, before wintry weather sets in with the possibility of frost.

Of the three divisions of vegetables: the leafy greens, the fruiting crops, and the root crops, the low-maintenance ones are:

- Leafy greens: Kale, leeks, spinach, Swiss chard, arugula, open-hearted lettuces, Asian greens, dill, cilantro, parsley.

- Fruiting crops: Broad beans, broccoli, cabbage, cauliflower, peas, cucumbers, pumpkins, squashes.

- Root crops: Beets, carrots, garlic, onions, radishes, rutabagas.

A healthy choice is unavoidable. If your favorite vegetables aren't there, it is probably because they are summer vegetables. If your soil is heavy, make a light, sandy soil mix in a deep banana box for carrots.

The easiest summer vegetables, sown or planted in spring, are:

- Leafy greens: Asian greens, kale, mustards, perennial spinaches, Swiss chard, perennial wild arugula, open-hearted lettuces, parsley.

- Fruiting crops: Eggplants, green beans, bell peppers, chilies, cucumbers, pumpkins, squashes, tomatoes. Overwinter eggplants, bell peppers, and chili plants in pots and plant out again next spring. A potted tomato can ripen indoors when winter strikes early.

- Root crops: Beets, carrots, radishes, rutabagas.

Vegetables grow in either or all seasons, but winter vegetables have dependable growth due to lack of scorching heat. Summer vegetables may bolt to seed early and have to be re-sown several times for continuous crops. This depends on your microclimate and the weather in any particular year. You will learn quickly what works and what doesn't in your plot. Adjust your planting next year.

There is an endless variety of vegetables in the three groups to experiment with, so plant one experimental crop each season. If an experiment doesn't succeed, all you have lost is some seed. Although there is no saying the seed would do better next year, you may as well give it a try, but don't let it take up space in the plot. Put it in a pot. If it germinates strongly, you can transplant seedlings.

Take photos before and after each season. Keep prints in a special food garden album. You'll be surprised when you look back in a few years at early snapshots of the bare beginnings of a food garden that has been sustaining you ever since.

SAVING SEED

Open-**POLLINATED SEED** is seed that has been grown with the aid of bees and insects in the open and will breed true to type, unless several so-called promiscuous species of the same family grow close together and the bees cross-pollinate one with the other. Familiarize yourself with the chapter on vegetable groups in Part Four (page 222) and either grow one variety per season, or space members of the same family wide apart in the garden to avoid cross-pollination and reaping seed producing a "cukin" or "pumpcumber!" If your only square is full of brassicas, cut the flower heads off all but the one you want to grow seed from. Cook all brassica flower heads as broccoli or in stir-fries. Learn more about cross-pollination from the Seed Savers Exchange (see Useful Addresses on page 317).

Saving your own seed is highly recommended because seeds grown in the conditions of your garden will do best when replanted there. Seed saving allows you to sow thickly—see Chard and *Brassica juncea* in Part Four, pages 243 and 236—and keeps open-pollinated varieties viable in your district as you share seeds with friends and neighbors. Sometimes, seed saving leads to self-seeding so that new plants come up in their own good time in the plot or compost.

The general rule for saving seed is to let pods and seed heads dry on the stalks. This enables seeds to take up all the goodness of the dying plant. You then cut off the seed, place it in a paper bag, and hang it in a dry, dark place for a few weeks. After this, you can harvest the seed from the pods or casings and store it in airtight, screw-top jars or plastic containers kept in a dark, dry, and cool place.

Reduce any humidity in seed containers with silica gel packets saved from vitamin bottles or photographic equipment. Humidity is a great spoiler of otherwise viable seed, either destroying or reducing the duration of its viability.

Don't keep seeds in the shed, for sheds get hot. Total seed-saving buffs keep their seed in glass jars in the bottom of the fridge. Find a shelf in the coolest room of the house for your precious seed collection, the food of the future. Use a closet shelf, for your seeds are more valuable than your clothes. Inside the door, pin a timetable of when to plant what. Also store seed catalogs here and a book on companion planting. Spread it all out on the bed for action.

When my beans start to bean, I tie a bit of red yarn around the fattest, longest beans, so that I don't pick those for the pot. These seed beans dry off with the plant. Red yarn also marks my best sweet corn cob.

When carrots wave strong, green ferns, indicating that the roots are ready for pulling, save the strongest, pushing a tall stick alongside it. Tie it up when it grows a stalk and let that one produce seed. Carrots flower like Queen Anne's lace, attracting beneficial insects by the thousands. Let the large flower heads dry until they are full of tiny, disc-like seeds. Further dry the heads indoors, then shake out in a bowl, and store.

All the brassica family (see Part Four on page 222) produce prolific tiny, round, black, or brown seeds in pods ½ to 1 inch long. Hang the pods in paper bags to dry. Only radish seeds are bigger. To plant radishes, break open the pods to release the seed. The others have to be winnowed, best done on a windless day. After a few weeks' drying, transfer one type of seed stalk at a time (like kale) to a pillowcase. Slap the pillowcase from left to right on a table or hard surface to break the pods. Soon you will have seeds and chaff. Go to the vegetable garden and stand beside a plot where you don't mind

a few self-seeded kales and take handfuls of empty pods from the bag, spreading them on the plot. The seeds will remain at the bottom of the pillowcase because they are heavier. Next, empty the pillowcase's contents onto a tea tray with a rim and blow gently across the tray, holding it above the plot. The chaff will blow off while the seed remains. A few seeds may jump down to take their chances. Shake the tray gently from side to side to separate seed from chaff between blowings. This is one of my favorite harvesting operations. You end up with fairly clean seed to store; it will be viable for several years. Winnow all seed above the same plot for a carefree escapee's Stir-Fry Plot (page 167)!

The cucurbit family of pumpkins, squashes, melons, and cucumbers have large seeds. Leave one fruit on the vine until the vine dries up. Open the fruit and scrape out the seed; wash and dry thoroughly before storing. Easiest are the pumpkins. Select your biggest, handsomest pumpkin, and when it looks ripe enough to eat, the seed is mostly viable

Refresh your stock annually or whenever possible.

after drying. A spell in the fridge may improve it. The other cucurbits are messier.

Even seeds from the pyramids have been germinated in the 20th century, but generally, there's no point keeping cucurbit seed for more than a couple of years.

Once you have a well-stocked seed bank, and not before, use old seed to grow a dense green crop on a vacant plot and dig it in. Or, let it grow and eat it. Or, save new seed from it.

Saving Your Own Seed and the Law

United States farmers are aware of the Plant Variety Protection Act of 1970 (PVPA) and Plant Patent Act of 1930 (PPA). Under these regulations, seed companies hold patents on seeds they claim to have improved, and farmers pay a series of levies to keep PVPA and PPA operating so that they may have access to the improved seeds. Growers are not allowed to share seed grown from these improved seeds with neighbors or other growers, as this violates the intellectual property rights of the seed company that owns the patent for the improved seed sold to the farmer. To assure future sales, global seed companies have created "terminator seed," which produces plants that cannot procreate. This com-pels farmers to buy new seed from the seed company each year. Presently, there is still a worldwide moratorium on ter-minator seed technology (see The Ter-rifying Importance of Growing Food on page 2).

Until the 1980s, there were some 7,000 small seed companies, each mak-ing a living from less than 1 percent of the market. Then, the first shadows of genetically modified and engineered seeds fell on this pastoral trade. Chemi-cal companies moved in to buy out these small traders. The aim was to produce value-added seed, sold with its own par-ticular fertilizer and pesticide. Once patents were taken out on these new seeds (mainly of commodities, like corn, soy, and canola), a seed company would control a part of the food-supply chain.

Before 1980, seeds were a universally free gift from Mother Earth that farm-ers and gardeners shared, swapped, and passed on to improve crops by select-ing future seed from their best plants. This was the world's best insurance to preserve biodiversity in food plants and avoid species collapse. Suddenly, seeds of important commodity crops that feed billions of people are owned by a company who controls what can and what cannot be done with them. In the hands of GM companies like Monsanto, DuPont, and Syngenta, "improved" seeds have become genetically modified or engineered seeds. As of 2007, these three companies held 44 percent of the global seed market, with one fifth in Monsanto's lap. The sale of transgenic seeds and traits made up almost 75 percent of Monsanto's 2007 profits.

The sharing of patented seed is now called piracy, even if the wind or a bird deposits it into your field. The US, Canada, and Australia have seen hundreds of prosecutions against farmers, including the bizarre prosecution in Canada of farmer Percy Schmeiser, onto whose land had blown some genetically engineered canola seeds from a neighboring farm, which then germinated. In the 1990s, he was saving his own seed and growing it on, whereupon Monsanto's seed police detected he was growing their particular brand of GE canola and was therefore guilty of patent infringement. Farmer Schmeiser claimed to know nothing of this seed but was convicted, and the seed company won that day in court. The Canadian Supreme Court's decision in favor of Monsanto in 2004 was followed by some ninety US farmers being similarly sued. Percy Schmeiser now travels the world for the cause of farmers' rights. Injustice makes activists out of people who just wanted to farm in peace.

Prior to 1987, when the debate over plant breeders' rights raged, it was feared that home gardeners would be prosecuted if they shared seeds with neighbors. It initially appeared to be the intention that all commercial seed would eventually fall under PVPA and PPA and hence were likely to become "value-added," with more pesticides to contaminate more soils, rivers, and ground water.[17] Organic growing with organically raised seeds is the only alternative.

When the PVPA was introduced, some people questioned whether the seed companies claiming these rights had paid royalties to the original owners of the seed they started with, meaning those farmers who had grown that seed or plant for generations through the ages. It appears that's not how it is done. One apparently goes to a third-world country and acquires plants and/or seeds cheaply and easily. One takes them home, alters them, and then markets them under PVPA or PPA laws (or the equivalent laws of the country in question) as new and improved seed burdened with intellectual property rights incurring fines when violated. The international seed industry is waging a global campaign to have all farm-saved seed declared illegal or subject to government royalties. Should they succeed, home gardeners may well be affected.[18] It is probably only a matter of time

The good news may be that on June 29, 2004, the International Treaty on

Plant Genetic Resources for Food and Agriculture became an international law. The Food and Agriculture Organization (FAO) described it as "vital in ensuring the continued availability of the plant genetic resources that countries will need to feed their people." This should preserve a greater variety of food plants and genetic diversity so necessary to keep intact the web of life that sustains humanity.[19] It looked as if the FAO recognized that having the world's seeds in the hands of just a few companies is a recipe for worldwide famine. The bad news is that the FAO didn't seem able to stop a new law in Iraq, as part of US reconstruction, that prohibits Iraqi farmers saving their own seeds, compelling them to buy seeds protected by PVPA from a US-based corporation that operates under "no competition" conditions. This could indicate that the genetic seed sources the FAO protects may not necessarily be preserved for the people who protected these resources for an untold number of generations. Ironically, the FAO had estimated in 2002 that 97 percent of Iraqi farmers, whose ancestors were the first farmers ever to grow and improve wheat, saved their own seed. Now most of these wheat varieties may soon be lost forever. It could be that the FAO's agenda is similar to the World Trade Organization's (WTO) push to make member governments adopt PVPA laws aimed at government control over all food seed sources.

The 2006 United Nations Convention on Biological Diversity's meeting in Spain debated lifting the moratorium on terminator seed technology, urged by the governments of Australia, US, New Zealand, and others. Brazil and India, on the other hand, have national prohibitions on terminator seed technology in place.[20] In March 2006, the UN Convention on Biological Diversity met again in Brazil and upheld the moratorium on terminator seed technology until the next meeting in 2008. "This is a momentous day for the 1.4 billion people worldwide who depend on farmer-saved seeds," said Francisca Rodriguez of Via Campesina, a world-wide movement of peasant farmers. "Terminator seeds are a weapon of mass destruction and an assault on our food sovereignty."[21]

During a 1992 summit for indigenous peoples held in Rio de Janeiro, the right of indigenous farmers over their crop genes was formalized, recognizing farmers' sovereignty over biological resources. More action is constantly required to make it work globally, but some countries have installed their own laws to protect indigenous seed.[22]

Indigenous seed may be easier to acknowledge than indigenous people when it comes to growing crops. Less than 4 percent of the world population is indigenous in the sense that anthropologists understand it, and most of them have lost their lands, so they are no longer growing food. Then, there are millions of people who were dispersed centuries ago, resettled elsewhere, and are living off the land. Obviously, they have developed local crop varieties. Even I, a rank immigrant from a tribe of migrants covering the five continents, developed a new variety of radish in my forest garden. Vegetable and fruit growers who put the better parts of their lives into working the soil they happen to live on, are, in my book, "indigenous" for the purpose of claiming rights over their biological resources.

Knowing all this, it's no wonder those who opposed the Plant Variety Rights Act and the Plant Breeder's Rights Act in Australia in the 1980s claimed that seeds were nature's gift to everyone, that nobody could own them, that all humanity had a right to use them to grow plants, especially food and medicinal plants, those that big companies want to monopolize. Patenting seeds is like patenting the air we must breathe, or taxing the rain that falls on our gardens.

Therefore, while these debates rage on about who has rights to seeds and who has not, be on the safe side, obtain heirloom variety seeds, grow them, and set up your own little seed bank. Learning from those who have gone before can, in this case, save our seed and food resources from being modified away by dollar-hungry corporations who take out contestable patents, have in-house lawyers to argue their cases, and don't mind spending a few million for a conviction to keep small growers cowed. Remember that few of the corporate managers have any innate knowledge or understanding of the art of growing food and preserving seeds. They are simply managers and may have started in the manufacturing of cars or cheese or basketball shoes. Those markets became saturated so they looked for other products to develop, and hey, people will always need food grown from seeds. So they hired scientists and financial wizards who, between them, came up with a plan to corner one or another crop in the world market. It's happened to coffee, it's happened to tea, it's happened to soybeans. They now have their eyes on broccoli.

From GARDEN *to* TABLE

ONE GREAT delight in my circle of friends is the "peasant lunch," a term we adopted to cover all probabilities and eventualities when serving an entirely home-grown meal. We sat around campfires in the earlier years, eating revolting communal stews concocted from tinned food brought by members of the archaeological team we worked with. No wonder we became foodies in later years, savoring the purest of foods, slowly and carefully prepared.

My early peasant lunches consisted of whatever vegetables and fruits were in season and dishes made with goose, duck, or chicken eggs. I might have bought cheese and cream, or added olives from a crate bought at the market and pickled annually.

Gradually, peasant lunches translated into meals from other cultures, using authentic recipes. Over the years, we have savored flavors from China (soy, spring rolls), India (chai, *paneer, laddhu*), Tibet (*tsampa, momos,* butter tea), Bali (chili, cilantro), Korea (pickles, roasted sesame seed), and the Middle East (salted lemons, almond mousse). Everyone contributes, often with no more organization than each person bringing a different course. Sometimes, a meal consists of starters, soup, salad, side dish, and dessert, omitting a main dish. And we have a wish list of countries whose cuisines we have yet to try in our super-mature years, when excellent food becomes the primary joy of life.

Fortunately, all great cuisines are based on peasant food and home-grown and farmers' market produce. We found that Korean cuisine uses the same seeds, spices, sesame oil, and rice vinegar for almost every vegetable, yet each dish tastes different. In Malaysia, just about everything is made with rice flour. For some cuisines, we buy new ingredients, but mostly we rely on our gardens and markets to travel the world at our table. Needless to say, the wines are local, although we went to some lengths to make Tibetan butter tea and Indian chai.

For everyday cooking, I lean on recipe books for the volume of green-leaf vegetables I dish up. Books can be found that deal mainly with antioxidant open-leaf vegetables, those that help fight cancer and heart disease, and which include many of the brassica family. Instead of

Eight carrots from 4 square inches!

The same carrots, washed up and ready for the table.

using greens as a garnish, a gesture, or a display bed for meat and fish, such recipes feature green vegetables as the main ingredient. In many cultures, most parts of the vegetable are used to make tasty salads, soups, and main dishes. One advocate for home growing, Mark Bittman, points out in his book *Leafy Greens* that leafy greens are easier to grow, have fewer pests than other vegetables, can

be started earlier, will last longer, and many will grow throughout the year in temperate climates.

Have I mentioned pride? Well, no. Pride in produce is ultimately due as praise for Planet Earth, for providing the raw ingredients for us to grow and place the very finest food on our tables. Humble food is undeniably the best-tasting food. Bon appétit.

ESSENTIAL UTENSILS

ANY VEGETABLE can be cooked on the stovetop, and many can be eaten raw, but with a few gadgets, you can get a lot more out of home-grown produce. Food gardens have times of overproduction. With a blender, a juicer, and a wok, you manage these times without waste. Buy during the sales and save dollars, or buy a combined blender-juicer, a cheap little machine giving years of service.

A blender enables you to make delicious soups, chutneys, and sauces with vegetables, fruits, and herbs. Experiment with blended, spiced-up cold cucumber or zucchini soups, apple and rosemary chutney, and fresh tomato sauce—simple additions to meals that you will not be without once tried.

A juicer is terrific when fruit ripens in the span of two weeks. Store unblemished apples and quinces on newspaper, in a dark, cool place. Bruised ones are best steamed, sauced, and juiced. I love that time of year when we drink glasses of fresh juice, concentrated goodness toning up the body.

People with cancer and those with digestive problems are often advised to drink vegetable juices. Why wait until you are ill? My favorite summer vegetable juice recipe is Cabbage Ribs and Co. Pick six big cabbage leaves, stripping the greenery for a stir-fry or chicken food. Cut lengthwise one large carrot and half a zucchini. Push cabbage ribs, carrot, and zucchini through the juicer with a knob of fresh ginger and a quartered apple. Or, add lemon or orange. You can use overproducing zucchinis at the rate of one every two days just by juicing.

The wok is a splendid invention from China, where it sits in a hole atop a brick stove. To use it on gas or electric stoves, buy a wok ring to steady it. Woks are for stir-fries, and stir-fries are for times of overproduction or underproduction, when a little of everything is enjoyed with rice or pasta, chutney or sauce.

Take a bowl and go for a walk around your Magic Square (or squares). Pick bits of everything, plus onion greens and a handful of mixed herbs. In the kitchen, wash, strip, chop, and divide all into bowls according to firmness. Assuming you have garlic and fresh ginger on hand, sauté these with onion in olive oil over fairly high heat. Pour in a little water or vegetable stock to create a steam cloud. Add the

Wok time: young broccoli, giant red mustard, beans, and zucchinis.

firmest vegetable, toss one minute, then the next firmest, toss, and so on, leaving tender greens till last. Add a squirt of soy sauce. Add chutney, sauces, grated cheese, or spices, and either cooked rice or pasta, for a very repeatable meal.

A spice grinder is another handy kitchen utensil, so useful for home-grown seeds of coriander, fennel, fenugreek, and dill—oh, the aroma! Or, get a cheap mortar and pestle from the Asian grocer and use elbow grease. Save brown paper bags and old pillowcases to dry spice seeds before threshing and grinding. Bring fragrance back into your life.

CUPBOARD SELF-SUFFICIENCY

CUPBOARD SELF-SUFFICIENCY is a natural companion to self-sufficiency from your square plot. By combining the produce of your square with the contents of a dry-foods cupboard, you will find it easy to prepare tasty meals of high nutritional value. Presently, we still enjoy the luxury of having a choice of imported and local grains, legumes, spices, and dried foods. Buy dry foods each time you shop. In the not-so-long run, you save money. You could stay at home for a month and never visit a shop for anything. And you can plant bought seeds and beans to grow and eat fresh, then dry the surplus.

Easy Party Dip

Cook chickpeas or orange lentils till soft, drain, and mash. Chop a large onion into a juicy pulp and stir through legumes. Mix in a tablespoon of paprika, taste, and add more, as needed. Thin down with yogurt. Serve with corn chips.

Garam Masala

For Indian curries, buy ready-made garam masala or mix your own from ground cardamom, coriander, cumin, cinnamon, cloves, nutmeg, ginger, fennel, fenugreek, black or white pepper, turmeric, and dried chilies. Store in a jar. For fresh garam masala, dry-fry seeds of cardamom, coriander, cumin, fennel, fenugreek, and mustard until they pop. Keep the lid on the pan. Mash in a mortar with drizzled oil, adding the other ground spices. Use fresh.

Chai Tea

Make your own chai—spicy Indian tea. In a glass jar, stir 3 tablespoons of cinnamon, a tablespoon each of ground coriander and ginger, a teaspoon of ground cardamom, and half a teaspoon each of five-spice and turmeric. Vary by using aniseed, clove, fennel, or nutmeg. In India, tea is boiled with milk, sugar, and a heaped spoon of this mixture, but you can just add a teaspoon to the pot with the usual amount of tea and pour on boiling water. Good to chase away a headache.

Mushrooms

Mushrooms are a healthy addition to any meal. Grow them yourself in a commercial mushroom box, buy fresh, or go for affordable dried mushrooms. Try varieties in small packets, as some can cause havoc with your personal plumbing. When you know which suit you, buy a humungous pack at a lower price. To use, boil fiftenn to twenty minutes, then slice and fry.

Shiitake mushrooms—also known as winter mushrooms or *dong gwoo* in Cantonese—recommended for people with cancer, are available dried, looking like small potatoes bursting out of their skins. Soak them for ten minutes in warm water, slice, and cook with vegetables. If you worry about what is in meat these days, replace it with small amounts of tofu, mushrooms, and beans. Freeze tofu overnight before use, as this opens the pores to other flavors.

Legumes

The food value of peas, beans, and lentils is so great that if you make it a habit to add them to meals three times a week, you'll soon find yourself turning away from less-nutritious foodstuffs and saving money. Beans come in all colors and consistencies. The softest are lima beans, which are good with homemade tomato sauce, but most brown and red beans will cook soft after a soak. Brown lentils go with almost anything. Fry small orange lentils raw until crisp before adding to pasta and rice.

The versatile chickpea—supplying protein, iron, and vitamin C—makes great patties, hummus, dips, and fill for soups and stir-fries. Soak chickpeas overnight, cook until soft, and make delicious chickpea salad with a blended sauce of garlic, olive oil, lemon juice, and a crumbed slice of bread. Add arugula, parsley, mint, and ground rosemary, and top with sliced tomatoes.

Buy dried fava beans to make your own falafel, if you can't grow enough. The hardest beans to cook are soybeans. After overnight soaking in just-boiled water, they need a long cooking time in fresh water. But plant them and you harvest fresh green soybeans called edamame, as gourmet as young fava beans and delivering all the benefits of soy. Store-bought soy products should be labeled as to whether they are GM-free or not.

Invest in a batch of fermented black beans to use sparingly in stir-fries or rice dishes. No cooking needed, and they keep well.

Reduce cooking time of beans and legumes by placing them in the freezer for a day. After soaking beans overnight, drain and rinse, boil vigorously in fresh water for ten minutes, then simmer till soft. Add pinches of aniseed, caraway, or fennel to the water to counteract flatulence.

Green mung beans sprout easily. Sprouted beans multiply their food value a hundredfold and can take the place of vegetables when your square is bare. Steep 1 to 2 tablespoons of mung beans in hot water and soak overnight, then rinse, pour into a glass jar, and cover with cheesecloth secured with a rubber band. Keep near the kitchen tap. Rinse and drain through the cloth several times a day. Soon, the beans begin to sprout. Kids love to rinse and watch them. After a few days, start adding them to salads, soups, stir-fries, pastas, and rice. Use as a sandwich filling with chutney or tahini for a fresh, crunchy snack. Start a new batch for a continuous supply. Try sprouting other beans and seeds: alfalfa, buckwheat, or fenugreek for curried sprouts.

Tasty Dhal

Rice and legumes combined are more nutritious than if eaten separately. One billion Indians can't be wrong eating rice, dhal, and vegetables daily. The incomplete protein of legumes becomes complete when combined with a grain.

For a tasty dhal, fry a cup of orange lentils in oil until lightly browned. Add 3 cups of water and bring to a boil. Chop garlic and onion to simmer along with it. Separately dry-fry on low heat pinches of seeds of cardamom, coriander, cumin, fennel, fenugreek, and mustard until they stop popping under the lid. Pound spices. Sauté chopped ginger, chilies, and ground turmeric and add to the lentils. When dhal is soft, add fried spices. Serve with rice, vegetables, and sliced cucumbers in yogurt.

An unripe pumpkin harvested with its last desperate flower after the vine shriveled up. It made a decent pumpkin soup with lentils and spices.

Oma's Haybox

My *oma* (grandmother) cooked in a haybox to save on gas. A haybox cooks rice, beans, and stews while you do other things. I have a lidded wooden box, painted ochre to double service as a rustic table or cushioned seat. It measures 20 × 20 × 15 inches. If you have a lidded box, fill six pillowcases with hay, padding bottom and sides, keeping one to place on the cooking pot. Spread newspaper on the table or floor. Bring beans, rice, or stew to a boil on the stove. With rice, wait until there is only water in the dimples of the rice. Whip the boiling pot onto the newspaper, wrap tightly, place in haybox, and cover with hay pillow. Close the lid and don't look for three hours. It keeps it hot for longer, even all day. You can also cook in bed! Place the pot in newspaper wrappings in a bed and pile pillows and blankets on top.

Flours

On the flour shelf, you will find besan, or chickpea flour, suitable for people on a gluten-free diet. It tastes nutty and is used for all floury purposes; for the self-raising kind, just add a pinch of baking soda or baking powder. Use it for sauces, tempura, and dumpling batter, or mix with rice flour (great for cakes) for a tasty pancake. In Indian cooking, besan is used in homemade sweets. Making *laddhu*, my very favorite confectionery, takes time, stirring continuously for 15 minutes, but lets you meditate on the amazing properties of chickpea flour as it metamorphoses spectacularly under your spellbound gaze.

For Italian dinners, buy polenta. Boil in water or vegetable stock, stirring constantly. Make it thick (2 cups of liquid to 1 cup of polenta) to set in a foil-lined form. Cool and turn out as a loaf, then cut in slices to grill or bake with olive oil. Serve with goat cheese, olives, and arugula, or with casseroles of tomatoes, bell peppers, and mushrooms. The ways of serving polenta are as numerous as cooks. You can do the same sort of things with couscous. Consult Moroccan recipes for combinations.

Sago

Sago is your next purchase. I knew a sago expert in Papua New Guinea, and am ashamed to admit I laughed on hearing he was off to a sago conference in Manila. How ignorant I was. Sago is the staple food for millions of people in Southeast Asia and Melanesia. I have eaten it fried as crisp pancakes, cooked with vegetables, and smoked in bamboo over a coconut-shell fire. All most satisfying. Sago has little flavor, but plenty of texture to combine with strong flavors. A friend recently revived the recipe for lemon sago. So simple it hardly needs a recipe, it became our favorite palate-cleansing dessert.

Sago swells to many times its dry state, so be prudent! Soak half a cup of sago balls overnight in 3 cups cold water with the zest of one lemon. Keep the lemon in the fridge. The next day, bring sago to a boil. Add the juice of the lemon, or two or three lemons, depending on how strong you like it. Aim for a consistency of thick porridge. Add small amounts of water, if needed. When sago balls turn glassy, taste. When soft enough to chew, add half a cup of white sugar and stir to dissolve, but don't drown the lemon tang in sugar. Pour into a bowl rinsed with cold water, cool, and then refrigerate. A marvelous dessert for people on diets. You can also make this recipe using oranges.

Grains

Buy brown and basmati rice in large bags. They taste nutty. I buy imported rice because Australian rivers can't sustain rice cultivation, but this may be different where you live. If your home is not mouse-proof, buy strong plastic, lidded buckets, or use a new rubbish bin. Also stock up on noodles. Rice noodles for the no-wheat lobby. Thick, thin, and hair-thin.

Pearl barley is a fine filler for vegetable soups and making barley water for upset tummies. At one time, no kitchen cupboard was without pearl barley, but pre-cooked grains sent it into exile. Roast organic barley in the oven and grind it to make tsampa, a staple food of Himalayan mountain people. Brew strong black Chinese tea with salt and butter or ghee, and stir into a bowl of roasted barley. A truly exceptional taste experience, and so sustaining. Grow your own organic barley on several Magic Squares.

Somewhere near the barley, you should find coconut milk powder for stir-fries and curries. Small luxuries go a long way. Also look for a packet of miso for nourishing soups. Miso is commonly made from soybeans or rice. Miso bouillon with finely cut herbs and onion greens is delicious.

Stock up on dried fruit and nuts for snacks, pilafs, cakes, and breads. Raisins, figs, dates, walnuts, and almonds can change plain dishes into festive food.

Have a wonderful time shopping the slow food way! The slowest of dry foods has to be soaked the night before—half a minute's work. Next morning, rinse off and pop in the fridge until you get home that night ready to cook. The quickest dry food is putting some almonds through a grinder, or toasting sesame seeds to sprinkle over freshly roasted vegetables. Your dry food supply waits in the cupboard for when you need it. Open the door and invent new combinations.

PART 3

THE MAGIC SQUARE PLOTS

A **NOTE** *on the* **MAGIC SQUARE PLOTS**

THE **3-FOOT SQUARE PLOTS** are graded according to the ease with which the plants grow in temperate climates. Salad plots start the list because lettuces, chives, and radishes are quick and easy to grow. These are followed by the Fava Bean Plot in autumn to give copious results for little work, while putting nitrogen back into the soil. Gradually, the plots get a little more complex and varied. Add or delete vegetables as you go.

If you are an apartment or condominium dweller, a few boxes on the balcony or patio will allow you to plant most plots in this book on an even smaller scale. A square plot translates into approximately four to five boxes. Boxes dry out quickly, so push them together and pack wet towels or newspapers around their sunny side in hot weather. Or, put up an umbrella during hours of blazing sunlight, or invest in a sun screen for you and your greens.

While your Salad Plot is growing, read Part Two (page 23) if you skipped it and make yourself familiar with the essential list of abbreviations on page xiv.

THE SALAD PLOTS

ALL MENTIONED salad vegetables and herbs are discussed individually in the List of Common Vegetables and the List of Common Herbs in Part Four (page 221). Varieties of lettuce are discussed under Lettuce; radicchio and endive have separate entries; see also Salad Greens.

Salad Plots are discussed in detail, because they are probably the ones you grow most often. Almost all green leaf vegetables mentioned are pick-and-come-again plants until they bolt to seed. If you want the easiest of all salad plots, buy a packet of mesclun seed, a mixture of up to a dozen salad greens. Sow half the packet, rake in, and water well. Sow pinches of seed through the season as space becomes available.

Home-grown salads can contain a dozen vegetables without a leaf of lettuce. Leaves of amaranth, beet, endive, giant red mustard, yellow mustard, radicchio, arugula, sorrel, spinach, bok choy, and mizuna, as well as cucumbers, peas, rutabagas, nasturtium leaves and flowers, carrots, radishes, salad onions, tomatoes, chives, bronze fennel, cauliflower and broccoli florets, borage, marigolds, and zucchinis all mix in the salad bowl. If fresh dandelion grows in your garden, use the leaves to add a delicious bitter twang and lots of nutrients. Then there are beans, beets (raw, boiled,

or pickled), and cabbage for coleslaw. These take a little longer to grow.

Try adding sprouting mung beans (which take up to a week to sprout, depending on temperatures), or succulent brown or lima beans to add bulk to winter salads. Or, toast croutons with crushed garlic and olive oil in a skillet and toss over the greens.

One quarter of a Salad Plot showing beet seedlings, cilantro, oak-leaf lettuce, new chards, and young nettle.

Herby salads are achieved by adding basil, chives, cilantro, fennel, mint, marigold petals, pennyroyal, salad bur-net, and tarragon. Look around an herb nursery and sniff the leaves. Small leafy herbs, like cilantro, basil, dill, and cara-way grow well between vegetables. Make a separate plot for herbs that sprawl—like arugula—in a border or under a tree with at least half a day's sun. Later in the season, take cuttings or seed from there to grow on as companion plants for vegetables, in the ground, or in mobile pots.

Seed saving: Let one of each variety go to seed. Stake tall plants.

A square plot can produce enough to provide three to four people with a small daily salad if you feed and water it well and keep plugging in seeds or seedlings. If artistically inclined, you could even paint with your vegetables by dividing the plot into triangles and growing dif-ferent colored vegetables in each with a marigold in the center.

Read Seeds and Seedlings (page 41) on raising seedlings and the unexpected benefits of toilet paper tubes. And don't forget about seed saving.

Salad Plot A

Spring & Summer

6 varieties of lettuce

6 bush beans

10 – 12 green onions in bunches of 3

2 – 3 cherry tomatoes on corners (staked)

radishes on the sidelines

1 arugula on the last corner

1 – 2 cucumbers in tub

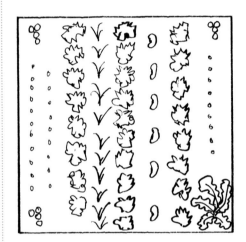

In early spring, dig the square with well-rotted manure and compost. Rake in B&B and lime if soil is acidic. Mix six pinches of lettuce seed varieties in a cup (romaine, butter head, green oakleaf, red

Lollo, mignonette, chicory). No need to keep these separate. Sow a row. If the weather is vile, or you want to protect seedlings from wildlife, sow in a deep box—such as a wine casket with a few drainage holes—that can be kept in a protected place until plants are large enough to be planted out. Sow one to two arugula seeds in one corner of the square.

Sow two or three cherry tomato seeds and twelve spring onion seeds in separate containers (a container can be a margarine tub with drainage holes). Plant six bush beans in toilet paper tubes stacked in a container, and two cucumber seeds in two toilet paper tubes standing in between containers. Choose dependable Lebanese, striped, or heat-tolerant Chinese cucumber. Place all in a warm, protected place. Water daily, twice if temperatures rise above 85 degrees. Seedlings should never dry out.

When seedlings are 2 inches high, transplant lettuces 4 inches apart, in three short rows 6 inches apart. When soil has warmed up and all danger of frost is over, plant tomato seedlings on the corners where they can be staked. Plant green onions in bunches of three, between lettuces. Plant bush beans between the lettuce rows. Plug in a dozen radish seeds here and there. When cucumber plants have four leaves,

replant them in a tub or large pot with plenty of CMC, next to the square where they can sprawl.

As plants grow, plug in compost where there is space. Pick outside leaves of lettuces regularly. Pick onion greens when young, and they will keep growing. Pick arugula all the time and, when it grows large, use leaves in stir-fries. Tomatoes take longer to ripen, so start picking as soon as the fruit gets a blush and ripen it on a sunny windowsill. Late, unripe tomatoes can still ripen inside or make green chutney. Freeze cherry tomatoes for sauce. Pick cucumbers young to keep plants producing.

A Salad Plot ready to go to seed but still providing plenty of pickings: endive in the background, four kinds of lettuce in the foreground, tomato on the right, and chicory on the left.

Salad Plot B

Spring & Summer

1 endive on one corner

3 lettuce varieties (oakleaf, butterhead, red Lollo)

12+ garlic on two sides

2 × 6 bush beans in two plantings

10 beets

2 – 4 mizuna on two corners

1 zucchini in tub

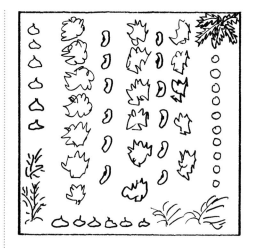

In early spring, dig the square with well-rotted manure and compost. In late winter, rake in B&B. Mix three pinches of lettuce seed varieties in a cup (butterhead, red Lollo, green oakleaf). Sow as in Salad Plot A (page 148), setting rows 8 inches apart. Sprinkle a few endive seeds in one corner and some mizuna seeds in an opposite corner. Break one knob of garlic into cloves and plant 3 inches apart on two sides of the square. Sow ten beet seeds 3 inches apart in one row. Beet seedlings produce more than one bulb and don't like being transplanted. Beans are best raised in toilet paper tubes or plugged straight into the soil but protected from rodents—see Pests and Predators (page 86). Raise one or two zucchini seeds in a pot in a warm position, or directly in a tub with plenty of CMC. When lettuces are 2 inches high, transplant 4 inches apart in alternate rows, parallel to the beet.

When the weather has warmed beyond danger of frost, plant 2 × 6 bush beans as in Plot A. Plug in compost as mulch where there is space. As plants grow, pick young garlic greens for salads. One month after planting first beans, plug in six bush bean seeds where there is space. Protect—see Hardware in the Food Garden (page 105). Repeat once more before mid-July.

Pick young beet leaves for salads, leaving plenty of crown leaves to feed the bulb. Pick endive and mizuna leaves as soon as plants grow vigorously. Pick zucchinis young to encourage continued production. Feed and water well.

Salad Plot C

Spring & Summer

2–3 choy sum on one corner

2 lettuce varieties (butterhead, red
   Lollo)

onions in a diagonal row

carrots in two rows along onions

mustard between lettuces

1 perennial spinach on other corner

1 miniature squash (such as patty pan)
   in a tub

In early spring, dig the square with well-rotted manure and compost and set up a tub or large pot for patty pan squash. In late winter, rake in B&B and sow two pinches of lettuce seed as in Salad Plot A (page 148). Sow a few choy sum seeds and a few perennial spinach seeds in two opposite corners. Make three diagonal drills connecting the other two corners, sowing the middle one with onion seeds 2 inches apart, and the other two with carrot seeds every ½ inch. Don't get the ruler out, just sprinkle between finger and thumb. Cover with ½ inch of soil, tamp down with a flat hand. Sow two patty pan seeds in a pot and raise in a protected position—the kitchen sill is fine—until all danger of frost is over and plants can go into the tub or large pots.

When lettuces are 2 inches high, plant out as in Salad Plot A. Plug in compost as mulch between plants. Plug in a dozen

mustard seeds between plants. Pick outer leaves of lettuces, choy sum leaves and flowers, and spinach. Pick mustard leaves from the bottom up; also use in soups and stir-fries. Pick some onion greens and the biggest tufted carrots.

Salad Plot D

Summer

3 bok choy

1 chicory

green chives, thin sprinkling of seed

1 romaine lettuce

1 cucumber on a corner

1 endive on a corner

fenugreek, thin sprinkling of seed

5 mibuna, pick early

4 mignonette lettuces

mizuna, sprinkle 10+ seeds,

    pick early

1 oak-leaf lettuce

4 radicchio (red)

20 – 25 radishes

1 arugula on a corner

1 sorrel

1 tomato, staked

nasturtiums, 3 seeds in a pot or tub

endive	bok choy	chicory green	cucumber
fenugreek	mignonette	romaine lettuce	chives
mibuna	radicchio red	oak-leaf lettuce	mizuna
sorrel	arugula	radishes	tomato

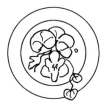

In early spring, dig the square with manure and compost. On the first day of spring, rake in B&B, then sow a cucumber seed and a tomato seed in toilet paper tubes. The other varieties are to be sown in open ground. Divide the square into sixteen squares of 25 × 22 inches. Next, sow or plant a different vegetable in each small square, such as four small lettuces or radicchios, a sprinkling each of seeds for fenugreek, mibuna, mizuna, small radishes, and three bok choy seeds. Sow large-leaved sorrel on corners. Grow arugula on an edge so it can flop outside the square. This is a basic salad plot, and it is pretty full. If you like more solid salads, you can leave out some leafy greens and plug in green beans or butter beans or rutabagas. Once plants are 2 inches high, add compost as mulch.

When the danger of frost is over, plant cucumbers and tomatoes on two corners kept free, where they can be staked. And the plus? A large pot with nasturtium seeds, placed next to the square to provide peppery leaves, edible flowers, and fake capers to pickle for the salad bowl. While harvesting plants from summer salad plots, plug in bush beans until mid-July. Water daily. And do save seed!

Salad Plot E

Autumn & Winter

baby carrots, light sprinkling of seed

9 Chinese rutabagas

cilantro, light sprinkling of seed

5 lamb's lettuce

1 daikon radish, on a corner

1 endive, on a corner

mizuna, sprinkle 10+ seeds, pick early

16 onions

parsley, light sprinkling of seed

1 arugula, on a corner

25 shallots

4 snow peas, on a 4-stick tepee

spinach, 1 perennial or sprinkle seed

1 tatsoi

6 winter lettuces on two small squares

1 salad burnet in a large pot

3 fingerling potatoes in a tub

endive	baby carrots	mizuna	daikon radish
Cilantro	Shallots	Chinese rutabagas	lamb's lettuce
snow peas	tatsoi	onions	parsley
Spinach	winter lettuces		arugula

Divide the square into sixteen smaller ones as in the previous plot. Sow one of each of the vegetables from the above list. Once the plants are 2 inches high, plug in compost as mulch.

There are two extras to try. Place a tub beside the square with fingerling potatoes cut into 2-inch pieces—see Potatoes in Part Four, page 260—for that firm potato salad with fresh cilantro. Also place a large pot in front of the tub, sown with a pinch of salad burnet seed—see List of Common Herbs on page 279—to hide the tub gracefully as well as grace the salad bowl.

If the parsley takes off, and you make tabouli, remember that a renowned Lebanese chef said that tabouli needs spices, especially five-spice.

Salad Dressings

Many a salad can be elevated to gourmet food by an imaginative dressing. But as taste is such a personal thing, the last word will never be written. You can hardly go wrong with a plain vinaigrette. Invest in good virgin olive oil and balsamic or wine vinegar; add pepper and salt to taste. Plant a lemon tree.

Try rice wine vinegar and the pleasantly acidic pulp of tamarind from the Asian grocer. Make herb vinegars by steeping any of the following in a small bottle of white vinegar for a month: thyme, oregano, rosemary, lemongrass, sage, tarragon, juniper berries, lemon balm, lemon and/or orange zest, Persian catmint, bergamot, nasturtium leaves and flowers, elderberry flowers, or marigolds.

Visit an Asian grocery for sauces: Japanese, Chinese, Vietnamese, Thai, Indian, Balti, Korean, and more. Check out your local grocery. Read the names, and if your taste buds start to salivate, read the label of the bottle that did it. If there are no objectionable ingredients (like MSG, palm and vegetable oils, aspartame sweetener, or genetically modified ingredients), buy that bottle. Organic soy sauce, garlic chili sauce, and mustard are a compatible trio. A few drops of sesame oil add a nutty flavor to any dressing.

Rudjak is an Indonesian salad made with either fruit or vegetables, with a unique sauce. For vegetable rudjak, parboil (for just a minute) florets of cauliflower, broccoli, sliced carrots, and green beans. Cube cucumbers and drain. Add frozen peas after draining. This is a basic version, and you can add whatever you grow, including zucchini. If you want more filling, add marinated tofu. For a fruit rudjak, chop bananas, pawpaw, cantaloupe, apple, pear, and anything not too juicy—even sweet cucumber.

For the sauce, mix half a jar (a whole one if feeding a tribe) of crunchy organic peanut butter with 2 tablespoons of white vinegar, lemon juice, or tamarind. Mix in 1 to 2 teaspoons of chili paste (*sambal oelek*) and 1 to 2 tablespoons of dark brown or palm sugar. These measurements are but a guide—add more of one or the other ingredient until you find the taste irresistible! If the dressing is too stiff, add coconut milk by the teaspoon, stirring vigorously until it is the consistency of a thick mayonnaise. The fruit or vegetable juices will thin it down further. Carefully fold the mixed fruits or vegetables into the sauce with two implements. Serve in a blue bowl, garnished with cucumber slices. Take this to a party to reap compliments.

For a more authentic rudjak sauce, fry onions and garlic in oil, adding chilies, shrimp paste, coconut cream, and crushed peanuts. Keep stirring before adding more coconut cream, lemon juice, and pinches of salt and sugar. This is also a thick sauce. Thin it down for a green leaf salad.

Another great standby for anything from a garden salad to a parboiled salad with cooked beans or a plain potato salad, is a yogurt-based dressing. Use plain or Greek yogurt. Crush several cloves of garlic and add thoroughly mashed coriander seeds, cumin, and black peppercorns. Add a good shake of olive oil, and dashes of sesame oil and orange essence to finish.

One of the simplest dressings is freshly squeezed orange juice, with or without a touch of lemon. Delicious on textured salads of apples, grated carrots, and zucchini, or on plain garden salads or grated carrots with fresh cilantro.

There is no end to the varieties of vegetables and herbs that can make a salad, nor to unique dressings. There is no excuse for an iceberg with mayonnaise from a jar. And if you live in wild parts, you may find additions in field and forest. Eating wild green leaves is the peasant's way, and we lost much more than a pleasant ramble through the fields when we started to live in big cities.

Mustard can be picked young for adding to salads, or used in stir-fries when bigger, dug in for green manure before flowing, or grown on for mustard seeds. Toasted seeds are great in dressings.

THE FAVA BEAN PLOT

Autumn & Winter

THIS PLOT follows the Salad Plots to return nitrogen to the soil, as all beans do. The fava bean is the only bean that will grow into the winter. Should there still be lettuces and seed-producing plants in the square, just plant fava beans in between and harvest the others by cutting their stems so as not to disturb bean roots. Add compost and OF.

25 fava bean seeds

4 stakes on the corners

furrows for thin sprinkling of

    carrot seeds

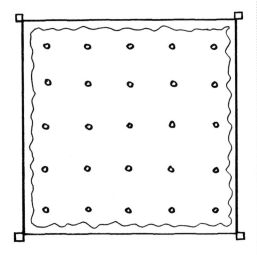

Leaving a 4-inch edge, push single bean seeds 1 inch into the soil at 20-inch distance, five across both ways. This gives twenty-five plants per square. Dense planting avoids stems breaking. If you have night prowlers, protect each seed with a plastic protector, either rings of PVC pipe or bottomless yogurt tubs. Push a piece of screening or pot scrubbers into these. Alternatively, place wire cages or dish racks all over the plot. See Hardware in the Food Garden (page 105).

Make shallow furrows around the edges and thinly sprinkle carrot seed. Cover with ½ inch of soil and pat with a flat hand. Water well. Cover these furrows with strips of old tea towel, held on the corners with stones, to aid germination of carrot seed and prevent ants from eating it. Peek after a week. When carrot seedlings are ½ inch high, remove strips, wash, dry, and store for later.

Once the fava beans have four strong leaves, remove protectors, and spread CMC between plants but not along carrot furrows. Soon, beautiful white and black flowers appear. Might the white cabbage butterfly with its black wing dots mistake these flowers for competitors? Try growing cabbages on an adjoining plot.

Place four stakes on the corners of the square and run baling twine or rope around the plot. As they grow, repeat this higher up to prevent outer plants breaking in the wind. Plants can reach 6 feet high. While the top is still developing flowers, finger-length beans appear near the base. Start eating the young ones whole. Picking helps the plant put energy into newer pods. Plants produce multiple pods. Pull baby carrots to thin out and serve with young fava beans.

When there are no more finger-length pods to eat whole, begin eating shelled beans twice a week. They also freeze beautifully, tasting as fresh as the day they were picked if frozen minutes after picking—a connoisseur's food out of season.

When harvest is over and seed beans have dried, cut stalks at ground level, leaving the roots with nitrogen-fixing nodules in the ground. In this nitrogen-enriched soil, you can plant green-leaved vegetables, of which there are more varieties than supermarket shelves reveal.

Seed saving: As pods grow bigger, choose the largest for seed. At four or five seeds per pod, tie red yarn around eight to ten pods. Let these dry on the stalk. But beware, during a heat wave they could dry to a sudden pitch black, which may cook the seed. Dried pods should be dried but not dead.

Only sixteen fava beans were planted in plastic rings with screening pushed in to prevent rats digging up germinating seed. Four stakes were used for roping in growing bean stalks. A denser planting of twenty-five would have provided better protection against wind.

THE OMEGA-3 PLOT

Spring & Autumn

YOUR INTAKE of carbohydrate-rich processed foods may deliver too many omega-6 essential fatty acids, which can lead to the so-called "modern lifestyle diseases." Get into balance with more omega-3s by eating two servings of leafy green vegetables daily with your main meal and a green garden salad with another meal or stuffed in sandwiches or bread wraps.

1 Siberian kale

2 broccoli (eat leaves also)

6 cavolo nero (Italian kale)

4 small green cabbages

4 chard

4 saag (Indian spinach)

4 perennial spinach

4 endives

3 bok choy

3 tatsoi

3 mizuna

3 mibuna

9 onions (eat straps also)

1 pot arugula

1 pot sorrel

1 pot parsley

1 salad box (alternate with garlic and
   start new salad greens seeds,
   as needed)

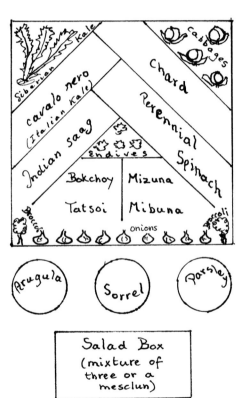

Choose winter-hardy varieties for autumn plantings. Raise seeds in toilet paper tubes while preparing soil with CMC, OF, and a sprinkling of lime. Harvest outer leaves from these plants as they grow. Douse with LS every two weeks. Plant one row of whole brown onions to harvest long green straps that give a lift to any dish or sandwich.

Cook kale, spinaches, chards, and cabbages quickly: steam, simmer, or stir-fry in olive oil. The first three are superbly tasty as purée: cook with onion and garlic until half wilted, cool, blend with a little olive oil and soy sauce. Make up for lost vitamin C with a good squirt of lime or lemon juice. For kale soup, see page 197. Serve steamed endive with white sauce and nutmeg, or use fresh in salads. Stir-fry mizuna, use young leaves with mibuna in salads.

This plot is planted so densely all year round that you will need additional containers. Sow seed of open-headed salad greens or a mesclun mix directly in a box or large pot. Sow another box when the first one has matured, and again if the season allows. If the season does not allow, bring salad boxes into a veranda or sheltered place so that you have salads all year. For salad dressings, see page 154.

Add three large pots for perennial sorrel, parsley, and arugula. These big yielders allow you to use green leaves by the handfuls. Sorrel gives another dimension to salads. Add it to cooked leafy greens for a sour touch, and try sorrel soup. Parsley makes delicious tabouli and is chopped into salads, soups, stir-fries, and root vegetable dishes. Arugula is not just a garnish. Try arugula salad, arugula soup, and arugula lasagna!

In spring, keep kales, chard, Indian saag, perennial spinach, and mizuna growing, and sow carrot seed in open places. Cultivate a new square to plant summer cabbages and broccoli with Chinese greens, spring onions, and a patch of cilantro. Start new salad boxes and replant finished boxes with garlic. Douse all with LS every two weeks.

At summer's end, the plot needs a rest from all that growing. Harvest what still grows as long as it lasts, while sowing a cover crop in between (peas, mustard, wheat) to dig in just before spring warms up.

Start a new Omega-3 Plot nearby to grow your favorite leafy greens.

To give your digestive system enough enzymes to digest all those greens, always serve some raw food with meals and packed lunches: sliced carrots, celery, rutabagas, red onions, apples, pears, arugula, or a tomato-laced tabouli. Good health!

THE ANTIOXIDANTS PLOT

Spring, Summer & Autumn

IF YOU NEVER grew anything else but this plot and picked three meals a week, the benefits to your health would be without measure. Antioxidants are essential to fight damaging free radicals in our bodies and help delay the onset of degenerative diseases. Fortunately, antioxidants in the form of green-leaved vegetables grow easily, tall, and fast.

1. amaranth
2. broccoli rabe
3. endive
4. mizuna
5. mustard
6. pea shoots
7. arugula
8. chard
9. spinach, perennial
10. turnip greens

In winter, swap some of the above for
    beets, bok choy, broccoli, cabbage,
    or kale

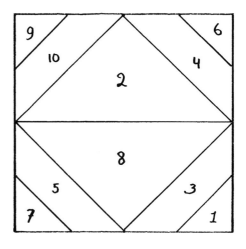

If you grew fava beans last season, cut stalks at soil level, fork in B&B, cover the plot with a thick layer of CMC, and water in well. Choose up to ten vegetables from the above list to try.

All brassica leaves are edible: pick lower leaves of cabbage, cauliflower, broccoli, brussels sprouts, and kale, and also the leaves of rutabagas, turnips, and Asian greens. Stir-fry or steam a weekly mixed bunch with some onions, ginger, garlic, and a little spice.

For a spring planting, don't choose beets, bok choy, or kale, but plug these in during early autumn if you want to keep this plot going through the first hard freeze. Raise broccoli in toilet paper tubes. All the others can be sown directly. Perennial spinach comes up in spring and grows throughout the year.

Pea shoots are young pea plants, picked at 4 inches for stir-fries. They only shoot once and are cut above ground. Sow a handful or harvest pea shoots from pea straw.

For easy germination, plant seeds in a handful of potting soil pushed into the compost layer. Ten different vegetables grow at different rates, but soon, you should be eating raw greens in vinaigrette, or steam up concoctions of ten different leaves for a taste sensation.

Whether you plug in winter greens or not, this plot is bound to continue into winter. So, for your next plot, you might just take out the garden fork and prepare another 3-foot square!

THE CURRY PLOTS

Autumn & Winter

WHILE CAMPING in Northern India, my travel companions and I ate a basic curry of cauliflower, carrots, potatoes, onions, and peas almost every day. Autumn and winter are good times to grow these vegetables. Because cauliflowers and carrots take time, grow a row of Japanese rutabagas as well. Daikon does well in curry and makes good use of small spaces. If you like more green, grow bok choy, kale, broccoli, fenugreek, and cilantro.

Curry Plot A

3 Siberian kale/broccoli or 6 bok choy

7 mini cauliflowers

fenugreek

red or brown onions on the diagonal

double rows of peas

carrots

20 rutabagas

8 daikon, pull young

cilantro

1 pot garlic

1 pot potatoes

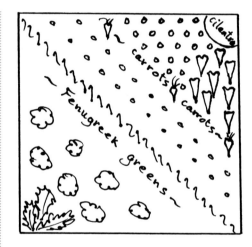

To grow gross feeders, such as the cabbage family and root crops, divide the square diagonally. Fertilize the gross feeders half with COF plus B&B. Dust the other half with B&B and add a layer of compost. Dust all with lime, and water well.

Sow broccoli and cauliflowers in toilet paper tubes and sow all others directly three weeks after soil preparation. On the gross feeders side, plant cauliflowers with your choice of bok choy, broccoli, or Siberian kale, and a row of fenugreek. On the diagonal line, sow red or brown onions; on the other half, carrots, cilantro, daikon, peas, and rutabagas. Plant small potatoes in a tub or on a small hill, and garlic cloves in a big pot.

Curry Plot B

6 mini cauliflowers

15 cilantro seeds

20 peas in a double row

50 carrots

30 rutabagas

fenugreek, sprinkle thickly

10 daikon radish, pull young

9 bok choy or 3 broccoli or
    Siberian kale

3-foot row of onions

Fertilize with compost and LS. Only
    manure rows 1 and 8 for cauliflower,
    bok choy, broccoli, and kale.

1 pot garlic

1 pot potatoes

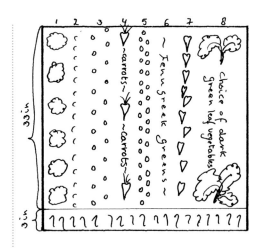

You can use an alternative pattern of 33-inch rows with a 3-foot row of onions as a border.

Read up on how to grow all these in Part Four (page 221). Douse seedlings with LS once a week and again after planting out for several weeks until they take off. Throughout the season, apply OF or B&B monthly.

Meanwhile, grind your own curry powder, just in case the blackbirds eat your fenugreek sprouts. All curry cooks have their own favorite combinations, so try the basic recipe for garam masala in Part Two (page 139), and vary it, to taste. With fresh garam masala, add the diced vegeta-bles, keeping the tender stuff till last. Add vegetable stock. Serve with rice and plain yogurt, garnished with cucumbers, cilantro, lemon juice, and pepper.

In the beginning, pick leaves of bok choy, broccoli, cilantro, fenugreek, kale, onions, and rutabagas to go with cooked chickpeas or sprouted mung beans. You either have to buy onions and garlic for curry day or do with the greens, as bulbs won't be ready till next season.

Other combinations such as beans, parsnips, and celery, are tasty, but the more absorbent a vegetable, the better it blends in a curry. In summer, the Curry Plot could grow versatile eggplants and tomatoes.

Seed saving: Come spring, let cilantro and fenugreek go to seed to dry for next year, and make garam masala.

THE BEANS PLOT

Spring & Summer

HERE WE ARE in fantasyland, in the realm of Jack and his bean stalk. You will remember this when your climbing beans grow beyond the farthest reach of your bean poles and when, suddenly, one morning, there hangs a whole handful of beans where you had not noticed anything yesterday. Beans like to surprise you.

This plot follows Curry Plot A (page 162) with its diagonal row of onions still maturing.

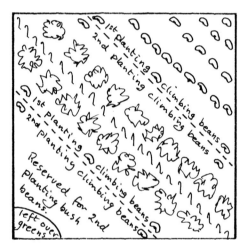

lettuces on either side of onions

trellises either side of lettuces

2 × 9 climbing beans on

trellises, 1st planting

18 bush beans, top right corner,

    1st planting

1 pot garlic

Later in the season: 2 × 9 climbing beans on other side of trellises, second planting eighteen bush beans, bottom left corner, second planting after removal of winter greens.

If you have flogged your square for two seasons, it is time again for a nitrogen fix. Grow early bush beans and slower-climbing beans with under-plantings of green and brown lettuces. Serve succulent garlic beans for dinner; make bean salads with radishes and almonds. Do remember that the scarlet runner bean prefers cool climates.

We are taking a risk here if last season you grew the Curry Plot and are left with that onion row on the diagonal and either kale or broccoli in one corner. Onions and beans are supposed to be incompatible. Test this, for there are gardeners who claim this companion plant ruling is baloney. When it's warm enough to plant beans—they don't even like chilly nights—start harvesting onions so that the acquaintance is kept brief. And if you grew Curry Plot B (page 163), where onions grow along one side of the square only, plant lettuces between them and the beans. Your garlic pot is still going.

Begin by raking in a light sprinkling of B&B on both halves. Cover with compost and water in well. Make shallow furrows on either side of the onions and thinly sprinkle mixed lettuce seeds, cover with ½ inch of soil, and tamp down with a flat hand. Water with LS.

Indoors, set up six containers with six toilet paper tubes each. Sow three containers with bush beans and three with climbing beans. Here, we enter fantasyland again, because choosing beans is pure myth. If you have joined the Seed Savers Exchange (see Useful Addresses on page 317), you will know that people make claims for their beans that border on the fantastic. Yet, by trying them out, you will find that some claims are true—all things such as soil and weather being equal.

The Ukrainian runner and scarlet runner bean sport bright red flowers. Others make do with mauve, purple, yellow, and white. Resolve to try them all out over the coming years, sticking to one bush bean and one climbing bean per year, and

learn to grow these well. If you are a bean lover—health be upon you—grow them every summer to revive a winter plot. Spend an hour rigging up a wire or bamboo trellis across the lettuces for the climbers, or poke in tall twigs.

When all danger of frost is over, plant out beans with at least four leaves, in their rolls, roots already hanging out. Dig deep holes, fill with water, drain, and push toilet paper tubes into the mud, firming the soil around them. Plant nine climbing beans between each row of lettuce and the trellises, totaling eighteen beans. Plant eighteen bush beans in the triangle not retaining winter greens. Water well and apply LS. Place shade cloches on new beans if planted in hot weather.

After one week, place CMC between rows. Set up the second sowing of eighteen bush beans and eighteen climbing beans in thirty-six toilet paper tubes. Or, if you do not have enough trellis, do thirty-six bush beans. Nurture these until big enough for bare ground. Plant 2 × 9 climbing beans on the outer sides of trellises and plant eighteen bush beans in vacant triangle after removing remnant winter greens. Place shade cloches, where necessary. Treat like first planting.

Plant out germinated beans until mid-July for a continuous supply. Keep harvesting lettuce leaves. Yes, they are in a slightly inconvenient spot between two trellises, but as they enjoy dappled shade, they'll be succulent and won't bolt to seed too soon.

Harvest last season's garlic—see Garlic in Part Four on page 249. Replant some in fresh soil, dry some, and pickle some. When bean plants are definitely finished, cut stems at soil level, leaving nitrogen nodules in the ground. May you have had your fill of beans!

Seed saving: Tie red yarn on as many bean pods as you will need next year and some to give to friends. Especially if growing heritage beans, ask friends to grow some so that the variety gains a foothold. Let one of each variety of lettuce go to seed. Some lettuce leaves are still quite edible when the plant is setting seed.

THE STIR-FRY PLOTS

STIR-FRIES ARE a wonderful way of using up summer's last greens, beans, and roots, old carrots, and celery stalks that mash in the wok with onion, garlic, ginger, and soy sauce. That's your basic stir-fry when the seasons flow into one another in your food plot. Serve with a bowl of rice, noodles, or roasted potatoes and pumpkin. If you grew the previous plot, autumn is waving its gentle wand. Cut old bean plants at soil level, cover the plot with a layer of CMC or COF, and water in well.

Winter Stir-Fry Plot

Autumn & Winter

CENTER:

4 stakes surrounded with twine

9 fava beans

4 × 3 snow peas under the twine

CORNERS:

3 flowering broccoli, 3 cabbages

5 mini cauliflowers, 3 cabbages

FIELD:

North: 9 bok choy

East: 5 tatsoi + 10 cilantro

South: 9 *Brassica juncea*

West: 5 mizuna + pea shoots

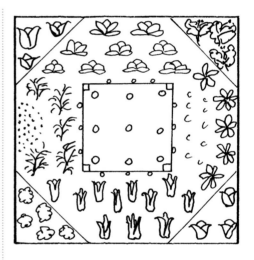

Raise three flowering broccoli rabe, six cabbages, and five mini cauliflowers in toilet paper tubes. Plant nine fava beans in a 3 × 3 bean square in the center, placing four stakes around them, tied with twine to prevent stems breaking in high winds. Plant 4 × 3 snow peas under the twine to climb up.

When seedlings have several sets of leaves with roots hanging out, plant broccoli, cauliflowers, and cabbages in the corners. Sow directly the spaces between center and corners with bok choy, mizuna, *Brassica juncea*, tatsoi, cilantro, and pea shoots. Rake in seed and tamp down. Pea shoots grow from thickly sown peas cut as shoots at 4 inches, or collect seed from pea straw.

When all are growing, scatter B&B. Water in well. By early winter, apply CMC and douse with LS every two weeks. Now put that wok on the stove twice a week for the pickings.

Use up end-of-summer greens, beans, and roots in a tasty stir-fry.

Summer Stir-Fry Plot
Spring & Summer

CENTRAL TEPEE OF TWIGS:

12 sugar snap peas on tepee

1 marigold in center of tepee

FIELD:

North: carrots, sprinkle thinly

East: 10 flowering broccoli rabe

South: giant red mustard, 3 mizuna
   or mibuna, sprinkle thinly

West: 10 Chinese cabbage

BORDERS:

green onions, sprinkle thinly

Since these plantings have different requirements, don't do anything to the soil except sprinkle lime around the four edges for green onions and in the central circle for peas. Then, cover the square with fresh compost.

Sow the following in individual toilet paper tubes: twelve climbing sugar snap peas, ten flowering broccoli rabe, and ten Chinese cabbages. Raise them on LS. Sow a whole packet of spring onion seed into two containers. The other vegetables are sown directly.

Build a tepee of tall twigs or bamboo (or from old blinds) in a circle of 15 inches diameter. This is a small tepee, so push twigs well into the soil and tie tops firmly so that it doesn't keel over in a wind gust. Plant marigold seed in the center.

Reserve a 3-inch edge all around the square for green onions. Divide the remainder of the square from inner edge to outer circle into four diagonal sections.

Sow carrots in one section and cover with wet tea towels. In another section, sow mizuna and/or mibuna with a few giant red mustard seeds. The remaining sections take flowering broccoli rabe and Chinese cabbages when seedlings have four to six leaves and roots are showing.

The peas may grow quickly. Cram twelve in a circle around the tepee. Green onions are planted out along the four edges when 2 to 3 inches high, covering white parts with soil, for they are modest and shy.

Since no manure was applied, make seedlings carry over with LS. Apply B&B to broccoli and cabbage monthly. Gradually pick one vegetable after another until your summer stir-fry contains the full complement.

Seed saving: Before you devour it all, remember seed saving. Tie red yarn on one tall carrot plant, one each of mizuna, mibuna, mustard, broccoli, and a handful of pea pods. When the seed peas have dried on the vine, cut plants at soil level. Enjoy the coming and going of happy insects buzzing around beautiful vegetable flowers setting seed.

THE ASIAN GREENS PLOT

Spring & Autumn

THERE ARE many green-leaved Asian vegetables that are worth growing, including bok choy, mizuna, mibuna, and tatsoi. Check Asian stores and seed catalogs and try a new one each season to find favorites.

CENTER:

red mizuna

NORTHWEST:

chinese chives

bok choy

NORTHEAST:

mibuna on the corner

Chinese kale or tatsoi

SOUTHWEST:

mizuna on the corner

chinese broccoli

Japanese greens

SOUTHEAST:

giant red mustard on the corner

chinese cabbages

3 pots for Vietnamese mint, cilantro, and
  fenugreek

In spring, plug in Japanese turnips
  where gaps occur

A very attractive peppery one is red mizuna, a tall, slender stalk with branches like fine seaweed and burgundy red-green leaves. It is long lasting

Red mizuna is an ephemeral herb that looks stunning in salads. It has a pleasant peppery taste. Let one go to seed, and it will pop up here and there next autumn so you should never be without.

Tatsoi.

for picking. Use raw in salads, sandwiches, roll-ups, and pastas for a punch. Red mizuna will seed itself through the garden from just one plant. Give some away and eat the others.

A number of Asian greens are mustard flavored and may come under the common name of *Brassica juncea*. All are tasty additions to stir-fries and steam pots. Grow some true mustard plants: yellow or giant red. Mustards improve soils and act as insect deterrents for nearby plants. Use leaves freely in cooking, as they lose their fiery sting.

Varieties of Chinese cabbage are useful vegetables, but keep slugs and snails at bay. They need compost around the base. Grow Chinese chives alongside to keep off insects.

Komatsuma, aburana, santo-sai and *hengsaitai* (Japanese) are all easy-to-grow brassica vegetables, happy with what's left in the soil after a heavily manured crop. They may also come by Chinese names. When you see a picture on a seed packet of a green leafy vegetable with tufts of four-leaved yellow flowers, it is a brassica.

Growing a number of brassicas together means that, if they flower simultaneously, bees will cross-fertilize them. The new seed may then grow a slightly changed plant next year: a green mustard with a red leaf rim, or something less attractive! Choose which seed to save in one season, and nip off all other flower buds. Don't throw them away! Not only do they contain nutrient value but most taste really delicious. I eat the tops and side shoots raw while gardening, then cut the stalk right down so the plant may grow leaves a little longer. If you have a bowlful, sauté buds in olive oil with a touch of soy sauce.

Grow a good cluster of flowering Chinese broccoli, known also as broccoli rabe, to extend your collection of Asian greens. Eat stem, leaves, head, and flowers, lightly stir-fried. Sheer goodness. And if you have space and energy, plant an Asian squash, herb, or cucumber without being able to read the name—just go by the picture and guess which season it would like!

THE BABY GREENS PLOT

All Seasons (Check seed packets for appropriate varieties)

THIS IS everyone's favorite plot for tender-leaved salads fresh from the garden into the bowl. Plant seed of spinach, red chard, perennial spinach, saag, Swiss chard, or other spinaches, to taste. Plant seed of red and green lettuces, non-heading varieties. All these are normal varieties of vegetables, scissor-harvested at 4 inches and left to regrow.

Growing baby greens becomes really economical if you save your own seed. Densely sow a whole packet of seed in a box, or several varieties in a 3-foot square plot, either mixed or in separate rows. Use good composted soil and apply liquid seaweed solution every two weeks.

Carefully mark the best two plants of each variety in a sunny corner to produce seed (this takes many months). Begin cutting baby leaves with scissors when about 3 inches tall. Plants will regrow several times. Keep snails and slugs at bay.

When seed-bearing plants grow tall, consider staking them against stormy weather. When the seeds have dried on the stalks, cut and strip seeds onto trays to dry indoors for another week or so. Lettuce seed dries on the stalk in a brown paper bag.

When bone-dry, store all seeds in brown paper bags in a dry place, or in plastic containers. Label with names and year: "Saag spinach 2012" or "Red chard 2013" or "Coral lettuce 2014." The seeds can now be used to sow more plots and boxes of baby greens. When you have used half your seeds, grow more plants for seed production. If you like greater variety, try mizuna and mibuna, or sow broccoli and kale seed for baby broccoli and baby kale; these add good flavor. Not all may regrow like the spinaches and lettuces do. Pick young leaves from these brassicas. Grow a nasturtium plant to add peppery leaves and flowers to the salad bowl. Health to you.

THE ARUGULA PLOT

Spring & Autumn

ARUGULA GROWS so profusely that it obviously is meant to be eaten or browsed by the mouthful. Forget one-leaf decorations. Arugula offers micro nutrients by the bowlful throughout the year. Being green leaves, they are bound to provide a generous dose of omega-3. Sow arugula (*Eruca sativa*) in autumn and wild arugula (*Diplotaxis tenuifolia*) in spring.

Make arugula salads. First, add a few leaves to lettuce salads, increasing the amount of arugula until you crave entire arugula bowls, writes garden writer and cook Theodore James Jr. about arugula. He adds mature leaves to creamed soups; they lose their bite when heated.

The two arugulas enjoy long-growing seasons in full sun, one during winter, the other in summer. Arugula launches its own seed, so it returns seasonally. They deliver a constantly renewing harvest of tasty green leaves that can be added to just about everything: sandwiches, salads, soups, quiches, stir-fries, omelets, frittatas, and pastas—as well as lending themselves to making many containers of pesto for the freezer.

If you love the taste of arugula and the textures of all of the above, why not grow these plants in separate plots of their own? Arugula self-seeds in the wild to grow more or less in the same place like good weeds do. But you can also make it part of your rotating 3-foot square plots.

My own arugula usually takes up 1 × 3 feet, plenty for a household of two. But if you plan to make pesto for the freezer to

Arugula leaves and flowers.

use at family feasts, a whole square plot is nice. If you like the peppery taste, you can add the cream-colored flowers to salads, salsas, pasta, and frittatas. When seed sets, wait for some to dry and fall, and pick some to store.

I grow the wild arugula in a large pot on the edge of the garden. It throws out long thin stems to 3 feet, covered in bunches of narrow, serrated leaves 4 to 8 inches long. The end of the stems become festooned with bright yellow flowers that are crowd pleasers to bees for several months whenever the sun is out. The bees pollinate vegetables and fruit trees in passing, so wild arugula plays an important role in backyard food gardens!

I'm suggesting you try wild arugula in a pot first, cut the stems right back in autumn when they dry off, and pot one or two seedlings that will pop up nearby, just in case. Don't bother to save the seed, but grow these seedlings on. All but one or two will be given away.

THE ROOT CROP PLOT

Autumn & Winter

I F YOU grew the Summer Stir-Fry Plot (page 168), there will be many plants still going to seed. This is a good opportunity to plug root vegetables in between. Root crops quietly mature in the earth while rain and wind lash taller plants. They mature at different times, so eat those that are ready. Leave out carrots if they grew here the previous season.

1 container onions in center

1 container leek, lower west

2 – 3 heads of garlic, upper west

Sow seed of beets, winter radishes, turnips, and rutabagas in rows, radiating from the center (see rutabagas, south) at distances appropriate for the size of the root vegetables.

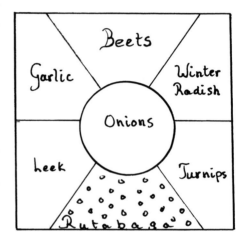

Sow one container of onion seed (red, brown, or white) and one of leek. Prepare square with a light sprinkling of lime. In soils that are poor to start with, root crops can't get ahead on nutrient left after a previous crop. So if your soil is poor, add a modest sprinkling of B&B; overdo it and you reap more leaf than root.

Mark out a circle in the center of your square for the onions. Divide the rest of the square into six sections. Sow around last season's seed-bearing plants and when these are finished, cut stems at soil level so as not to disturb root crops. Sow winter radishes, turnips, beets, and winter rutabagas in four sections. In order to mulch for winter, sow in short rows radiating from the center, and mulch in between. Break enough garlic knobs into cloves to plant the fifth section and cover thickly with straw.

When onions and leeks are 2 to 3 inches high, plant them in the circle and last section, respectively. Mulch between rows with CM. As the other vegetables come up, mulch them also with CM. Once the plot is up and growing, douse it once with LS. That should be enough.

You can eat the leaves of onions, garlic, turnips, rutabagas, and beets, as well as young radish leaves, but don't rob a plant of its crown. Pick lower leaves gradually for a weekly feed before pulling the roots.

Seed saving: Tie red yarn on your best plants. Save one leek, beet, rutabaga, and turnip and three onions (braid together to avoid flopping). Let garlic tops die down, pull, then tie in a bunch or braid, after storing a few knobs in a dark cupboard for replanting in autumn. To let one winter radish go to seed brings a glory of mauvy-pink flowers, but it is a big plant. Choose a radish on the edge of the plot and gently guide it to flop sideways, for it can take as long as the garlic for the pods to dry. Pick young radish seed pods to pickle in vinegar with olive oil. Should you produce big beets, pickle a few sliced into jars and add to your home-grown food store.

THE PASTA/PIZZA PLOTS

THESE ARE the favorite plots of many a busy cook because bland pasta is so amenable to being married to these pronounced flavors for a quick and healthy meal.

CENTER:

onions maturing

Top half, left to right:

1 container red onions

1 arugula

3 eggplants

LOWER HALF, LEFT TO RIGHT:

3 chilies + chives, sprinkled thinly

3 bush tomatoes + 1 basil

3 bell peppers

3 fingerling potatoes in a tub or on a
small hill

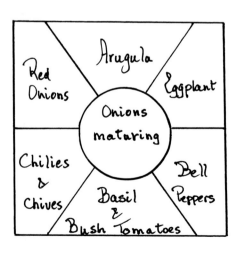

Pasta/Pizza Plot A
Spring & Summer

There are half a dozen plants going to seed in all directions of your square. As these plants dry off, they don't use nutrients, so you can plant around them or harvest what seed there is and pull them out. Avoid watering the onions in the center when the tops are drying off. Alternatively, prepare a new square for pasta/pizza vegetables and herbs and sow a summer Bean Plot (page 164) in the old Root Crop Plot (page 176).

In spring, sow three seeds each of eggplant, bell pepper, chilies, and bush tomatoes in toilet paper tubes. Sprinkle a pinch of basil seed in a pot and red onion seed in a container. As none like frost, keep damp and warm under glass or indoors. If you don't want to raise basil from seed, wait till the weather warms up to buy a plant.

As previous seasons have used up any goodness you put into the soil, prepare your plot as for gross feeders. Apply

CMC plus OF or B&B. Preserve the division in six sections.

Sow arugula directly and early—it likes cool nights but may bolt to seed in summer. Chives are sown directly. Prepare a tub or hill and plant potatoes; mulch with compost and straw.

When the weather warms up, plant out red onion seedlings. As nights grow warm, plant eggplants, bell peppers, chilies, and tomatoes—protect with plastic, if in doubt (see Hardware in the Food Garden, page 105). Plant basil between tomatoes. Douse all except last season's onions with LS. As plants grow up, push in mulch to preserve moisture, as these plants hate drying out.

This plot can be used in so many ways, apart from roasting the fleshy vegetables. A mushroom and fingerling pizza with chives, arugula, and goat's cheese goes down really well. You can cut eggplant slices and vine-ripened tomatoes to sun-dry on a tray under muslin. Bell peppers can be dried, or preserved in glass. Basil can be frozen. Make tomato sauce.

If cold weather sets in, dig up eggplants, basil, bell peppers, and chilies with root balls, pot them up, and bring indoors. Feed with LS. Rather than design a new plan to follow this Pasta/Pizza Plot, continue to sow where there is space for a winter plot.

Pasta/Pizza Plot B
Autumn & Winter

Rake in some B&B between still-growing plants. If you grew the Stir-Fry Plot (page 167), the onions have now been harvested. Flop one arugula plant over the edge to produce seed.

Around the old arugula, sow lots of cilantro for Thai dishes. Plant garlic where no onions grew previously—this is where a garden notebook comes in handy! Sow Asian greens and giant red mustard in all other spaces. Apply compost. Plug in a few chard seeds for ricotta torte and vegetarian lasagna.

Those who love asparagus with pasta or pizzas should dig a separate permanent plot, because asparagus are perennial plants, producing for decades. See Asparagus in Part Four (page 231) and plant roots in autumn, applying thick CMC.

THE WILD GREENS (HORTA) PLOT

All Seasons

THIS IS a made-to-measure crop for a food garden developed one square at a time. Since ancient times, the Greeks have gathered horta by climbing rocky mountains after autumn rains to pick a multitude of edible wild greens for the pot. If your environment does not have such abundance, you can sow a Horta Plot. Until you know how much horta you will consume, prepare one square and divide it into four quarters with a trowel. Sow one quarter every two to three months, choosing seasonal varieties.

Go to the spice cupboard with a deep bowl. Put into the bowl a teaspoon each of yellow mustard and coriander seed, and add generous pinches of buckwheat, caraway, dill, fenugreek, and any whole spice seed you have. From your seed collection, add three or four seeds each of bok choy, *Brassica juncea*, Chinese cabbage, kale, mizuna, giant red mustard, arugula, French chard, tatsoi, and any other fast-growing greens, plus a sprinkling of chive seeds. Go outside, mix seeds, and rake lightly into one quarter of your plot. Water in well. The mustard will be up in a week, shading the others. By the time you start picking this plot, seed the next quarter. Pick leaves and tops of mustard, lots of arugula, Chinese greens from the bottom up, and stems of spicy greens, leaving the roots to shoot again.

Enter the kitchen with a bowl heaped with greens. If your natural environment sports edible greens like dandelion, nettle, or milkweed, add these. Greek cooks put it all in a pot of boiling water to simmer for five minutes before they drain and fry it. A lot of the goodness remains in the water, which women take as a health drink.[23] I prefer to wash, drain, and roughly cut the lot and throw it half wet into the wok to quickly stir-fry with a dash of olive oil, and onion and garlic to taste. Or steam the horta. The volume goes down rapidly. You get two small heaps of dark greens with a powerful yet velvety, spicy taste. Combine horta with bland sweet potato or tofu, or use in an omelet. Eat horta the Greek way with chunky fresh buttered bread and olives. I would have put the Horta Plot at the head of the list, because it is my mainstay in a new garden with unimproved soil. While other vegetables took time, we were eating horta six weeks after moving in, almost as soon as radishes. Through winter, I add shredded cabbage leaves. At any time, I add anything green to the horta fry-up.

The Greeks also serve horta cold. Boil greens a few minutes in water with salt, tough ones first, tender ones last. Drain, then rinse in cold water. Swing them dry in a tea towel before chopping finely and serving on a flat dish. Sprinkle with salt, pepper, olive oil, and lemon juice. Or go Greek-Korean, using oil, chili salt, rice vinegar, and toasted sesame seeds.

Although this is intense companion planting, pick the plot clean seasonally to grow peas or beans followed by a root crop for rotation purposes. Set one square aside for next year's horta. Quickly grown food carried straight from the garden to the kitchen and eaten within the hour is as good as it gets! You and those you feed will burst with health after a year on horta. They fed Olympians on it!

Seed saving: Let one of each kind of green go to seed so that the plot becomes self-perpetuating.

THE AZTEC PLOT

Spring & Summer

THE HEALTHY DIET of the Aztecs was based on companion planting. Aztec staples were corn, beans, and pumpkin or squash, all shallow-rooted plants. The beans climb up the corn stalks, shaded by their broad leaves, and the pumpkin or squash vines ramble underneath keeping everyone's roots cool. Read up on these in Part Four (page 221).

After so much crop rotation on one square, why not let the horta grow on into summer, and if you have not done so yet, dig up another square for a new experiment. The Aztec combination can also grow after a winter's Fava Bean Plot (page 156). But it is not a pick-and-come-again plot. You will pick beans first, corn late summer, and squash in autumn. So consider sowing a Salad Plot (page 147) as well, or plug seeds into the Horta Plot (page 180).

1 marigold in the center

4 small pumpkins or squash

16 sweet corn

16 climbing beans

4 stakes on the corners

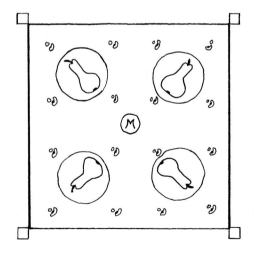

What still succeeds in Mexico's climate may not flourish where you are. None of these plants stand frost, but some varieties take cold nights better than others. Instead of sowing all seeds simultaneously, plant squashes first, sweet corn next, and, lastly, beans when spring warms up. Use a plastic roof, or re-seed if plants fail.

Three weeks before planting, prepare the soil as for gross feeders with CMC and a sprinkling of lime to please the beans. As you do for fava beans, pound stakes on the corners to rope corn stalks in when 18 inches tall.

Fill four toilet paper tubes with potting soil, plant four pumpkin or squash seeds, germinate under glass or indoors.

Four-year-old Emile's accidental Aztec Plot: sweet corn, zucchini, and beans.

Raise with LS. If rodents are a problem, also raise sixteen sweet corns and sixteen climbing beans in toilet paper tubes indoors until 4 to 6 inches with a good set of leaves. Plant out when the danger of frost is over. Raising plants before that date gives you a head start.

If you prefer to sow directly when all danger of frost is over, push sixteen sweet corn seeds 1 inch deep in four rows of four. Plant sixteen climbing bean seeds next to each sweet corn. Place PVC rings or bottomless yogurt tubs over both, preferably with screening (see Hardware in the Food Garden on page 105). Place four rings with pumpkin or squash seeds equidistant between the sweet corn, and put a marigold in the center because you can't have enough of them. Sprinkle organic fertilizer between rings and water in well. Douse with LS. When all plants are up and away, top dress with CM. The Aztec Plot supports a lot of growth, so rotate LS, B&B, and OF every two weeks.

Expect several pounds of beans depending on variety, thirty-two corn cobs, and ten to twenty squashes, depending on how well the bees pollinate the flowers. If you have any doubt about bees, hand-pollinate by picking a male flower (the one without the swollen base at the stem) and pushing it full onto a just-opened female flower (with the swollen base at the stem), rubbing them well together. That's getting physical, and it works.

Seed saving: Tie red yarn around your best cob and best beans. Let them dry on the stalk. Leave one pumpkin or squash drying on the vine, scrape out seeds, rinse well, and leave to dry in a dark place. Sweet corn seed does not remain viable for long—use it next spring.

THE PEA PLOT

Spring & Autumn

MY SECOND JOB in Australia was pea picking in late winter. These were bush-podding peas, whereas now we have tender snow peas and sugar snaps, which tend to grow well in early spring. Generally, peas don't fancy hot summers, but if you live in cool or snowy regions, you may have to plant peas in early spring for a summer harvest. Know your own mini-climate or experiment with seasonal sowings of pea varieties until you learn what does well when and where you are.

Peas are as exciting a crop as beans. Flowers of white and pretty colors climb high or huddle demurely, bush style. Lime your plot. If you don't have rodents, sow direct three weeks later. Otherwise, sow seed in toilet paper tubes. Protect with wire, racks, or cages until plants are 3 inches high. Plant bush peas densely, six across the square, thirty-six plants in all. For climbers, push a tepee, wire trellis, or tower into the ground—see Hardware in the Food Garden (page 105).

When plants are up and away, apply B&B or OF, and douse with LS. This should be enough to keep them developing. To add to pea dishes, plant mint in a pot and place on a paver to stop roots from sinking in. In case of overproduction, snap-freeze peas.

THE MELON PLOT

Spring & Summer

I USED TO sprinkle melon seeds in a corner during the busy spring planting season, to discover two months later that nothing had come of them. One year, I decided to pay attention to melon seed, raising six seedlings of Hale's Best and Amish melons in toilet paper tubes in a cold frame. I prepared the bed with cow and horse manure covered with compost. When the weather was warm enough, I planted the seedlings and applied B&B.

I watered daily and deep. "See," I grinned to myself, "the other seeds must have been taken by the birds." By midsummer, the vines sported a few dozen melons the size of tennis balls. At summer's end, they all died.

For that, I blame the weather—it was the hottest summer in living memory, after the driest winter. I began wondering about melon growing in Afghanistan, Israel, and the Turfan Depression in Central Asia, places renowned for extreme temperatures. The fame of their melons spread far beyond their borders. The Turfan Depression is the lowest lying land on the globe, with average summer temperatures around 120 degrees. Their melon farmers irrigate. I took note of places in Australia where melons have been grown commercially. They are hot places, too.

So I tried again, using Percy's plastic roof (see Hardware in the Food Garden, page 105) to keep seedlings warm during spring, feeding them pig compost. Edible melons were almost mine, but when they ripened, the wildlife ate them!

Next year, I'll dig a ditch in a sunny spot, layer it with manure, B&B, compost, and straw and drench it, to imitate the Turfan Depression. I may experiment by sticking water-filled plastic bottles with drip holes in the caps upside down in the soil to irrigate, applying compost, LS, and OF, and pinching out the tips of the vines when the melons have set. The sight of melons in your own garden is worth all that.

For watermelons, I am tempted to try the same method, but I also know they love to spread their roots through undisturbed compost heaps that get watered. Don't come to me with tales of people who just spit out a few seeds from the veranda and eat melons all summer! They aren't telling where they spat. As for not sharing my melons with the wildlife, I'll try a cage held down with bricks to keep those rats out. Best of luck to us.

THE CHINESE MELON PLOT

Late Spring & Early Summer

NO, **THIS IS NOT** about how to grow a melon variety from China, but how to grow melons the ancient Chinese way. It comes from a 1958 collection of extant sections of ancient Chinese books, going back to the 2nd century BCE and collected by Professor Shih Sheng-han, on all aspects of making a living from the soil.

A farmer could learn everything he needed to know from these ancient manuals. Because in our society we come to organic farming anew, after a century of dallying with chemical agriculture, much of this sounds terribly modern, for instance, soil conditioning with green manures.

Melons originated in Africa, entered Europe as the Roman Empire ground to a halt, and were introduced to Asia from there. A Chinese description of raising melons dates from the 6th century CE, but was copied from 1st century BCE writer Fan Sheng-chih!

1 earthenware jar

1 tile to cover jar

4 melon seeds

10 spring onions or shallots

First, locate the warmest spot in your garden, sunny, well protected from wind, perhaps against a wall. If necessary, build a south-facing suntrap from a wooden crate on its side, open at the top, lined with 21st-century silver foil or other reflective material.

Preferably plant melons where beans grew previously (such as winter broad beans). Make a shallow pit in the ground, 9 inches across and 3 inches deep. Mix one *shih* of manure (my guess:

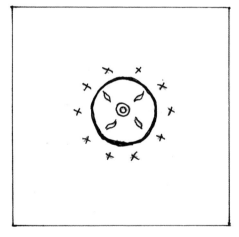

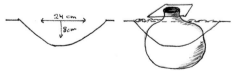

The ancient measurements of a hole 9 × 3 inches are not sufficient for dry conditions.

one bucket) with an equal amount of earth. Place an earthen jar (unglazed) in the center of the pit, with the mouth at ground level when manure and soil are returned to the pit. Fill jar with water and cover with a tile. When water level drops, fill the jar up to the rim. Plant four melon seeds around the jar. Plant ten shallots or spring onions around the jar and the melon seeds.

Mulch the shallow "saucer" around the jar, and water it well after sowing. The jar should keep the melon roots cool and provide seepage; the shallots give biochemical protection. Towards the fifth month, when the melons ripen, the shallots can be pulled. Place ripening melons on a tile and protect from rodents and birds by wrapping each fruit in layers of orange bag netting.

I picked some ten melons the size of tennis balls from two plants that came up in rough compost from a store-bought melon seed. Without transplanting, they did the best they could where they fell, but were sweet and lovely tasting. Easy to germinate, melons do well in warm summers, if given extra care.

THE ESSENTIAL HERB PLOT

All Seasons

HERBS ARE WILD PLANTS. They have survived numerous climate changes, grazing by megafauna and microfauna, and land degradation caused by humanity. Still with us, they offer concentrations of micronutrients, and omega-3s because they are green-leaved. Use them daily. Herbs have medicinal qualities. Scientists are at last becoming interested. Garlic, onions, oregano, and thyme are antibiotics. So are chilies and many spices used in curries.

Dry bunches of herbs before they set seed, by hanging upside down out of the sun. Rub off the stalks, store in jars, keep in a cool dark place. Use dried herbs for cooking and mixing herbal teas.

Some herbs are invasive and can get out of control, the gardener's nightmare. Instead of ending up with an overgrown herb wilderness, grow your chosen herbs in 10- to 12-inch pots in a round plot. Push pots an inch or two into the soil. If the herbs root through the drainage holes, they will still be contained by the pots. Stuff mulch between and around pots, and it looks ever so pretty. Only mint and lemon balm must be placed on a saucer, as their roots really mean business when they sniff soil. Garlic needs more than a pot; give it a plot.

Chives: Leaves and white and mauve flowers are edible. Can be divided. Cut finely and sprinkle on everything.

Lemon balm: This refreshingly fragrant relative of mint is very invasive. Grown in a pot on a saucer and pruned regularly, it looks great. It will seed itself, so pull seedlings out. But use lemon balm daily in your greens pot, stir-fries, and fresh juice drinks.

Garlic: Classed with herbs as it is used in small quantities in cooking. To grow good bulbs, plant cloves in the soil or a box in autumn and cover with thick straw mulch. Harvest in spring when straps start losing their color. Braid the straps of five bulbs and hang up in a cool, dark place to dry.

Mint: There are so many. Choose one for mint sauce and one for mint tea (peppermint or Moroccan). Place pots on saucers so no roots can escape and overrun your estate! Prune down when flowering starts, so that bees can't cross-fertilize different mints.

Oregano: This plant also spreads when planted in the ground, but not as relentlessly as mints. Mine didn't do well in a pot, but seeded itself beside the pot. I am keeping an eye on it. Use in Mediterranean cooking. Dried oregano is more concentrated. Dry in bunches, strip, and rub down.

Parsley: Grow flat-leaved Italian for fine cooking. Curly parsley is bulky enough for tabouli. Both parsleys go to seed in their second year, then die. Let the best plants produce seeds, dry, and save a little, but sow a new bed immediately. After a month, it will peek up.

Rosemary: A rosemary bush is decorative and too big for a tiny herb plot or pot. Plant it in an ornamental border. Pick a 4- to 6-inch branch daily. Strip leaves off branch and chop finely. Cook with greens or pasta dishes and experiment. It has powerful benefits. Take cuttings before pruning the main bush, as they sometimes die.

Sage (*Salvia* sp.): Buy *Salvia officinalis*, the medicinal one, to make a gargle for sore throats and drink as medicinal tea. Although probably not a true salvia, I also grow the large, light-green plant with masses of light-blue flower tufts

An ongoing greens plot surrounded by bottles of water.

for cooking with greens or adding to a creamy pasta sauce. Pluck a top with ten leaves, strip, and cut finely. Also good roasted. This one lives in a large pot beside the apple tree.

Tarragon: There is French, Russian, Mexican, and more. My Mexican is a woody perennial, growing in a 10-inch pot in a sunny spot with periodic shade. The plant falls dormant after flowering, when I pull a few rooted pieces to pot on. In summer, pick freely and dry enough to tide you over the cold months. Delicious in just about everything, but especially with eggs.

Vietnamese mint: Essential for *laksa* and other Vietnamese dishes, this ele-gant plant has pointy leaves with a burgundy center. Being tropical, it needs a warm spot and may not survive frost. It does well in a big pot in part shade. Must not dry out.

Lemon balm, mint, rosemary, and sage: These make a good mixed herbal tea. I add to that my favorite fatigue fighter yarrow (flowers and leaves). Dry tea herbs in bunches, strip, dry off on a tray, then store. If you have a lot, fill pretty jars and surprise your friends. Nose around your local nursery's herb collection. There is always something new—or very old—coming on the market.

THE SOUP PLOTS

OLD-FASHIONED SOUPS with no names used to be made with a soup bunch of carrots, parsnips, shallots, and parsley. These were sold door-to-door from a basket at Newcastle in the early 20th century by a Chinese market gardener.[24] Now, mixed roots for soup come in plastic packs without the greens, which sell in different packs.

All soups are good for you, even if only for the deep comfort they spread in our bodies. In the Soup Plots, plant your choice of green herbs to add to soups made from leftovers. What cook doesn't have tiny leftovers, if not on a daily basis? Fight food waste with healthy soups! Save tiny leftovers in a container in the freezer (see Preserving and Using Home Produce: Freezing on page 308).

Soup Plot A

Autumn & Winter

CENTER:

1 container of onions in two triangles

1 – 2 knobs of garlic

1 – 2 Siberian kale

NORTH:

carrots, sprinkle lightly

EAST:

20 – 24 beets

SOUTH:

1 sorrel and 5 drumhead cabbages

WEST:

1 container of leek

1 tub or small hill of potatoes

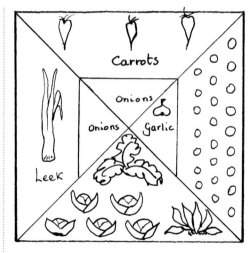

Also recommended are herbs from the Essential Herb Plot (page 189). Three weeks before planting, rake lime into the square. Divide into four quarters. Prepare one quarter for gross feeders with CMC and B&B.

Sow five drumhead cabbage seeds in toilet paper tubes. Sow one container each of leeks and onions. Plant potatoes in a tub or on a small hill, and mulch with straw. Sow beets, carrots, garlic, and Siberian kale directly. Plant out leeks and onions in shallow ditches as explained in Leeks (page 253) and Onions (page 256). Plant one sorrel plant, or a few seeds in a corner of the cabbage quarter. When plants are up and away, douse with LS to give them a boost. The cabbages are planted tightly, so pick outer leaves as they swell.

You are still eating pumpkin soup from the freezer compartment, blended from summer's last pumpkins. Soups are meals par excellence to freeze and pull out in a hurry, served with bread, cheese, and salad. Your cupboard holds lentils for lentil soup. Make a hearty blend with lentils, pumpkin, and cumin. Maybe you grew celery and are a bit sick of celery soup from those leafy heads. A little celery goes a long way, and it's great for your health if organically grown. There are still pickings in the square for a mixed vegetable soup. Once all that is gone, we are into winter soups, one-pot meals that do not need a dollop of fattening cream on top, because that would mask the good taste of vegetables grown especially for winter. Serve with fresh buttered bread. Garnish with fresh herbs. Apart from making soup, you can also eat the greens of beet, kale, and sorrel, and fry cabbage with garlic and onion greens.

The vegetable stock used in the following recipes can be made in bulk and frozen in meal-size portions. Roughly cut carrots, celery, and onions to simmer in water until soft. Cool, blend, store, and freeze. For clear stock, drain first and use vegetables as puree. Alternatively, save vegetable offcuts (roots, peels, onion skins, pods, herb stems, and such) and freeze until there's enough to boil a pot of stock—add fresh herbs.

A bouquet garni that will enhance any soup is made with a bay leaf, sprigs of parsley, two cloves, half a teaspoon of cumin seed, and some peppercorns tied in a square of muslin for easy removal. Or tie other combinations of parsley sprigs, rosemary, sage, and thyme in a bunch. These bouquets can be used fresh, made ahead of time and frozen, or dried in a dust-free place.

Soup Plot B

Any Season

TOP ROW:

leeks

BOTTOM ROW:

whole onions

FOUR MIDDLE ROWS:

shallots

carrots

parsnips

turnips

LEFT BORDER:

thyme

parsley

tarragon

RIGHT BORDER:

sage

nasturtium

oregano

3 POTS FOR FRESH TOPPINGS:

cilantro

cumin

chives

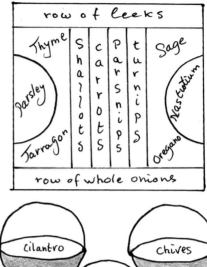

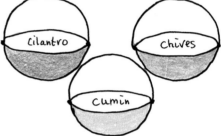

In spring, plug in Japanese turnips and sow more carrot seed where no carrots grew before.

Plant a patch of parsley, a pot of celery herb (use sparsely), a few nasturtium seeds on the corner so plants can sprawl (pick the peppery leaves), tarragon, sage, oregano, and thyme. Plant whole onions to grow green straps. A box of sorrel is an asset for many a soup.

Anyone with a freezer compartment can make tasty vegetable stock and store it, rather than buy a packet. Chop a large carrot, a few sticks of celery, and half a leek, and boil in plenty of water for an hour. You can add a slice of onion and a turnip. Frugal cooks freeze cut-offs from any such vegetables until there is enough to boil up. Cool the pot, strain off the liquid, and pour into ice cube trays.

On the day you need a hearty soup to restore your sanity, get out a stockpot and a soup pot. Break out three or more blocks of stock and melt in a little water to form the base of your soup in the stockpot. Tell yourself: "I made this. It does not come out of a carton. It has no preservatives." Retrieve cooked leftovers from the freezer, tip into the stock to melt on a low flame. Cool sufficiently in a bowl to put the contents through the blender. Add an extra stock cube, if necessary. Set aside.

Go outside and pick a handful of fresh herbs, a few leaves of sorrel, and some onion straps. Strip and finely chop herbs and straps, sauté briefly in the soup pot with some olive oil and a drizzle of sesame oil. Rotate pan to avoid burning. A wonderful aroma arises. You feel good already. Just as the herbs curl up a little, pour the blended soup into the soup pot and reheat, stirring the greenery through. Season with salt and pepper or a squirt of soy sauce. Voilá. Serve with grilled cheesy dreams of whole-wheat bread and farmers' cheese. Add a little salsa of freshly cut tomatoes and red onions, no dressing, just salt and pepper.

The beauty of this leftovers herb soup is that it is never the same. Much depends on the quantity and spicing of leftovers. You can vary the fresh herbs each time. Add fresh young kale for a change, finely chopped; or a handful of frozen green peas, and wait for the requests for second helpings.

This plot can be extended by adding other herbs to make the Essential Herb Plot (page 189).

Herbs growing between the vegetables.

Winter Soups

BORSCHT

Sauté raw, grated beets with sliced leeks, onions, celery, shredded cabbage, and garlic. Stir frequently until vegetables are reduced. Add vegetable stock. Boil for several hours. Traditionally served with sour cream added just before serving, so put a dollop on top with a sprig of dill. Also excellent served chilled with plain yogurt, dill, and diced cucumbers.

CABBAGE SOUP

This soup is famous in European novels for leaving a nauseating stink hanging in the stairwells of crowded tenements. Let's start anew with this noble vegetable that has saved many people from starvation, and was the mainstay of my hardy ancestors.

In the midst of the Dutch famine in the 1940s, a compassionate enemy soldier gave me a large green cabbage. It was so heavy that, as a ten-year-old, I could not carry the bag but had to drag it a mile through the snow during curfew hours. I could have been shot for this cabbage but I got it home, and it fed us for a week. Unforgettable things happen in wars.

Finely shred a quarter drumhead. Sprinkle with half a cup of wine, cover and set aside. Grate two or three potatoes, sprinkle with a splash of vinegar, cover, and set aside. Sauté a big diced onion in olive oil. Add 2 cups of vegetable stock, grated potatoes, and a teaspoon of caraway seeds. Simmer twenty minutes. Whisk until smooth. Add salt and crushed black pepper. Add shredded cabbage and bring back to a boil. Simmer until cabbage goes limp, but is still al dente. Serve with sesame bread sticks.

FRENCH ONION SOUP

Ditch those packets and chop onions into rings and sauté until translucent. Add black pepper and vegetable stock. Turn on the oven. Cut a French loaf or two baguettes into slices and toast one side under the broiler. Place half the bread in an ovenproof pot and grate hard cheese over it. Pour in the hot soup. Cover with the rest of the bread and more cheese. Brown a little in a hot oven before serving this French lunch.

Another recipe starts the same, with sautéed onions. Stir in a few spoons of flour, add enough hot milk for a soup, then pepper and salt. Cook and stir. In a separate bowl, beat some egg yolks and add soup one spoon at a time until it is fifty-fifty. Then pour the egg and soup mix into the soup while whisking. Reheat without letting it come to a boil. Serve with fried bread.

GARLIC SOUP

Contrary to the powerful sensation the name of this soup brings to the taste buds, it is a gentle soup. Crush six to twelve cloves of garlic and boil in vegetable stock with as varied a bouquet garni as the garden provides: parsley, bay laurel, tarragon, thyme, oregano, fennel, and rosemary are good. Boil for an hour to extract flavors. Add salt and pepper. Beat one egg, slowly pour into soup while whisking, but don't boil. Serve with cheese sandwiches, fried, grilled, or plain.

LEEK AND POTATO SOUP WITH SORREL

Slice leeks and potatoes. Boil until soft. Cool and blend soup while adding salt, black pepper, and a pinch of fenugreek powder. To serve, reheat. Meanwhile, lightly sauté a handful of chopped sorrel in a tablespoon of olive oil and stir into the soup just before ladling it into bowls. Serve with boiled egg slices on crackers.

SIBERIAN KALE SOUP

Coarsely chop leaves of Siberian kale and simmer with one chopped onion and garlic cloves until soft. Cool and blend. For a punch, blend the onion raw. Add soy sauce, to taste. Reheat this delicious green soup and serve with cheesy dreams—cheese sandwiches fried on both sides.

Summer Soups

CUCUMBER AND YOGURT SOUP

A lovely soup for late summer gluts of cucumber. Cook cucumbers in water, cool, and blend. Mix in plain yogurt. Serve chilled with dill or arugula and a dusting of cumin or ground coriander. Also make this soup with zucchini.

GAZPACHO

This is a famous Spanish dish and a main meal. Mix a few slices of bread with olive oil, a little vinegar, garlic, and 2 cups of stock. Add chopped tomatoes, cucumbers, bell peppers, and onions. Blend or mix well, carefully adding cayenne pepper. Add salt and chili to taste. Serve cold with chives. Adding crushed walnuts tastes good, though maybe not very Spanish.

THE PICK-AND-COME-AGAIN PLOT

Spring & Summer

B Y NOW, you may have a collection of seed packets for all sorts of pick-and-come-again greens. Check which can be planted in spring and summer. Since you may have grown onions, garlic, and leeks for the Soup Plots (page 192), and these continue into early summer, plug in seeds of Asian and other summer greens while harvesting the older vegetables as time goes by. Plug in non-heading lettuces and raise one cucumber plant and one or two cherry tomato bushes in toilet paper tubes. Scratch B&B between plants and douse seedlings with LS.

This plot will give you ingredients for stir-fries, soups, quiches, and salads, if your way of cooking and composing meals takes into account what grows at a particular time. This is all you can do while the allium family is drying off. But nothing stops you from digging up a new square if you haven't done so yet, to grow your favorite starchy staples. And if you have done so, there should be space available.

Endive and perennial spinach take up one sixth of a square, yet provide interesting greens for most of the year.

THE STARCHY STAPLES PLOT

Spring & Svmmer

SWEET CORN grows well after a winter crop of fava beans—leave the stakes in place—or after crops that were well fed. If the plot is new, treat with CMC or COF. Plant seeds in a square grid 6 inches apart, denser than for the Aztec Plot (page 182)—6 × 6 seeds may yield thirty to fifty cobs, if you feed and water plants well. Use braided baling twine or pantyhose to tie around stakes to keep stalks standing in high winds. Apply B&B when cobs start forming, and keep up the watering. Harvest when the silk dries off. Should rats eat ripening cobs, cut waxed paper plates once to the center, place one under each cob upside down, staple the cut section, and wind a strip of sheeting around the stem to keep the plate in place. Or, cover each cob with an orange net bag. Cobs can be frozen. Dry the best cob on the stalk for seed, and use within a year.

Potatoes are prolific croppers. One plant can produce up to 1 pound of potatoes, depending on the variety and soil fertility. You will get much more from one square than from the tub we've used to grow fingerling potatoes for salads and pizzas. Choose a bigger potato this time. Whereas fava beans and sweet corn can be alternated for a few years, never grow potatoes in the same place for at least five years, to avoid root rot. Apply manure and straw.

Sweet potatoes grow mostly in tropical to subtropical climates, but in temperate regions, try sprouting a tuber indoors, then plant it in a sheltered, sunny spot. Water daily but assure good drainage. If the plant produces plenty of vines above ground, you can pick leaves and crunchy fry them for a delicious green vegetable. Apply a thick cover of CM after planting. Read more in Part Four (page 268).

THE ROTATING MONO-CROPS PLOT

All Seasons

MANY PEOPLE take pride in growing one prolific crop really well each season, rather than bother about diversity. As long as you can buy a range of locally grown organic vegetables, your square can grow the fillers.

Begin in spring with a plot of sweet corn. Follow this in autumn with fava beans. Follow this the next spring with potatoes, and the following autumn with peas. Read up on their cultivation in Part Four (page 221) or in previous plot plans. After harvesting, snip bean and pea plants at ground level, chopping up and digging in the plants as green manure. Such a sequence returns some of the nutrients the crops take out, but in the fifth season, it is best to grow a grain or a green crop, like mustard, to dig in. Or, cover the square thickly with CMC and B&B and grow shallow-rooted lettuces, Asian greens, or horta through summer and winter, before returning the plot to the sequence, starting with sweet corn in the fourth spring, but omitting potatoes for another four years.

THE INTERLACING PLOT

Spring & Autumn

THIS IS another gem from 6th-century China, still practiced today. Professor Shih Sheng-han calls it olericulture. The Webster's Dictionary defines that as "the cultivation of edible plants as pot herbs," but the professor talks about the "Interlacing Plot System" grown in open ground. Pot herbs may also be herbs for the cooking pot.

The problem to be solved, he writes, is "how to obtain the maximum number of individual plants in a unit area of land, yet eliminate the ill effect of overcrowding, and to avoid temporary vacancy as far as possible."

CENTRAL DIAGONALLY

5 Tuscan kale

5 Siberian kale

LOWER LEFT CORNER

3 mibuna

UPPER RIGHT CORNER

salad greens

20 beet seeds

7 broccoli plants

row of rutabagas

row of bok choy

row of radishes

row of carrots

4 – 5 choy sum plants

row of turnips

This book is full of interlacing plots! I confess that overcrowding was less of a worry than unused space. The professor advises that the Interlacing Plot grows well-chosen sets of different plants that are harvested successively with as little as possible "mutual interference."

Examples are spring onions or bush beans planted among melon vines, as commended by the compiler of the first agricultural almanac in the 2nd century CE. Chia Ssu-Hsieh in the 6th century

CE adds his combinations of onions and parsley, turnips and hemp (hello!), and turnips among mulberry trees.

If you look around your garden, you will find spaces not as well occupied as they could be. Take into account how deep the roots of the plants you combine will grow, how wide the plants will become, whether they need the same water and fertilizer treatment and like the same soil, usually neutral at a pH of 6.5 to 7, as well as their share of sun or dappled shade. If planting under a tree, consider whether the tree has deep or surface roots.

I successfully "interlaced" the wine tub in full sun that contains my mulberry tree. As garlic is a good companion for most fruit trees and likes soil deep enough to develop bulbs, I planted thirty cloves in the surface soil of the tub. Both mulberry tree and garlic plants looked happy. I harvested thirty garlic bulbs—and the generous crop of mulberries is not garlic flavored! It's now re-sown with carrot seed.

I interlaced cauliflowers with cilantro. Both grow in the cool season, so just plant cauli seedlings and rake coriander seed through the soil between them. The cilantro did better than the cauliflowers.

Another combination was high-rise broccoli with small Japanese turnips. Pick the lower leaves of the broccoli to give the turnips some sun. Wash and cut leaves and stir-fry in olive oil with a kaffir lime leaf, garlic, and thyme. Delicious on toasted bread or pasta.

Great interlacing patterns can be made by planting root crops like onions, scallions, radishes, and carrots among high-rise plants like broccoli, kale, and choy sum. Plant in short rows so you can find the shorties at the back. Beet, turnip, and rutabaga benefit from shallot and carrot companions. As they all take a fair while to grow, I interlaced them with quick-growing salad plants whose outer leaves are constantly picked. Or try bok choy, mibuna, and radicchio.

If interlacing appeals to you—and it should appeal to anyone with little space—sit down with a companion planting book and your garden notebook. While the rain pours down outside, or the sun bleaches the skin off the fences, educate yourself on the plants that grow well together. Write down combinations to try through two planting seasons: autumn and spring. Hang up the list near the back door, or in your seed cabinet, and let the experiments start.

Professor Shih warns "to avoid temporary vacancy." The moment a thin row of shallots or radishes has been harvested, recondition the soil with fresh compost and a little B&B, and plug in lettuce seeds or seedlings. When carrots come out in meal-size bunches, replant with bok choy or kale. As long as the soil is kept supplied with nutrients, there is no reason you can't plant continuously, all year round.

Should there come a day that all the vegetables in the interlacing plot are reaching maturation, let it happen, eat marvelous meals of the combinations, pick seed-head salsas, then sow a green manure crop of mustard seed (a good handful), and turn that in before it starts to flower. Another month later, apply old manure and fresh compost, and the plot is ready to be planted with whatever you choose, as it has undergone considerable crop rotation already.

THE ONION AND GARLIC PLOT

Autumn & Winter

F YOU grew starchy staples and peas, there ought to be enough nutrients left to grow a root crop. Maybe you are too busy this year to pay attention to the food garden. But you can save much money without spending much time by setting out an onion and garlic plot. Decide how much garlic you want and how many onions. Clean the soil and draw a dividing line. Divide a packet of onion seed over two containers and break heads of garlic into cloves. Buy a handful of shallots to plant direct and triple in volume.

To save maintenance time, plant garlic in rows and transplant onions in straight drills when 3 to 4 inches high. Mulch thickly on top of the garlic and between onion drills. Douse with LC. The only work left to do is weed the onion plot while seedlings are struggling up. They look like grass but they don't feel like grass between the fingers, much less smell like grass. This once-only weeding job cannot be avoided. Do it when straps are 5 to 6 inches above ground, then cover soil between rows thickly with CM.

Water the square if rains should fail, and douse with LS once a month. You can harvest onion and garlic straps to flavor many a meal. You are having a winter off from food gardening, yet saving money and eating home-grown produce. Plan to have more variety next season!

THE GINGER OR GALANGAL PLOT

Spring

YOU MAY want to grow either ginger (*Zingiber officinale*) or its close cousin galangal (*Alpinia officinalis* or *Alpinia galanga*). Ginger has a stronger taste. Some sources say it originated in Jamaica. *The New Oxford Book of Food Plants* says it "evolved in South-East Asia but is never found in the wild state," but there is also Indian, Chinese, and African ginger. Since the ancient Greeks, Romans, Indians, and Chinese all had it millennia ago, who can know for certain? I saw ginger growing wild on the big island of Hawaii, along the road leading from Hilo to the top of the volcano Mauna Kea, where the rainfall is notoriously high. Like all roadside plants, they grew on rain and sun and sometimes received not enough of one and too much of the other. The flowers are fragrant and gorgeous.

My own gingers and galangals near the water tank are as wild as they come; they seem to thrive on neglect. The part eaten, the root or rhizome, grows partly above ground. Using ginger and galangal is a daily affair in Asia. It is part of the trio that starts off any stir-fry: garlic, onion, ginger, or galangal. Galangal is milder. India is named as its country of origin. The plants look like ginger, but galangal has a pretty mahogany red sheen to the skin of the root.

A warm spot in the garden, partly sunny with a few hours shade, will grow ginger and galangal. As they grow tall, you can plant them as background or along a fence as a screen. In spring, make a rich mix with compost and humus, buy a root or two and push them just below soil level. Water well and initially cover with a thin layer of straw mulch. Never drown them, but don't let them dry out, either. Shoots will appear and grow into strong green stems with narrow leaves. When these have become a bunch that pushes above the soil surface, you can cut a piece off for the kitchen. Keep using it because, when summer ends, you may have to pull up the entire plant to divide it and harvest the bigger roots. Chop stems and leaves for the compost, and grow young roots in pots in a warm veranda to go out in open ground next spring. Process or use the rest.

Ginger and galangal keep in a cool, dark place, in the fridge, can be frozen, or preserved. Preserve finely cubed ginger or galangal in honey. Peel, cut, pack

Galangal in flower. Galangal and ginger plants grow in pots by a water tank that provides shelter and reflected warmth.

into jars, and dribble with honey until covered. Use these preserves for baking and desserts. Small jars make great presents. Over time, the honey becomes ginger mead!

If you live in cold climes, you can grow both ginger and galangal indoors in 1-foot pots filled with potting soil and humus. Buy a few roots, push just below soil level, and water in well. Place in a sunroom or enclosed veranda, keeping pots just moist. Cut off a chunk when needed, but harvest when they burst out of the pot. Replant the best piece and use the rest as above.

Do not plant a whole 3-foot square with either plant, unless you mean to use it frequently. One root of each will do, in the ground or in pots, until you know how much you are likely to use. Make these tasty roots part of your life, and you will add another health plus to your tasty meals.

THE ANTI-CANCER PLOTS

KIDS OBJECT to strong-tasting vegetables. So do some adults. Brussels sprouts and broccoli used to taste bitter, but this has been bred out to make these vegetables more palatable. The old bitter taste was caused by glucosinates that helped the plants ward off pests, and also helped the human immune system ward off the formation of tumors. That is how the brassica family, especially broccoli, became known as cancer-fighting vegetables. There is evidence that modern vegetables have less vitamin and mineral content than old varieties. The epidemic of cancer in a bewildering variety of forms has been blamed on an equally bewildering number of possible causes. But since the maintenance of our bodies and immune systems relies largely on what we ingest, we should perhaps take note of these findings.[25]

It seems that by altering vegetables for modern tastes or for longer shelf lives, the plants' innate protection mechanism has been reduced. Subsequently, genetically modified crops have been bred to make them pesticide resistant so they can be sprayed against pests. Waste no time, but return to the old varieties available from seed banks (see Useful Addresses on page 317).

Anti-Cancer Plot A

Spring & Summer

For a spring and summer Anti-Cancer Plot, plant Chinese flowering broccoli, green summer cabbage, and kale. Raise broccoli and cabbage, in toilet paper tubes while preparing soil with CMC, OF, and lime. Plant broccoli and cabbage 8 inches apart. That's crowded, but you'll pick outer leaves for stir-fries. Sow seed for several kale plants to make green soup—see the Soup Plots on page 192. Douse all plants with LS.

Also eat yellow/orange vegetables to bolster the immune system. Read up on carrots, pumpkins, and squashes in Part Four (page 221). Sow carrots direct as instructed; raise pumpkins and squashes in toilet paper tubes as in previous plot plans. Plant out when danger of frost is over.

Feed monthly with B&B, OF, and LS in rotation. If there's space, plug in seed of summer-loving Asian brassicas—see An A–Z of Vegetable Families (page 222).

Anti-Cancer Plot B
Autumn & Winter

In mid-summer, raise half a dozen brussels sprouts in toilet paper tubes to grow on into winter. Sow seed for new kales, winter broccoli (slice the thick stems and cook with florets), cabbages, and Asian brassicas preferring cool weather. Grow winter or all-season carrots and daikon radishes (see recipes under Daikon in Part Four on page 263). Sow a row of beets, for all red vegetables and fruits are cancer fighters.

Apart from eating brassica vegetables three or four times a week, make meals with one green and one yellow/orange vegetable, and add red fruits and vegetables whenever you can. Prepare these foods in several ways—fresh, steamed, in soups or salads—so the body gets a steady supply of disease-fighting nutrients. Do not discard outer cabbage leaves, but wash and simmer with onions, garlic, and caraway seed. These leaves are the best of the cabbage. Make cabbage rolls with grated daikon, fresh cilantro, or fenugreek and marinated tofu. Steam beet greens. Use all stems of kale, broccoli, and cabbage for juicing, adding apples, carrots, or ginger for flavor. Blend beet juice with carrots. Health!

BERRY PLOTS AND HEDGES

Autumn

ALL BERRIES prefer cool weather. For growing notes, see Easy-Care Fruit Trees and Berries on page 293. Appropriate netting not dangerous to wildlife may be necessary, therefore plant hedges that can be reached from both sides. Berries are superior foods providing immunity boosters and disease-fighting and health-restoring minerals and vitamins. Red and blue berries are cancer-fighting fruits.

Presently, blueberries top the list of anti-cancer fruits, followed by blackberries, a disappearing species due to spraying by landholders. If you have a stand of blackberries on your land, and you can keep a goat, let her prune it after fruiting. Goats know what's good for them. The bushes grow back to fruit copiously. Dig out seedlings where you don't want them. The main reason for the spread of blackberry seedlings is neglect of unattended land. If they get into your garden, either dig them out or cut them down continually. Regular edge trimming for three years eradicates them. Should you have acres of blackberry bushes on your new country block, mend your fences and get another goat. But don't contaminate the neighborhood and waterways by broad-acre spraying.

A thornless blackberry is available from nurseries. It grows like topsy on a support and can be pruned into shape. Also consider raspberries and other brambles such as youngberries. Youngberries bear large, juicy fruit and will grow vigorously on lower wires between espaliered fruit trees. Extreme heat can kill them. Plant them where they get shade in the heat of day. Apply deep mulch and rocks to keep roots cool. Water during dry spells.

Raspberries need a string support between stakes. Train new shoots espalier fashion for easy picking.

Berry bushes with thorns are best kept away from vegetables. Plant bushes so you can cultivate the soil around them. Or, plant a freestanding berry hedge, spacing bushes according to their labels. Include one or two of each variety, let them fight it out, and pick your three-berry mix straight from the bushes. My partner grew up in North America. One day, picking over a large wild blueberry bush, he sensed someone else was picking the other side. Peeking around the bush, he came face to face with a large brown bear! The bear was more interested in the berries than in other pickers, so that expedition ended well. See Blueberries on page 297 for requirements.

Gooseberries are delightful if ripened on the bush. They are thorny and perennial.

Strawberries live the low life in semi-permanent beds. As they need netting, make a bed the size of your cage or netting. It's a nice idea to plant strawberry borders, but long borders are hard to protect from birds. Even under netting, millipedes come for dessert. Read up in Part Four (page 306) for important directions.

Consider strawberries in their natural environment of dappled light in forests and hedgerows, partially shaded in richly mulched, well-draining soil, surrounded by nutritious weeds. Hard to imitate. Commercial strawberries grow in open fields, through slits in black plastic sheeting on rows of heaped-up earth made weed-free with chemicals. They need to be fed and watered heavily to produce the three large annual crops that make them commercially viable. They keep every latest wave of human immigrants in part-time work, picking, packing, and cultivating.

Mulch strawberries with pine or fir needles to improve the flavor.

THE PUMPKIN PLOT

Spring & Summer

THE PUMPKIN takes an important place in our diet. It used to be the sloppy yellow one you had to have alongside your greens. With luck, it was baked pumpkin. As innovative cuisines gained popularity, the pumpkin took off in the form of a golden soup, adorned with herbs, spices, cream, and chives, whose popularity has not waned. Roast pumpkin turns up in convenience foods—baguettes, tarts, pizzas—and chefs' gourmet creations.

Now that the seed of many old-fashioned varieties is procurable, everyone can find a favorite pumpkin, although the Queensland blue and the Chianti-bottle-shaped butternut will deservedly remain favorites for their sturdy flesh and keeping qualities.

An experimental summer delivered the good keeper Queensland blue pumpkin, Japanese pumpkins, and some prolific yellow squashes.

The ideal growing medium for pumpkins is the compost heap. Question is, how to leave a compost heap undisturbed for half a year to allow pumpkins their place in the sun? Compost heaps provide a variety of nutrients and preserve moisture with good drainage. All these the pumpkin vine appreciates. Pumpkins have been known to grow in long-term heaps, those you throw the rough stuff on.

Present climate changes leading to hotter summers must be taken into account. Planting three pumpkin seeds in a small hill and pulling out the two weaker seedlings may still work in cooler and wetter parts. But on the plains and in dry places where water is scarce, grow pumpkins in a thickly composted and manured bed. In semi-desert climates, grow them in a ditch.

Cutting three 3-foot ditches side-by-side gives a compact situation, where all water expended is kept in the family, whereas one long ditch of 9 feet tends to dry out on both sides. In the three-ditch square, the middle ditch may do best. Dig 12 inches deep. In late winter, fill ditches with layers of soft weeds or green leaves and stalks, manure, compost, OF, or B&B, and straw mulch. The green matter decomposes quickly; all layers will mash to form the feeding ground, with applications of LS or OF as pumpkins are forming.

Start off only one variety of pumpkin seedlings in nine toilet paper tubes as described in the Aztec Plot (page 182), three plants per ditch. Of course, they will clamber all over each other and sprawl beyond the square. But as long as you place straw, planks, or tiles under forming fruit, it should not matter. When there are several fruits on a vine, pinch out the tips. This tells the vine to stop having babies and put its energy into the ones it already has. Steam the tips and young leaves, flowers and all, in coconut cream, and serve as a vegetable.

Shade is important in very hot weather. With three ditches on one square, it is easy to place a shade cloth or hospital gown over the plot, holding it down with rocks. Remove cloth at dusk. Or construct a four-poster tepee wound with shade cloth.

Don't pick pumpkins too early. When stems start drying out and are obviously unable to feed the fruit any longer, cut pumpkins with a 2-inch stem. Place on a table or bench in an airy place outside to harden off. Blend immature pumpkins for soup and freeze. Immature pumpkins have an immature taste, but mix with lentils, herbs, and spices to give edible results.

Seed saving: From the best one— the biggest and most mature—wash the seed, dry it for several weeks out of sunlight, and store in a mouse-resistant container.

THE PERENNIALS

All Seasons

READ UP on these vegetables in Part Four (page 221) for more details. Perennial vegetables are ideal for the busy person who often does not see the garden in daylight until the weekend. These vegetables can look after themselves better than annual vegetables. Make sure you want them where you plant them, because they mean to stay more or less forever. They do not fit into the pattern of rotating vegetable plots. Here are a few indications of how little work is involved.

Artichokes are easily grown from seed in late summer, or offsets from a nursery. The plants make a great hedge, but after harvesting—spring to summer—they must be cut to the ground to rise again. They are not choosy about soil, although better soil breeds better chokes. Mostly, they require mulch and an application of CMC and B&B in late winter, before they fruit in spring. Give weekly waterings in summer as they grow back. When new plants form at the base, these can be cut off with a spade and planted out.

One packet of seed gives a good hedge, and that hedge will give you another hedge in time. And so on to the neighbors! For seed, let one choke turn into a thistle-blue flower and don't cut down till it is dried on the stalk.

Asparagus is for the patient gardener, but worth every juicy bite. Dig soil a spade deep. Grow from seed sown

Artichokes are an underrated, decorative, and easy crop to grow along a sunny fence. A perennial vegetable, the plants can be divided each year to establish a hedge.

in autumn, or plant crowns and cover with CMC and thick mulch. Do not eat any spears for two years, and then only a few, before picking meals in the fourth year. Never clear-fell them.

They survive on an annual big feed and weekly watering.

Perennial spinach and sorrel, both spinaches, can be grouped together and cooked together. Both grow through all seasons, both survive on a twice-yearly feed and watering in dry times, and both increase by division or dropping seeds. Cut seed stems if not needed. They are a great standby.

Rhubarb grows from crowns, and one or two plants are enough for most families. As the (toxic) leaves grow big, two plants take up half a square, so it is advisable to plant rhubarb out in the garden to look decorative. Rhubarb also needs a good feed before the growing season, a rich mulch, and weekly watering.

THE SPICE COMPANIONS

Spring, Autumn, & Winter

THE ADVENTURE of a spice plot is that you would never have seen some of these plants, even if you cook with spices. A spice plot does not have to fill a whole square; a quarter will do, or even a handy strip by the kitchen door.

Just as you grow coriander and fenugreek from seeds bought in the grocery, so with other spices. Rake seeds into the soil in small patches or tiny rows and stick in name tags, as they tend to look alike.

Caraway, cumin, and dill look similar when young. Like cilantro and fenugreek, these green herbs are all great seed producers. Fennel grows enormous, so plant just one, and separately. Don't let seed spread to the neighborhood—cut off seed heads before seed drops. Mustard soon towers over others and is bet-ter grown among vegetables. Buy *kalonji* or "onion seed" (visibly related to love-in-a-mist) from the Indian shop.

Duck into shops of various cultures for seeds in little packets. Ask what they are used for. Try them out in the kitchen and plant a few. Some, being tropical, may not respond, but other fresh spice greens make delicious additions to small meals of a few vegetables, noodles, roasted pumpkin, salads, blender soups, or bread sprinkled with olive oil and cheese. Gourmet eating made easy.

THE STINGING NETTLE PLOT

Spring, Autumn, & Late Winter

NETTLES? AREN'T THEY A WEED? They fooled you, too, didn't they? Stinging nettles have developed one of the best defenses against being eaten by man or beast. A child who unwittingly picks a stem of hairy nettle gets such a shock and rush of tears that, as an adult, she goes circles around nettles. If the child could recognize a dock weed (*Rumex* sp.), she would pick a leaf and vigorously crush it to rub the juices into the affected hand.

A plant from the northern hemisphere, stinging nettle (*Urtica dioica*) has spread to southern continents through human migration. Wherever nettles grow tall and deep green, the soil is rich and fertile. Used over the centuries for medicinal purposes, it was and is an ingredient in peasant cuisine in the form of nettle soup and recipes calling for fine spinach. Nettle tea, from fresh or dried leaves, but with no sting, has a velvety taste. Rich in nitrogen, nettles are a soil food, a compost activator, and make excellent compost "tea" to spray on vegetables. For those who eat nettles, it provides vitamins, proteins, potassium, iron, calcium, and omega-3s. Flowering nettles attract beneficial insects to your garden.

Nettle is the designated food for certain species of butterflies and moths. Nothing else eats nettles in the raw. This virtual pest-free existence make nettles a good crop. There are still some farmers who grow it to make linen after soaking the stems. Experiment: soak nettles for a few weeks until leaves have dissolved. Drain liquid where you want to grow the next crop. Dry stems and thrash the nettles on a stick with many headless nails and you have the basic ingredient for a rough sort of linen.

Even before the age of garden gloves, curious humans found that nettles were actually food.

Toss young, leafy stems in olive oil or in a stir-fry for a delicacy on your plate. The heat of cooking destroys the sting.

Saved plants will eventually flower and set seed. As seed starts drying, tie paper bags over the tops to stop seed dispersing. Re-sow a patch nearby or a vegetable bed needing restoration. Keep this routine going: always harvest the bulk of the nettles and save seed of the best. Don't let it blow about the neighborhood to people who think it is a weed and get out the toxic spray.

Although most animals will avoid a nettle patch, wild nettles could have been polluted by traffic fumes or farm sprays. But should you be so lucky to have nettles in your backyard, this is the way to maintain that plot of rich and tasty food. Just water them when conditions are dry, and if they look pale, apply chicken manure, and water in well. They will soak up the nitrogen. Leave some of the best plants untouched to collect seed. Gradually eat your way through the others. A famous Melbourne restaurant has nettles stir-fry on the menu, so what are you waiting for?

THE EDIBLE FLOWER PLOT

Spring & Autumn

FLOWERS PERFORM many functions in the food garden. They attract bees that will pollinate fruit trees and other flowering crops and attract beneficial insects that will control not-so-beneficial insects. They also exude their own unobtrusive chemicals that will protect food plants and fruit trees, and thus become valued companion plants. Spring and autumn are the best seasons to sow new flowers, but check seed packet advice.

In the edible flower plot, sow caraway, cumin, cilantro, mustard, dill, borage, chives, marigold, nasturtium, tarragon, and just a few carrot seeds.

It is easy enough to plant the right companion plant under a fruit tree. But it's not always possible to plant the right flowers with the food plant that needs it, because food plants come and go, turning up here and there through the seasons.

I solve this by letting marigolds (*Calendula officinalis*, not the frilly French marigolds) seed themselves to come up where they will, pulling up excess plants, but saving seeds. I harvest the flowers for salads and also dry petals for baking biscuits and cakes. They brighten a green garden like little else will. Nasturtiums grow well on an asparagus bed after the vegetable goes dormant. Pick flowers and leaves for salads, and pickle the seeds as fake capers.

Arugula flowers are peppery and good enough to nibble while gardening.

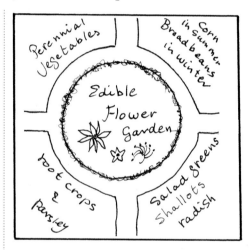

Strew them on pasta, salads, and salsas. Fold them in avocado filling for rolls. The flowers of the brassica family (cabbage, kale, mustards, Asian greens) tend to be all of the same yellowish hue. These yellow tops make delicious side dishes sautéed in olive oil. No spicing needed, unless you like a toe of garlic in it. Borage has blue star flowers with black pistils— eat only the petals. Endive and chicory going to seed produce heavenly blue flowers that look good on salads. Purple chive flowers are edible, too, if you don't mind an oniony flavor.

Bees and insects are attracted to a plethora of colors and fragrances. So if your food garden is more than a few square plots, why not make one in the center, the Edible Flower Plot, for you and your winged friends. Make it round, surrounded by a path and then a larger circle of the plots it serves.

Leave the marigolds rambling through the vegetables. In the Edible Flower Plot, grow borage, nasturtium, dill, caraway, cilantro, cumin, and one flowering carrot. The colors here are orange, blue, yellow, white, whitish pink, and cream. For winter color, add Mexican tarragon with its stalks of deep golden flowers, and in summer, mauve or red-flowering bergamot for fragrant herbal tea. If you can place in the center a 6-foot tripod of three branches or bamboo stems and rake in a handful of sweet pea seeds underneath in autumn, you can look up at some of nature's more divine flower hues against a blue sky come spring.

Once planted, the plot will re-seed itself. Whenever there is a bare spot, just sprinkle in a few carrot seeds, because when carrot goes to seed, it towers above all the others, so you can pull what is too much and eat the carrot, leaving one to rise and display its large umbels. Carrot leaves are a chemical factory in themselves; nothing ever eats them, but the flower is visited. Stand there on sunny mornings and watch the traffic!

Marigolds (*Calendula officinalis*) should ramble through any food garden. The flower petals can go by the handful in salads, cake batter, rice pilaf, or on top of soups and baked dishes. Petals can be dried and stored for later use without losing color. Marigolds are plant companions and renowned pest controllers. The plant also has medicinal value.

PART 4

DESCRIPTIONS
of
FOOD PLANTS

An *A–Z* of VEGETABLE FAMILIES

L EARNING TO recognize which plants are related makes it easier to recognize their seedlings and meet their needs. Individual species of plants belong to a genus, a group of plants having characteristics in common. A genus, in turn, belongs to a larger family of genera, but, in practice, the word family is used for genus, like the peas and beans family.

A quick read of these three pages gives you much information in a nutshell to acquaint you with the nature of vegetable plants, so you can choose accordingly. They are grouped under their family, sharing specific growth habits.

Aizoaceae/ice plant family: New Zealand spinach (Warrigal greens).

Alliaceae/Allium/lily family: Around 500 species of chives, leeks, onions, and all sorts of shallots—grow from seed. Grow garlic and bunching onions from division of bulbs. Grow day lilies (*Hemerocallis*) for lily buds. All produce one seed ball per stem.

Apiaceae/Umbelliferae/carrot family: Grow from seed. Flowers range from white and pinkish to yellow. These plants hold their seeds in "umbels" like flat umbrellas, helipads for beneficial flying insects. Let them set seed throughout the vegetable garden in spring, and predators will come in enough numbers to keep pests in check. Caraway, carrots, celery, chervil, cilantro, cumin, dill, fennel, parsley, and parsnips are friends to food plants under attack.

Asteraceae/Compositae/sunflower family: *Artemisia* species (the wormwoods). Some are grown from cuttings, but the following are grown from seed: chamomile, chicory, dandelion, endive, lettuce, salsify, scorzonera, *shungiku* (chrysanthemum greens), sunflower, and tarragon. Yarrow can also grow from root division. Asparagus, globe artichokes, and Jerusalem artichokes are perennials grown from crowns or roots.

Brassicaceae/Cruciferae/mustard family: This large family grows seeds in small pods like mini peas. Most have yellow flowers with four petals forming a cross. Includes many Asian greens and all gross feeders loving richly manured soils. Kale and brussels sprouts like a touch of frost. Although most brassicas

Protecting brassica plants from cabbage white butterfly is achieved by indicating that the territory is already occupied. Invisible thread such as fish line would work even better.

can be grown throughout the year, they do better when planted late summer/autumn to grow through winter/spring. They tend to go to seed in hot weather, although some remain edible throughout summer. Most of the flowers and seed heads are edible: bok choy, *Brassica juncea*, broccoli, brussels sprouts, cabbage, cauliflower, Chinese cabbage (*petsai*), collard, cress, horseradish, kale, kohlrabi, mustards, choy sum, radish (white and mauve flowers), arugula, rutabaga, tatsoi, turnip, watercress. Swirl seed heads in a wok with sesame and olive oil.

Chenopodiaceae/goosefoot family: Beets (leaves edible), Swiss chard, English spinach, perennial spinach, red orach, rainbow chard.

Convolvulaceae/morning glory family: Sweet potato (*Ipomoea batatas*), originally from Peru. Prefers warm weather and are liable to become unwell when nights are cold.

Cucurbitaceae/gourd family: The genus *Cucurbita* comprises twenty-five species. There is pumpkin on one end and zucchini on the other end. In between are cucumber, gherkin, gourd, marrow, melon, and squash. The terms gourd, squash, and pumpkin are often used interchangeably, depending on local usage. One gardener's butternut pumpkin may be someone else's squash. All are vines, rambling or climbing. Sow late spring through summer.

Fabaceae/Leguminosae/pea family: The nitrogen fixers. Beans and fenugreek (eat bulb, or use leaves and seeds in curries) grow from late spring through summer. Broad beans and most peas from autumn through winter/spring. Direct sowing. When harvesting, cut plants at ground level, leaving roots with nitrogen nodules in the soil.

Malvaceae/mallow family: Okra. Tropical/subtropical and needs a long frost-free season or a greenhouse. Grow from seed.

Poaceae/Grass family: Comprises most grain crops and sweet corn (all beloved by grazers). Grow sweet corn in summer to fix nitrogen.

Polygonaceae/buckwheat family: Buckwheat (from seed), rhubarb (grow from crowns). Both love summer in high altitudes.

Solanaceae/nightshade family: These plants mostly grow in spring/summer. They have five-petaled flowers—white, mauve, and purple—with prominent yellow anthers. The family includes eggplant, Cape gooseberry, bell pepper, chili, goji berry, pepino, potato, tamarillo, tomatillo, tomato, and inedibles like tobacco and belladonna. The latter indicates that toxic solanins exist in all solanum plants to various degrees. They are believed to aggravate arthritis. A Solanaceae-free diet may make a difference to a sufferer. That said, tomatoes are claimed to be essential in the prevention of prostate cancer. But any potatoes showing green patches, from exposure to light while growing, are toxic and must not be eaten by humans or animals.

Urticaceae/nettle family: Stinging nettle, essential plant food in compost and a delicious wild vegetable (stir-fry in olive oil), or herbal tea. Tibetan sage Milarepa (11th century) lived most of his life in a cave on a diet of mainly nettles. A much maligned food worth growing.

SUMMER, WINTER, *and* ALL-SEASON VEGETABLES *and* HERBS

Summer Vegetables and Herbs

Summer vegetables and herbs are mostly sown in spring, although repeat sowing of quick-growing vegetables like radishes, lettuce, and beans are possible until it gets very hot. (For "under glass," read also "behind glass or plastic or indoors.")

Since local climates differ considerably, the starting dates of spring and autumn will vary accordingly. However, the following lists are useful when planning twice-yearly plantings.

PLANT	NOTES
Amaranth	Leaf, some are grown for grain, sow direct
Arugula	Early, outdoors
Basil	Tropical, after frosts in late spring to early summer
Beans	After frosts, repeat sowings until mid-summer
Beets	Plant spring, summer, or autumn
Bell peppers	Start under glass, plant after frosts
Broccoli	Summer variety
Brussels sprouts	Plant mid–late summer
Cabbage	Summer varieties, plant early
Carrots	All seasons variety
Cauliflower	Summer varieties, not in hot climates
Celery	Start early indoors
Chard	Sow thickly for young pickings
Chilies	Start under glass, plant after frosts
Cucumbers	Start under glass, plant after frosts
Dill	In shade, or wait for early autumn
Eggplant	Start under glass, plant after frosts
Globe artichokes	Sow seed in pots, transplant in autumn

Lettuce	Summer varieties, part shade
Melons	Start early under glass, plant after frosts
Mustards	Will bolt (run to seed) early in hot climates
Onions	In cool climates, sow spring onions and other small varieties in early spring
Potatoes	Mulch thickly
Pumpkins	Start under glass, plant after frosts
Radishes	In between other plants, or mix with carrots
Rhubarb	Mulch, regular watering
Snow peas	Plant early, only in cool climates (check packet)
Squash	Summer varieties
Sweet corn	Sow direct when soil warms, re-seed failures
Sweet potatoes	Start indoors, plant after frosts
Tomatoes	Start under glass, plant after frosts
Zucchini	Start under glass, plant after frosts

Hardy butternuts for small families.

Winter Vegetables and Herbs

Winter vegetables and herbs are sown middle to late summer and into autumn while the soil is still warm. Establish perennials like artichokes, asparagus, rhubarb, sorrel, perennial spinach, and strawberries in early autumn.

Fruit trees are best planted in early winter while trees are dormant, but citrus trees should be planted when soil is still warm or in spring—consult your local nursery.

PLANT	NOTES
Arugula	Annual, save seed, grows on till early summer
Asian greens	Greens and flowering tops
Asparagus	From crowns
Beets	Greens and beets
Broad beans	Beans and tops
Broccoli	Flowering stem
Cabbage	Most varieties
Carrots	All-season variety
Cauliflower	Winter varieties
Celery & celery herb	Stems and leaves
Chard	Grow rainbow colors
Cilantro & coriander	Grow as a fresh herb or for the spicy seed
Dill	Greens and seed
Endive	Hearting variety
Fava beans	Plant in autumn
Fenugreek	When seedpods dry, harvest seeds for curries
Garlic	Plant while soil is still warm
Globe artichokes	Plant roots
Kale	Eat leaves and flowering tops
Leeks	Plant in a row while soil is still warm, transplant when 4 inches
Lettuce	Winter varieties, like radicchio, lamb's lettuce, oak-leaf
Mustards	Including giant red
Onions	Plant sets or seeds in a row, transplant when 4 inches
Parsley	Seed or division, biennial, re-sow every second year
Peas	Winter peas, or check seed packets

Radishes	Including daikon
Rhubarb	Plant crowns
Rutabagas	Japanese
Snow peas	Check seed packet for climate directions
Spinach	English, perennial and others
Strawberries	Late autumn to early spring
Turnips	Purple top

All-Season Vegetables and Herbs

All-season vegetables and herbs are best sown in spring and autumn, as most seed-lings won't take off in summer's heat or winter's dread. Some appear in previous lists as summer or winter vegetables, but can manage in all seasons. Others have special "all-season" varieties.

PLANT	NOTES
Asian greens	Most leaf vegetables
Beets	Greens and beets
Broccoli	Depending on variety
Broccoli rabe	Flowering stem—winter and mild summers
Cabbage	Depending on variety
Carrots	All-season varieties
Cauliflower	All-season varieties
Chard	White or rainbow stems
Herbs	Can be planted any time, except tropical ones, although cilantro, dill, and arugula do well in the cool season
Jerusalem artichoke	Plant roots
Lettuce	Romaine, mignonette, radicchio, and mesclun mix
Mustards	Including giant red
Radicchio	Red or green
Rutabagas	Japanese
Turnips	Purple top

For more on how the weather affects growing, see The Seasons (page 116) and Climate, Weather, and Microclimate (page 119).

COMMON VEGETABLES:
HOW *to* GROW *and* USE THEM

NLESS OTHERWISE STATED, these vegetables are grown from seed. Some food plants are known as both vegetable and fruit, like melons. Some large herbs are also known as vegetables, like sorrel. Brief cooking suggestions are included, especially for lesser-known food plants.

General Growing Notes

COLORS

Green vegetables contain chlorophyll. Carotenes are found in orange and yellow vegetables like carrots, red bell peppers, melons, pumpkins, sweet potatoes, and tomatoes. Anthocyanin colors red-purple vegetables and fruit; these are important in preventing cancers. They range from red and blue berries, cherries, and plums, to purple Siberian kale, red-brown lettuces and radicchios, red cabbage, and beets. It has been claimed that antioxidants in reddish plant foods eradicate harmful free radicals ten times faster than do green vegetables.

OFFICINALIS

Plants carrying *officinalis* as their second botanical name were used as medicine before modern pharmaceuticals appeared. Some *officinalis* plants are once again being used in medicines after a period in exile.

LIME

Soils that are acidic rather than alkaline need a dusting of lime, particularly when growing peas, beans, and onions. But amaranth, eggplants, blueberries, celery, and potatoes don't like lime.

NITROGEN

Found in commercial fertilizers and concentrated manures, such as poultry manure. Nitrogen generates abundant

Asparagus is for the patient gardener, as you must not pick any spears for the first two years.

growth of foliage. Reduce applications for fruiting crops after plants are established, or they will grow more leaf than fruit. Fruiting crops are eggplants, beans, broccoli, brussels sprouts, bell peppers, cauliflower, cucumbers, pumpkins, squash, tomatoes, and so forth.

For root crops, like beets, carrots, onions, parsnips, rutabagas, and turnips, very little nitrogen goes a long way—too much, and you eat leaves. Peas and beans fix nitrogen from the soil, leaving enough behind for root crops if pea and beanstalks are cut off at soil level rather than pulled up.

SOWING SEASONS

Sowing seasons are only a guide. Across the country, there are vast differences in climate and elevation. Climatic conditions have become unpredictable, and freak weather occurs everywhere. Watch seasonal cycles where you live, and be prepared to sow again if first sowings fail due to bad weather. Keep a garden notebook.

STAPLE VEGETABLES

These are described here in greater detail than more experimental varieties. Consult seed catalogs for organic seed of more unusual varieties, or try aquatic vegetables in a pond or a water pot.

List of Common Vegetables

AMARANTH
(any variety of the *Amaranthus* genus)

Sow in spring, after frosts have ceased. A prehistoric plant with a variety also known as love-lies-bleeding. Amaranth grown for its leaves is sometimes known as Greek spinach, although similar amaranths appear in Southeast Asia, Africa, and the Caribbean.

These tall, green-maroon plants have a counterpart (*A. caudatus*) grown in South America for its small grains that are ground into flour. There are more varieties, with maroon to yellowish feathery flowers, producing the best leaves or best grain, and all are very nutritious. Pick young leaf tips for salads or mix mature leaves with milder spinaches. The plant doesn't like lime, fancies a little nitrogen, and accepts poor soil. Being drought tolerant, self-seeding, and easily removed where not wanted, amaranth's glorious colors would grace a bare spot in an ornamental garden.

For a first crop, sow the fine seed indoors in a tray and transplant at 3 to 4 inches. Plant outside after frosts cease, keeping a few reserves in pots. Success in the garden means self-seeded plants next year, but do harvest some grains. This is a plant whose time is yet to come.

ARUGULA (*Eruca sativa*)

Sow in late summer. From the Mediterranean. Also rocket or Italian cress, roquette, rughetta. There is also a perennial wild arugula (*Diplotaxis tenuifolia*) with long serrated leaves, a self-sowing sprawler with a milder taste. Arugula has moderate water requirements, grows profusely, and produces enough lobed leaves to be treated as a tasty standby vegetable. The only gardeners complaining about arugula's fecundity are those who restrict its use to decoration on salads or risotto. The plant is easily pulled up where not wanted, appears disease free and bug resistant, and loses its bite when cooked, making it suitable for soups and stir-fries.

Arugula is still a wild plant, like sorrel. It grows in the cool season, going to seed when the heat arrives, self-seeding freely so that, by autumn, you can start picking lush, deep green leaves. It starts small, barely higher than a lettuce, but can shoot up suddenly, which may have given rise to its English name. One plant produces hundreds of tiny, pale-cream flowers, and sets thousands of seeds in tiny pods. Although arugula can be relied upon to drop enough seed to re-seed itself, pick enough dry pods to store for a thickly sown arugula bed in spring or summer.

Arugula can withstand some warm weather and still provide handfuls of fresh leaves for salads and pastas. During overproduction, make amazing arugula soup served with a dollop of yogurt. Chickens love a meal of arugula. We all need arugula. It is one of the antioxidant green plants that boost our immune system, keeping us young. Let it set seed in at least two places because the flowers attract good insects.

ASPARAGUS (*Asparagus officinalis*)

Plant crowns in autumn or sow in spring. Companions: nasturtiums, parsley, and tomatoes. A perennial indigenous to Central and Western Asia, Europe, and North Africa. The Greeks have cultivated it from ancient times, and the English pluck it along their coasts.

Asparagus has male and female plants. The females are slim and pretty, too thin to cook, and produce tiny vermilion-seed berries. The familiar fat spears come from the male plants. Buy male crowns and be done, or buy seed and raise a mixture. The female spears are tasty enough raw, and the seeds will produce more plants. Spears are broken off underground at the point where they can still be snapped by hand.

Fork over a deep bed of extra-good soil in autumn, as asparagus are perennials and remain permanently where planted. Shore up the bed with planks or sleepers to hold layers of compost and straw mulch. Sprinkle lime three weeks before planting crowns deep enough to cover with compost and thick layers of animal manure and pea straw. Plant nasturtium seeds in pockets of soil in the straw to grow a groundcover on autumn rains. This bed is permanent, so the rest of your Pasta/Pizza Plot (page 178) needs another square. I have seen an asparagus bed that had been producing spears for sixty years and gave no sign of quitting. It is something you pass on to the kids or the next owners of your property.

The test as to whether you are serious about your love for asparagus comes when the first spears appear in spring, because you must not pick any spears for the first two years. Just let them grow and die down to build up the crowns, otherwise they will never be vigorous. Remember the origin of asparagus in the steppes, where plants need to gather courage to establish themselves. In the third spring, you may pick a few spears here and there, mainly the female ones. Leave the rest till the fourth spring, then have a feast! But never pick the bed bare, as this exhausts the roots.

After the harvest is over, push nasturtiums to the edges and cover the plot again with compost, manure, and straw.

Nasturtiums usually drop enough seeds to recover the plot.

Chefs boil and steam asparagus spears in bundles, standing them up to their waists in narrow pots of boiling water. They garnish them with sauces and herbs, cheese, or eggs, or include them in frittatas and fancy dishes. My asparagus seldom reaches the table. Like the nomad I am, I pick it fresh and nibble the juicy spears as I work in the garden. Try that before rushing to the cookbooks.

BEANS (*Phaseolus vulgaris*)

Plant late spring after all danger of frost is over. Companions: feverfew and marigold. From South America as well as the Mediterranean and Middle East (*Vicia* spp.).

A few are perennial, dying down late summer and returning in spring. There are climbing and bush varieties and many different-colored flowers, pods, and beans. Old World beans have mostly black and white flowers, the best-known being fava beans. Fava beans and the scarlet runner bean have separate entries below, as they thrive in different conditions from most other beans.

The history of beans and their travels between the Old and the New Worlds is quite fascinating. Choose from borlotti, blue lake, broker bean, lima bean, noodle bean, redland pioneer, French bean, Spanish runner, stella bianca, snake bean, to name just half of those I've tested. Grow climbers on a tepee, trellis, or wire cylinder. Green soy beans grown from dried soy beans are called edamame, a nutritious addition to rice, salads, and vegetables. Beans are the peasant's great standby.

The Seed Savers Exchange (see page 317) offers many old-fashioned varieties never seen in shops, as do small seed companies. Plant a few dried beans from European and Asian groceries, like borlotti beans. Buy packets of different beans, cook, and taste them, and if you like them, plant some. See Useful Addresses on page 317 for more on seeds.

Apply lime to the soil three weeks before planting, but don't overdo the B&B. Plant seeds in toilet paper tubes at the same time. In a wildlife-free zone, you can plant beans directly in the soil after frosts. Otherwise, beans sown directly are likely to attract night-feeding prowlers who dine on the sprouting beans. To foil freeloaders, germinate beans indoors, in a cold frame (aired during the day), or under a wire rack—see Hardware in the Food Garden (page 105). Prepare four margarine containers with six toilet paper tubes each, filled with seed-raising mix or potting soil. Push in four different types of beans,

bushing and climbing. I love the way beans pop up a week later. First, the bent swan neck pushes up the earth, then two leaves unfold, remarkably big for having been folded up inside a small bean only days before. Start preparing their plot, away from onions and garlic. Soon, the next set of leaves appears, and, when you lift out the rolls, you will see root growth protruding already.

Do not plant out until they have four well-developed leaves and roots are hanging out. Dig a hole slightly deeper than the roll, pour in water, push the roll into the wet soil, and pack earth around it. Surround with CMC. As they grow, provide initial B&B between plants and douse every two weeks with LS. It seems a long wait for flowers, but once they appear, beans are not far behind. Pick twice a week to encourage production. Steamed fresh beans are delicious on the plate, in salads, almost raw in a garlic-chili-coconut dressing, and in stir-fries.

Plant new beans every month, as long as three months of warm weather can be expected. Climbing beans take longer to fruit than bush beans, hence sowing times are critical. Cut old plants at soil level to leave nitrogen in the ground.

Grow more beans than you need and dry them on the stalk. When bone dry, shell and store in jars for winter. Soak overnight and next day rinse and cook in fresh water for delicious bean dishes, soups, and salads. Vegetarians eat beans and lentils instead of meat for excellent protein. Combined with rice, their food value increases dramatically. Next time you want to give a friend a present, make a little box with four to six different bean varieties. Your friend may thank you years later!

BEETS (*Beta vulgaris*)

Plant spring, summer, or autumn. From Europe and Western Asia. Apply lime on acidic soil, but no nitrogen fertilizer—use LS. Sprinkle wood ashes around plants, but never coal ashes. Beets belong to the same family as chard, and leaves can be eaten two or three times before harvesting the root. Beets come in colors of purple, bright red, gold, white, or red-and-white stripes. Golden beets have a delicate flavor, but white beet is soapy to some taste buds. Choose from round, long, and flat beets. In common with other red-colored fruits and vegetables, red beet contains betanin and rates high in anti-cancer diets, especially as a daily serving of fresh beet juice.

The seeds, like chard seeds, produce two or three seedlings each. Plant seeds 4 inches apart to allow for two or three beets to grow sideways. They don't fancy being unraveled and transplanted. A hundred beet seeds fit on a square, but by planting ten seeds to grow twenty-plus

beets and repeating two months later, you will get a continuous supply. Beets like compost with animal manure, but using poultry manure will produce more leaf than root. Withhold nitrogen fertilizer to prevent forked roots. This goes for most root vegetables. Harvest beets as they grow, pulling the bigger ones. They can remain in the ground a long time before setting seed and getting woody.

To pickle, boil beets in the skin until a fork just goes in, but don't let them get soft. Cool, then rub off the skins. Cut into slices and pack into jars, alone or with onion rings and black peppercorns. Pour in a good vinegar, close the jar, and leave for one month.

Beets served hot are delicious. Boil beets as above, cool, and slip off their skins. Grate the beets coarsely and put aside. Finely cut an onion and some parsley and fry in olive oil. When the onion just browns at the edges, add grated beet and toss until thoroughly heated. Sprinkle salt, pepper, lemon juice, and a little sugar and stir again. Serve with potatoes, as a hot salad on mignonette leaves. Or pop mustard seeds in olive oil, sauté onions, garlic, and ginger, and add ground cumin, grated raw beets, and chopped beet leaves. Toss well before adding coconut milk to simmer until tender.

Try a dip made of boiled and pureed beets, mixed with yogurt, salt, pepper, and ground cumin, served with wedges of fried pita bread.

Saving seed from beets can take two seasons. If you also have chard setting seed, protect the beet flower head with a tied paper bag to prevent cross-pollination.

BELL PEPPERS (*Capsicum annuum*)
Solanaceae family. Also known as sweet pepper or capsicum, they originated in South and Central America. Paprika is a milder and thin-fleshed variety. Choose from Hungarian, Italian, Japanese, Russian, Portuguese, or American. There are yellow, orange, red, purple, and black bell peppers, but they all start off green. Sow seed early under glass or indoors, and feed LS. Build up the outdoor plot with CMC. Plant out after frost ceases and days are truly warm. Keep up feeding every two weeks with LS or OF, and always water well. If your summer is short, cover plants with thick straw to overwinter, or transplant into pots and bring indoors. They can be returned to the ground next spring. Pick bell peppers for size rather than color to keep the plant in production. They can be eaten raw, grilled, baked, or fried. Preserve bell peppers by pickling in oil and vinegar.

BITTER MELON (*Momordica charantia*)
Sow late spring to summer. Also known as bitter gourd or *foo gwa*. This native to India and southern China is not so much a melon as a warty, bitter-tasting cucumber. Growing on vines, it likes warmth, good soil, and B&B. I've only grown it in a greenhouse at 2,000-foot elevation, where it climbed delightfully up the rainwater pipe against the sunny side of the house. The ferny leaves of bitter melon are lime green, their aroma heady and addictive.

The fruit is picked unripe when pale lime green. Let them ripen for a feast of color, as they turn a rich yellow-orange, split open, and reveal bright red seeds. At this stage, they are no longer edible. I thought growing bitter melon was worthwhile just for the aroma and visual delights! When traveling in Lahoul, in Northern India, I thought I saw bitter melon vines everywhere, but they turned out to be hops, a cash crop.

Use bitter melon sparingly in Asian stir-fries, and they can be pickled. The seeds must be removed, as they may cause a purge. To reduce the bitterness, Asian cooks blanch them for a few minutes in boiling water. Alternatively, cut, sprinkle with salt, and leave twenty minutes, then rinse off. Prepare with salt, pepper, sugar, and vinegar, or serve with green onions and black bean sauce. Or, add to fresh chutney with bland and sweeter ingredients, including garlic.

BOK CHOY
(*Brassica rapa* var.*chinensis*)

Plant autumn, winter, spring. From China. When bok choy first became available, I gave some seedlings to a friend who soon exclaimed: "I don't know how we lived without bok choy!" It can be grown in all seasons, but bolts to seed quickly in hot weather. This versatile Chinese vegetable has crisp dark green leaves shaped like a ping-pong paddle with a strong white central rib. The entire rosette makes a great wok meal, but it is more economical if you pick outer leaves from several plants until they go to seed. Use also in pastas, soups, and salads. A bok choy stir-fry with garlic, ginger, onions, and a handful of other leaves such as amaranth, giant mustard, or the like, makes a fine meal with rice noodles and crispy tofu.

Avoid early bolting by providing manure and water. Let one plant set seed, and next season, sow thickly for a bok choy carpet.

BRASSICA JUNCEA

Plant in autumn. From Japan. Add manure and lime, feed LS. Sold under this botanical name in Japanese seed packets, as well as by local seed companies, *Brassica juncea* stands for a group of mustardy Asian greens ranging from mild green to burgundy. All are favorites with me if grown quickly and picked young, excellent for steaming or adding to winter salads. Sow a half or quarter square by raking in seeds and patting down. Water regularly, and when plants are 4 inches high, begin pulling the biggest, making room for others to grow. Eat it twice a week—you will buzz with energy. Save the best plant for seed, tying red yarn to it.

BRASSICA VARIETIES FROM ASIA

These include bok choy, *Brassica juncea,* Chinese flowering broccoli rabe, kale, cabbage, giant red mustard, mibuna, mizuna, choy sum, and tatsoi. Also see separate entries.

Alan D. Cook of Brooklyn Botanic Garden Record's publications, writes that no matter how proficient you become at raising Asian radishes, yard-long beans, cucumbers, and water chestnuts, "you can't be a good Asian-food gardener if you can't handle the *Brassica rapa* gang."[26] The problem lies with the quick-bolting habit of Asian brassicas when the weather changes to warm and/or humid. In Guangdong Province, China, where the climate is more often warmly humid than cool, I observed bunches of flowering broccoli, cabbage, and kale on sale everywhere. In cool weather, brassicas don't bolt. By not waiting, but cutting and eating before they do so, you get more value, and the flowering tops are excellent.

Sow regularly. The best way to get on with the *"Brassica rapa* gang" is to sow varieties at different times and record the results in your garden notebook, remembering the best season for each variety—easy. Not that I do this. I sow them all year round as fillers for spaces coming to hand, and use them as (and when) they please to come for salads, stir-fries, seed, and chicken food. Adjust planting times given for Asian brassicas to your own microclimate. Experimentation is advisable.

BROCCOLI
(*Brassica oleracea* var. *italica*)

Plant summer, autumn, or spring, depending on the variety. Companions: cilantro, dill, young nasturtium. From Europe, especially Italy. By preference, a cool-weather plant. Varieties include heading, sprouting, green, purple, Italian, or Chinese broccoli rabe (with long edible stems). Commercially grown broccoli normally needs a flavored sauce or a generous helping of grated cheese, but home-grown broccoli has a taste all its own.

A gross feeder (see Plant Food and Soil Food on page 63) broccoli needs plenty of organic matter. Lime the soil if acidic. I mention broccoli in the chapter on attitude (page 19), as it is half wasted when growers only cut the head. This cancer-fighting brassica can be eaten all year round with regular plantings and picking of the plentiful side shoots, if also fed and mulched well.

Plant in late summer to get it on its way by winter, developing rosettes of blue-green edible leaves and a gorgeous head. The art is to judge the state of swelling in hundreds of individual buds and pick the head before any lose their deep coloring, but not before it has reached maximum size. When the first yellow flower appears, there's not a day to spare. At moments like, this you will remember that growing a variety of food plants is one of the most intelligent things a human can do in life.

Yet I am duty-bound to report that broccoli side shoots with half the buds in flower are easy pickings, eminently edible, and good for you as well as tasty. But edible stems must be cut shorter as they go woody. Use shoots raw in salads. Sauté stems and florets in olive oil, adding lemon juice, salt, and pepper. Should you care more for stems than heads, grow Chinese broccoli rabe with edible leaves and flowers. As long as it is picked tender, broccoli is suitable for almost any mixed-vegetable dish. Try zucchini, broccoli, and grated carrots, with a Vietnamese-style dressing, or soy sauce with Dijon mustard.

When the plant flowers profusely, give it a severe pruning, saving the best flower head for seed, and you will still pick shoots for another month. Make sure no other brassica (see An A–Z of Vegetable Families on page 222) is setting seed simultaneously, as they may cross-pollinate. Cover one with a tied paper bag, if necessary. Strange new varieties don't necessarily combine the best of both parents.

BRUSSELS SPROUTS
(*Brassica oleracea var. gemmifera*)

Sow late summer to early autumn for growing in the cool season. Originated in Belgium. Said to be the latest development of the cabbage, brussels sprouts first appeared only a few hundred years ago in Belgium. They look like mini cabbages clinging to a tall stem with an open, cabbagy head. I have been spectacularly unsuccessful with this vegetable so far and plan to make it a special project next year. My sprouts opened up, perhaps due to too much nitrogen, but we still ate the heads!

BUCKWHEAT (*Fagopyrum esculentum*)

Sow in spring. From Central Asia. Buckwheat can be seen growing at very high altitudes in Asia, where it is sown in late spring and matures through the short alpine summer, which can still include snowfalls. I have grown it through sunny winters to accommodate its liking for cool climes, yet one frosty winter, it died. It can grow on poor soils. Try it out if your climate approximates a Himalayan summer—hot days, cool nights. Or do small test sowings every season.

This increasingly important plant is not a wheat at all; it is gluten-free. The small grains are ground up to make flour for pancakes, noodles, and mixed baking flours. The reason I list it under vegetables is twofold. The triangular leaves can be eaten as a tasty spinach. Second, buckwheat is an excellent cover crop to grow on a bare plot. Harvest the seed or dig in the plants before seed sets. The plant has whitish to rose pink flowers. Buy seeds from small seed companies or try buckwheat from health shops. Use cooked buckwheat in soups and as filling for a colorful winter vegetable salad, using a rudjak dressing (see page 154).

CABBAGE
(*Brassica oleracea var. capitata*)

Plant autumn, winter, spring, or summer varieties. Native of Southern and Western Europe. Companions: plant celery herb, mint, pennyroyal, tomato, sage, and southernwood to confuse predators, with aromas of chamomile, sage, southernwood, and thyme to repel cabbage moth. (Place the mint in pots between cabbages so that it doesn't get any ideas of taking over the plot.) Generally, they like cool weather. Choose from green, white, red, savoy, and sugarloaf cabbages.

Summer and winter varieties are planted respectively in late winter and spring, or late summer and autumn. A cabbage is a gross feeder (see Plant Food and Soil Food on page 63). It can also sit still and wait until the time is right. And that also goes for its cousins, cauliflower and broccoli. Cabbage seedlings can sit for two months without developing until the weather or other conditions change to their liking. Then they take off as if they'd been waiting for a starting signal—which, of course, they were. They still develop a head, even tardy specimens. Never abandon a cabbage, and it will not abandon you.

Sometimes, winter is too warm, no rain falls, the soil dries out, and you hope the cabbages will get by on dew. Then a few will suddenly bolt and produce seed heads out of a well-developed plant. Use them as broccoli, steaming the seed heads. The plant will produce shoots for a while. Pick leaves for chicken or worm food, saving the ribs for juicing with carrots and ginger. Thus, a cabbage that missed its vocation is still a very edible plant.

Although modern cabbages grow all year round (check seed packets), water deep in summer or they won't produce. They are easier to grow with winter rains. Grow plenty and pick outer leaves for stir-fries, saving the plant's energy for the cabbage head.

The main enemies are cabbage moths, pretty white butterflies with black spots. They lay eggs on the underside of the leaves, and the grubs eat the cabbage head hollow. When you pick and cut the head, all you find is a gray mess in wrappings. Heartbreaking, I assure you. What to do? Some years ago, a viewer sent in a clever idea to a TV gardening program. I tried it, and it worked for me.

Plastic butterflies protect cabbages from the worst damage cabbage moths can do. They spell out "territory already occupied." Outer leaves have been attacked but the heads are firm and clean. Include a pot of mint as a companion plant.

Hammer in four stakes around your cabbages. Cut butterfly shapes from a white plastic container and fasten at hand-width intervals to thin thread. Tie the thread to each stake, crossing diagonally through the middle of the square in both directions. I have used Styrofoam twists from packaging as butterflies before, but have learned to avoid the edible kind made from corn as the birds make short shrift of these.

Why would it work? The answer appears to be that the cabbage butterfly is territorial. Seeing the plastic butterflies, it thinks the patch is already taken and flies on. I have used the method several years in succession after half my cabbages were eaten hollow, and although cabbage-white butterflies dance around my garden, they've left the cabbages for me. I have no idea where they now procreate, but not in my cabbages, thanks to an unknown gardener passing on a great idea.

CARROTS (*Daucus carota*)

Sow spring to autumn, or an all-season variety. Companions: chives, cilantro, lettuce, onions, radishes, sage, shallots, and violets. By mixing all these seeds together, you can have your entire salad growing in one spot, as none of them need much nitrogen. Leeks and parsnips are carrot buddies, too. Originally from Afghanistan, Pakistani carrot seed produces a deep orange carrot with a purple top, close to the original. Great source of carotenes. Only feed a little OF. Choose from long or stumpy, pale or deep orange.

Old garden geezers will tell you growing carrots is dead easy, but many a gardener has troubles with this indispensable root vegetable. The main requirement is deep, light soil so carrots can penetrate downwards. If you have concrete soil and no supply of sand to lighten it, go up instead of down. Dig over one quarter, then knock the bottom out of a waxed cardboard banana box, or use a tub. Fill with potting soil, preferably lightened with sand and a pinch of lime. Be careful with nitrogen—it produces forked carrots. Don't overmanure carrots, although they may need a top dressing with OF when reaching adolescence.

Sow half to one packet of carrot seed per box. Conventional carrot wisdom dictates they must be thinned out. Thinning out seems such a waste. Just when a healthy little plant has surfaced, it gets pulled up by the roots and thrown on the compost because it hugs its neighbors. Instead, mix carrot and radish seed, pulling the quickly maturing radishes to leave room for carrots to take up.

Carrots seem able to postpone growing until room becomes available. Carrots tell you when they are well developed underground by developing a large tuft of greenery above ground. By carefully pulling those large tufts—pushing back smaller ones—you make room for others to grow. If the soil sinks from watering, top off with compost to prevent carrots turning green.

Germination is guaranteed by covering soil after sowing with a tea towel, T-shirt, or jute bag. Fit the carrot plot to the size of the cover. Water well and in two to four weeks, green sprigs will push up. Remove the cloth when sprigs are ½ inch tall. Now cover with wire, to keep off the birdies. Sow one tea towel of carrots per month to always have three to four plots on the go from which to pull. Collect deep boxes with strong corners, tea towels, T-shirts, and old racks, and you shall eat baby carrots, sweet and juicy.

When the carrots go woody, give the biggest one its head and reap the seed. The flowers are as pretty as Queen Anne's lace. Carrot tops will be greedily eaten by geese. In former days, farming families seem to have eaten them, too. You can replant carrot heads, after cutting short the tuft, to grow several small carrots.

If you were born during the last half-century, you may never have savored real carrot taste. Carrots used to be yellow and purple in 16th-century northwest Europe, and the Dutch developed orange carrots. But modern carrots must grow faster and taller, rendering them rather tasteless. Restaurants use them mainly for color and fill, scarcely for their unique taste.

Pakistani carrot seeds I bought from a small seed company hardly came up or they started dying off. Those sprigs found themselves in the wrong place and climate, and were, perhaps, only a few generations removed from their source. I raked the ground and grew something else. The following winter, a strong carrot plant rose between the broccolis. The Pakistani. Did I pamper that carrot! As it grew huge, I staked it. As it burst into flower, I fed it. I talked to it daily in plant lingo. When the weather warmed considerably, the seed heads formed and dried off. As they ripened unevenly, I harvested heads for weeks, drying the seed indoors by daily stirring.

That home-grown seed produced seedlings that decided to grow in my garden. The resulting carrots were a deeper orange with purple tops, tasting like prewar carrots. There are Japanese and Nepalese carrots also promising better flavor. Do not grow them simultaneously if you want to save seed.

CAULIFLOWER
(*Brassica oleracea* var. *botrytis*)

Companions: cilantro, cumin, dill, lemon balm. Originally from Italy. From the Mediterranean, but widely grown in India where hot-climate varieties have developed. In the Indian Himalayas, I came to appreciate curried cauliflower. Winter, summer, and all-season varieties are available, as well as purple and mini caulies. They are gross feeders, needing plenty of organic matter like CMC and lime. See Plant Food and Soil Food (page 63).

Cauliflowers are real teasers. They grow large gray-green leaves, then fold them inwards so you can't see what's happening inside. After months of tending, you begin to think they're having you on. Nothing seems to be happening. Then one day, you see a snow-white or creamy bit of cauliflower peeping between the leaves. If you then go away for a two-week vacation, you may return to find that the whole lot has collectively matured or bolted. Therefore, plant half a dozen periodically throughout the year, and keep an eye on these most secretive of all brassicas!

Cauliflowers can be petulant about when they form a head, usually for lack of choice food. Once, I left an unproductive one in a bed where it wasn't in my way, just to see how long it would take to make up its caulie mind and head up. The year came and went, and she still stood there in full leaf, barren. It became a contest. She had time? Well, so had I. Then, in a very cold winter, she started to bulge, and after an eighteen-month pregnancy, produced a respectable medium-size cauliflower. It was difficult to cut her down after such a long contest of wills. Perhaps I should have let her go to seed for a breed of long-life caulies. Instead we enjoyed her valiant effort one chilly winter's day and she tasted very good. One cauliflower to remember.

When a caulie ripens in warm weather, snap the great outer leaves and fold over the flower head to protect the color. You can tie the leaves at the top. Keep up manure and water. In autumn and winter, they grow slower but more happily. Raise one seed per toilet paper roll, and plant out when the roots come out the bottom. Never sprinkle seed in a container, because you disturb the roots when transplanting, and they may go dormant.

Depending on your microclimate, sow seed from late summer until late spring. Should three caulies bolt in one week, make thick cauliflower soup with cumin, and freeze. Dilute as needed. Peel and slice the thick stem for stir-fries—tender and tasty.

CELERIAC
(*Apium graveolens* var. *rapaceum*)

Sow in spring. This relation of stalk celery produces ball-shaped roots with a delicious celery flavor for soups and stews in the second year. Grow like any root vegetable, in light soil with CM and LS.

CELERY (*Apium graveolens var. dulce*)

Sow in spring. Companions: bush beans, tomatoes. From Europe and Asia. See also Celery Herb on page 281. The celery we know best is stalk celery, obtained by blanching wild celery by heaping soil around the plants to grow longer stalks. But growing celery in a trench and filling in as she rises is easier and holds the water better. Dig a 12-inch deep ditch, fork in CMC, plant seedlings, or seed in more compost at the bottom, and gradually refill the ditch as plants grow. The stalks are eaten and the leaves are excellent for stock, soup, or stir-fry.

CHARD (*Beta vulgaris*)

Plant any season. Companion: parsley. Also known as silverbeet. From Europe and Western Asia. The homesteader's perennial standby, these tall, green plants have hung around many a backdoor for a quick grab of green to add to a stew, soup, or casserole and, these days, a quiche. Chard is tough and survives neglect. Trouble is that when it does,

the leaves become as edible as old slippers. Yet the plant possesses the means to overcome this and be a true gourmet vegetable. Read on.

Chard comes with stems in plain cream, deep red, golden yellow, orange, and purple. Those with thick, white stems and broader leaves tend to be known as French or Swiss chard. Chards have a fine taste, and the stems can be steamed or baked as a separate vegetable and served with a piquant sauce. Steam green leaves with a bouquet garni, touch of lemon or a lime leaf, and black pepper.

Chard going to seed is a sight. A heady aroma of honey issues from a plant that may be 5 feet tall. The stem becomes a trunk with hundreds of branches bearing rows of seeds. You don't need that much. Prune lower branches to feed the main seed head. Maturation takes time, and you can't grow much under this chard tree, as its roots spread far. When seeds start drying off, cut them quickly, as hanging in the sun for weeks won't improve them at this stage. Hang seeds in an old pillowcase or paper (never plastic) bag on a shady veranda for wind drying. After a few weeks, strip the seed off. You will fill a shoebox. Share some out and, with the rest, grow chard in gourmet style.

Prepare half a square, or whatever size your protective cage is (see

Hardware in the Food Garden on page 105). Dig in plenty of manure or other organic matter and B&B. Take a handful of seed and rake thickly through the bed, patting it down with your hand. Push under any seeds still showing. Place the cage over the bed and water in. Soon, you'll see a forest of young chards standing shoulder to shoulder. Start picking a bunch of the larger leaves when 6 to 8 inches long. These have short stems and take but minutes to steam to superb tenderness. The manure will keep this bed going quite a while, providing tender greens even during heat waves. To ensure continuous supply, plant a batch three or four times per year. Never eat old-slipper chard again!

Since I started growing gourmet chard, I've noticed that one plot inter-growing with parsley was much less nibbled by tiny snails than one without. This may work where you are. Trim parsley regularly for soups, stews, and tabouli, and let only two stalks go to seed.

Use this gourmet chard instead of spinach in recipes for quiche and spinach loaves. Dice and steam leaves and drain. While still hot, stir in a few eggs, herbs, and spices, and firm up with breadcrumbs until the mixture sits comfortably in a baking dish. Bake in a moderate oven. Add to a basic spinach loaf: onions, garlic, capers, and beets, chopped nuts and citrus zest, zucchini and carrots, and grated white radishes or mashed potatoes. Replace breadcrumbs with cooked rice and rice flour or chickpea flour—see Cupboard Self-Sufficiency (page 139). Get creative with chard.

CHICORY (*Cichorium intybus*)

From the Mediterranean and Western Asia, where it grows wild, and the brilliant blue flowers make a nice change from the usual yellow of roadside herbage. Linnaeus, who cataloged all plants in a comprehensive system, found that the chicory flower opened and closed with the regularity of clockwork.

Italian cooks, accustomed to many varieties of chicory, sauté the young leaves with garlic in olive oil. For the salad bowl, pick leaves before the plant sets seed and always from an unsprayed location. The Italian chicory "rossa" adds purple stripes or blushing greens to a salad—see Radicchio on page 262. Blanched chicory is popular in Western Europe as witloof or *chicons*. Apparently, certain chicory roots, tossed in a box with earth and covered with a layer of manure and sand, will start shooting within a month to produce what is known as Belgian endive, a tender, greenish white salad vegetable. Ground chicory root makes a pleasant coffee substitute. Chicory is not choosy about soil; an underrated vegetable.

CHILIES
(*Capsicum annuum* and *C. frutescens*)
From South and Central America where they grew wild thousands of years ago. There are hundreds of varieties, hot or mild, red, yellow, or purplish black. Long ones are milder. The tiny bell pepper *frutescens* is hot-hot-hot, grown in the tropics, and turned into hot sauce and cayenne.

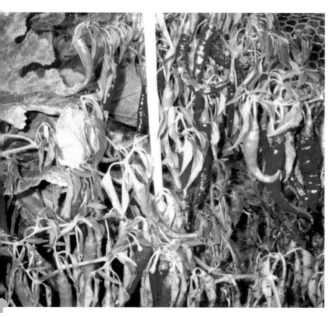

Jalapeño chilies in Paul Zabukovec's seaside garden, with "Goldrush" zucchini in the background.

Start seed off under glass in spring. The seedlings are very small and may get lost in a garden bed still full of cabbage giants and garlic. Tease them out and plant two to a small pot and fertilize. After a few days in the shadehouse, they come out in the sun and, once they show four leaves, they can be replanted into a plot in full sun. Add CM plus a dusting of lime. After harvesting, use chilies fresh, removing seeds and white lining, or string them up to dry in the shade. Pickle chilies in vinegar and oil, or store in the freezer. Plants can be overwintered indoors.

CHINESE CABBAGE
(*Brassica pekinensis*)
Sow all seasons. Also known as *pe-tsai*, *wong bak*, *Shantung*, *Tsientin*, Nappa, or Manchurian. There is a short variety, but the 12-inch long, light green, crisp, tightly folded cabbage is the most versatile Chinese vegetable of all, used in all manner of dishes. Its delicacy results from quick growing in rich soil with plenty of water. Hence, it is a matter of experimenting to find what the optimum seasons are in hot, cold, dry, and wet climates. In some areas, shade may be beneficial. Build up soil around plants to blanch the leaf base. Experiment.

For a sweet-and-sour dish, fry red bell peppers, onions, and shredded

Chinese cabbage. Sprinkle with dressing of soy sauce, rice vinegar, and sugar.

CHIVES (*Allium schoenoprasum*)

Sow autumn to spring. Companions: cabbage and lettuce. Also garlic chives (*Allium tuberosum*, mauve starry flowers) with flat stems and mild garlic flavor, Chinese chives (*Allium odorum*, white starry flowers), and Chinese garlic chives (*Allium tuberosum*). Native of the Northern Hemisphere. Chives repel aphids and are easy to grow. Cultivate like onions. European chives have purple spiky flower heads. Plant seeds, or buy a pot of chives, split the clump, and grow more. Find yourself adding chives to almost everything from salads, soups, and roasted vegetables to dainties like deviled eggs.

CHOY SUM
(*Brassica chinensis var. parachinensis*)

Sow in spring. From China. Chinese greens with pretty yellow flowers that are eaten with the juicy stems. Sow fairly thick as it is a quick grower, and you will pull whole plants, although it sprouts again if you use parts only. Steam, stir-fry, or mix in salads.

COLLARDS
(*Brassica oleracea var. acephala*)

Sow late summer. Native to Europe. A cousin of kale with a strong cabbage flavor. Cabbages and kales have finer flavor, but collards grow so readily that if you have trouble growing anything, try them. Water and feed well, picking leaves from the bottom up. Use young leaves for salads or sauté with onion greens, ground cumin, and quartered kumquats.

CUCUMBERS (*Cucumis sativus*)

Companions: bush beans, radishes, lettuce, savoy cabbage, sweet corn, sunflowers, and stinging nettle. Use horse manure compost.

Possibly originated in the Himalayan foothills and was already growing in ancient India, Egypt, and Greece more than 3,000 years ago.

Although lovers of hot weather, cucumbers like protection from scorching heat, either from taller plants or shade cloth. This prolific producer diversified as it spread across the globe over centuries. Choose from green, yellow, white, crooked, straight, long, short, round, striped, horned, and baby-skin smooth. Or go by country: African, Armenian, Chinese, Dutch, German, Italian, Japanese, Lebanese, Russian, Syrian. Or by flavor: apple, lemon, or . . . cucumber!

Grow only one variety per season if you save seed, as varieties cross-pollinate. Cucumbers grow well on a trellis or draped over a cane chair, saving space and preventing mildew—thanks for that, Chris Watters!

Sow seed in toilet paper tubes behind glass; apply LS. Prepare bed with CMC in a warm spot with dappled shade, in a poly tunnel, or under a plastic "roof." Plant out when the danger of frost is over and plants have several leaves on a strong stem. Avoid root damage. Keep up LS, mulch, and water as fruit forms, to make the difference between a sweet cucumber and a bitter one. You'll be amazed how many cucumbers one little vine produces. If vines are long and many, pinch out the tips. Pick cucumbers twice a week, or they'll stop producing. Some gardeners claim that two vines are more than enough. Plant herbs and flowers to attract bees for pollinating. To save seed, let one cucumber ripen fully on the vine. Wash seeds before drying.

If your red onions ripen in cucumber time, make a salad of the two with a dressing of rice wine vinegar, sesame oil, and tamari or soy sauce. German immigrants brought cucumber pickle recipes to America. After sprinkling sliced cucumbers and hard onions with salt and leaving overnight, they went into jars with oil, vinegar, black pepper, and mustard seeds. If you like sweet pickles, try oil, vinegar, sugar and spices, mustard, celery seed, ground cloves, and turmeric.

EGGPLANTS (AUBERGINE)
(*Solanum melongena*)

Sow in spring. Companions: green beans. Also known as aubergine, the eggplant hails from India. By nature a tropical perennial, eggplant will still grow in temperate zones in warm spots. If the summer is short, or elevation causes cold nights, grow them in pots and bring indoors to mature. Eggplant does not like lime, but needs extra nitrogen. Choose round, egg-shaped, long-thin, or lavender varieties. They are a popular choice for home-cooked dinners.

Start seed off under glass with LS. Prepare the bed with plenty of horse manure and compost. Plant out when the weather has truly warmed up. Tie plants to short stakes when growing and protect from strong winds.

Writer Rana Kabbani wrote the following Syrian recipe for eggplant dip in Antonia Till's book *Loaves and Wishes* (see page 316).

Roast three eggplants over an open flame, sprinkle with salt, and cool, before scooping out the flesh and blending it with a little olive oil, garlic, and Greek yogurt. It should taste smoky. Serve with hot bread.

ENDIVE (*Cichorium endivia*)

Sow in autumn. Known in ancient Egypt and Greece and related to chicory (same blue flowers). Several varieties—all easy and hardy.

Apply LS plus a dusting of lime. As a kid in Holland, I had a love-hate relationship with endive, which in that damp climate grew into large bunches, like non-heading lettuce. Mum used to wash, cut, and cook it with just the last rinsing water hanging on, and serve it with a white sauce sprinkled with nutmeg. I gradually grew to like it, but its bitter tang is not for young children.

Appreciate endive as a salad vegetable, picking outer leaves while young so that half a dozen plants are plenty. Later in the season, pick the yellow hearts. Endive is easier to grow than related witlof, which has to be blanched (see Chicory on page 244). To get new plants, rub a handful of dry seed heads between your hands and rake in. This will ensure endive coming up in its own good time.

FAVA BEANS (*Vicia faba*)

Plant in autumn. Also known as broad beans. From the Middle East. Fava beans help control wilt virus and can be planted after tomatoes. This native of Afghanistan and Western Asia became the main bean throughout the Mediterranean, Middle East, and North Africa until Columbus discovered the land of other beans. Known since Neolithic times, the cooks of the Levant ground fava beans to create falafel, now a global fast food. The post-nouvelle cuisine movement rediscovered young fava beans to garnish spring dishes. Flowers are white and black, or red.

The versatile fava bean, the only bean that grows in the cold season, can be eaten at all stages: first as young, finger-length pods, steamed with oregano; then as shelled beans when not too old. You can even tip prune the plants when they are in full flower and toss the tender leaves in a stir-fry. Later, shelled beans can be frozen.

Finally, dried shelled beans can be reconstituted or ground up to make falafel. Dry them in the pods on the plant. After soaking and cooking, coarsely puree beans with an onion, a raw potato, garlic, chili, and parsley. Add pepper, salt, cumin, and coriander. Enjoy your own falafel made with home-grown ingredients!

Boil, steam, or fry fresh fava beans from one to four minutes, depending on their age. Serve with pasta, seasoning, olive oil, quince paste, and sour cream. Team beans with sweet potato mash, or roasted carrots with lemon and Italian parsley. Or, serve with crumbed goat cheese. Some cooks peel the skins off beans after cooking, which is like eating only the heart of the artichoke. The skins are flavorsome and good roughage.

If last summer you grew the Aztec Plot (page 182), or just sweet corn, plant fava beans in autumn to put some nitrogen back in the soil. Plant five seeds every two weeks in autumn for a staggered harvest.

FLORENCE FENNEL
(*Foeniculum vulgare* var. *azoricom*)

Companions: appears to be a loner and may inhibit other plants. Probably from the Azores. Grows less than 20 inches high (for tall field fennel grown for seeds and foliage, see Fennel on page 282).

Florence fennel needs rich soil with added lime to form the half-submerged fleshy leaf base, the most edible part. The flavor has a hint of aniseed, favored in Mediterranean cooking. Eat steamed with pasta or as a salad with orange slices and chives. Try raw with cherry tomatoes and a cool dipping sauce. Cinquaterra cakes from Genoa are flavored with fennel. When Florence fennel forms seed heads, cut off all but the central stalk to produce seed.

The ferny foliage is used as bedding for colorful foods. Place freshly picked leaves on a blue platter, arranging cubed cheese, tomatoes, olives, and red onions on top. Serve al fresco with crisp bread and good wine.

GARLIC (*Allium sativum*)

Plant in autumn. Originally from Central Asia and cultivated in ancient Egypt and Mesopotamia, now worldwide.

Garlic is a natural antibiotic, protecting you from colds and infections, and is indispensable in most vegetable dishes. The price is high enough to consider growing this delicious condiment yourself. To get 100 knobs from a 3-foot square, plant cloves 3 inches apart in ten rows of ten. You will be able to use the greens, use garlic young and fragrant, serve whole baked garlic, and store a few plaits at the end of summer! Grow enough garlic for cooking, drying, pickling, and replanting. Grow different varieties in boxes filled with compost, placed on underfelt.

Do not buy imported garlic to plant out, in case of disease. Search farmers' markets for organically grown garlic, even if they carry names of waves of immigrants. Russian garlic is the biggest and mildest. Red Italian has a fine taste. Try Vietnamese, too. Save the best of each for replanting.

In autumn, fork over a plot one spade deep, adding B&B. Break up bulbs and push cloves half a finger into the soil, spaced 4 inches apart in both directions. Dust soil with lime. Cover with CMC and a thick layer of teased-out straw. Water in well. Green spikes will appear soon. As most garlics don't fully mature until the tops die off, the ground may be occupied for the best part of the year, but start using bulbs from spring onwards.

Sometimes, I grow so much garlic that full-grown bulbs left in the ground start shooting as many spikes as they have cloves. These I use as a whole bunch in stir-fries for a delicious young garlic flavor. Garlic just bulbed and not yet fully cloved tastes mellow. Simmer three sliced bulbs in oil, green tops included, before adding other vegetables. Use green tops for soups and salads. Use fresh or pickled garlic to make traditional Mexican salsa. In a mortar mash four or five garlic cloves with half a teaspoon of sea salt; add finely chopped onions and tomatoes, fresh chopped cilantro, lemon juice, and black pepper. For a really hot one, use minced red pepper.

Store garlic in net bags hung in a cool, dark place or between newspaper in a box in a dark cupboard. When some start to sprout, it is time to pickle the rest. No need to peel. Just rub off loose skins and place whole bulbs in jars. Fill up with white vinegar, and top with olive oil. The taste remains great and the vinegar is fine for salads. Garlic braids of three to five bulbs are a welcome present for friends who like cooking, so you can never grow too much.

GHERKINS (*Cucumis anguria*)

Gherkins are from Africa and possibly traveled to the New World with the slave trade. They are cultivated in the West Indies and Eastern Europe, which exports gherkins. Seed can be bought specifically for varieties suitable for pickling due to prolific cropping and texture.

To pickle, sprinkle gherkins with salt and leave overnight. Dry off. Pack in jars with bay leaf, chili, peppercorns, dried ginger, fennel, and dill—whatever you fancy. Evidently, one grape leaf per jar gives a gourmet touch. Pour on white vinegar and a layer of olive oil, closing the lid tightly. Save jars with plastic lids for pickling, as these don't corrode.

GIANT RED MUSTARD
(*Brassica juncea*)

Sow autumn to late winter. From China. This stunning plant prefers cool seasons, yet will grow any time, although it bolts to seed quickly in summer. The leaves are the most superb burgundy-maroon and green with fine nerve undulations like a map of rural Guangdong Province.

The taste is pleasantly hot. One leaf cut in strips makes a personal salad or a piquant addition to mixed salads. Use shredded in pastas. One plant produces so many leaves that you can afford to cook it as spinach or in stir-fries, where it loses its bite but still adds flavor. A head of yellow flowers attracts good insects. Cut off side shoots to let the central stem produce seed.

GLOBE ARTICHOKE
(*Cynara scolymus*)

Plant roots in autumn or sow seed in spring. This high-fiber perennial grew in North Africa where Roman conquerors learned to enjoy it in the 1st century. The Italians have been cultivating artichokes for at least six centuries. The French eat them cold for lunch, with vinaigrette, or hot with garlic butter.

Globe artichokes are thistles, and, if not picked, will produce a brilliant blue flower followed by seed. The globe is the flower bud.

Seed is available from small seed companies and germinates easily in late spring to summer. When seedlings have two good leaves, pick them out, plant in individual pots (in part shade), and start feeding LS. If your soil is acidic, work in lime three weeks before planting out in autumn in a composted bed, and when the plants have six leaves. They grow to be tall, handsome plants of decorative value, looking great along a picket fence, and will produce globes the next spring.

I pick from the first day of spring until the beginning of summer. Once a week, pull off decaying leaves and lay these as mulch around the plants. If night prowlers gnaw stems underneath the globes, pull an orange net bag over the top, and tie it down.

When all globes are harvested, cut down the stalks for the compost heap. Cut off leaves and arrange between the plants. Place fertilizer underneath and top with straw. Soon, new plants will sprout from the old stumps, and the whole process will start again.

The following year, carefully slice off new plants with a spade, including a piece of root, and replant elsewhere to ensure continuous supply of this Old World delicacy. When cutting down old stalks, some may separate with new white shoots under the earth. Carefully saw the stalk into as many pieces as there are shoots and plant each in a pot with compost. They will soon form new plants to be set out where there is space to grow. Thus, you continually renew your stock and create designer hedges of these toothed, gray plants of classical elegance.

I drive past a farm where, one year, they had a marvelous 6 × 30-foot stand of globe artichokes. At the end of the picking season, the whole hedge disappeared. I wondered why they would dig up this superb stand. But next winter, it was back in the same spot. I concluded that, in typical farm-management style, the farmer mowed the stand down after harvest! However, setting out a new hedge every few years is a safeguard in case old roots with deep fissures rot in wet winters.

To prepare artichokes, boil the globes in plenty of water. I like eating the inside of the bitter stems as well and cook these separately in the same pot. Rich people only ever eat the hearts of artichokes, which is what you buy in tins. But apart from the stems, the outer leaves have much to offer.

Boil globes for thirty minutes, then with two forks pull off a leaf, and scrape the inside with your teeth. If you can't scrape yet, boil till tender. Each leaf has a tasty, fleshy base. Peel off each leaf, dip in vinaigrette or garlic butter, and scrape with your teeth. Green and purple globes taste the same. This is real peasant food, slow food, to be enjoyed. As you come to the innermost parts of the globe, the whole leaf can be eaten, but it is the heart—after removing the "choke" of hair that covers it—that is your reward for approaching it so slowly! To eat the classical way, cut in halves and remove the heart and soft leaves to eat with lemon juice, olive oil, and sea salt.

JAPANESE VEGETABLES

Japanese greens available as seed tend to belong to the hardy and easy-to-grow Cruciferae/Brassicaceae group of vegetables. Gourds, pumpkins, and root crops are also available and more will no doubt appear. As the text on seed packets is usually in Japanese, use garden sense and experiment with planting times and LS. See also Brassica Varieties from Asia (page 236).

JERUSALEM ARTICHOKE (*Helianthus tuberosus*)

From North America. This root vegetable gives some people unfortunate bowel symptoms. But if you have tried them without ill effect, do obtain a root, cut it in pieces, and plant. Soon, you will have lots of edible roots. Any piece left in the soil will grow again, like horseradish, which is so hard to get rid of it can take over entire plots. If your garden thrives on neglect and sweet chaos, think twice before planting Jerusalem artichokes. Boil and eat like potatoes.

KALE (*Brassica oleracea var. acephala*)

Sow in autumn. Native to Europe. Named varieties of this non-hearting cabbage plant exist, including ornamental ones. One of my childhood delights was *boerekool met worst*, a Dutch one-pot winter meal of potatoes mashed with finely cut curly green kale and a smoked sausage on top. My love of the invigorating taste of kale remains, and I grow green curly and Siberian purple kale. Kale needs to have a touch of frost to taste really good. By planting in late summer or autumn, they just catch a night frost when they are ready to eat.

Siberian purple kale is not curly but scalloped. It can stand low temperatures, but, strangely enough, is also quite happy in summer, even surviving heat waves. It is more tender than the somewhat tough curly kale. The leaves lend a wonderfully engaging taste to horta, salads, soups, or stir-fries. The young seed heads can be eaten as broccoli shoots. Whereas curly kale grows to broccoli height, Siberian kale can reach 6 feet, setting thousands of seeds in order to survive Siberia's winter. The seed keeps well. Use it to grow a green crop for digging in or chicken food.

Pick leaves young—wonderful stir-fried in olive oil with ginger, garlic, and onions. For Siberian kale soup (not purple but green) that even my grandsons used to eat with relish: cook leaves with an onion, cool, put through the blender, and season with soy sauce. This soup stands alone in terms of nutrition as well as having a convincing taste impossible to describe. When served to guests accustomed to pale soups with dollops of cream, some are likely to break into praise songs. As Siberian kale is not always available in shops, you have to grow your own to experience this amazing vegetable, also known as Russian red kale.

To grow kale, allow a quarter of your square. This big, beautiful, decorative plant may need staking. No one need go hungry as long as we grow on the seeds of Siberian kale.

KOHLRABI
(*Brassica oleracea var. gongylodes*)

Sow in all seasons. From Europe, but also grown in China (*gai lan tau*) and Vietnam. Prepare soil with CMC and lime. Kohlrabi can develop rather quickly and goes woody if left to linger, so pick them young. A greenish white or purple swollen stem base is the part normally eaten, but young leaves can be used in stir-fries. A taste all its own. Use in soups, as a cooked vegetable, or eat raw.

LEEKS (*Allium porrum*)

Sow late summer to autumn, and don't count on using that plot for more than half a year. The Egyptians grew leeks in 2000 BCE. Leeks can be expensive as they occupy ground for so long. But they are easy to grow from seed, planted out like onions. Apply CMC and lime.

Don't wait for the tops to dry off as with onions. Harvest leeks when young and tender, when medium sized, and when tall and fat. If you see the flower bud—a papery sheath containing a ball of mauve sparklers—you're almost too late, as they get woody, but you can still make a batch of concentrated leek soup to put in the freezer. Let the best leek go to seed. When black seeds begin to pop from the sparklers, these are ready to be cut and dried. Old leeks pulled up may have little bulblets at the base. Plant them between cabbages and lettuces, as they take time to become "leeklings."

Leeks in seed are quite decorative.

Make leek-and-potato soup or use sweet potato; dress it up with a dollop of yogurt garnished with chopped chive stems and young flowers, onion greens, or arugula. Use leek with other greens in dhal and pies, or as a vegetable with hard-boiled-egg sauce.

LETTUCE (*Lactuca sativa*)
Sow in all seasons. Companions: beets, cabbage, carrots, onions, radishes, and strawberries. From Asia Minor and the Middle East. Small seed companies may carry more than a dozen varieties: hearting and non-hearting. Some lettuces grow better in winter (butter lettuce, romaine, oak-leaf), others in summer, so you can eat lettuce all year round. Easily grown from seed. As commercial lettuce is grown with human-unfriendly chemicals, it's worth growing your own.

The smaller, non-heading lettuces are picked from the outside while they keep growing; ideal for the single vegetable gardener. A packet of mesclun mix contains some of the following: green curly, coral leaf, coral curly, romaine, butterhead, oak-leaf, green and red mignonette, Lollo rosso, radicchio, rabbit's ear, lamb's ear, and more. See also Chicory (page 244), Salad Greens (page 265), and Radicchio (page 262). To make the plot look pretty, sow lettuce in a small bed, then transplant, alternating red/brown varieties with green ones. This is basic kitchen gardening, where the eye wants to be pleased as much as the taste buds.

Size is important when planting out lettuces. Romaine is tall and erect. Once I saw Romaine 24 inches tall in an organic garden supplying restaurants. Start picking before they become so big. Other lettuces are ground hugging, good for borders until they send up seed stalks with tiny yellow flowers. Lamb's ear or mache is the smallest, sprawls, and is not a true lettuce. Radicchio, the tough, bitter, and beautiful Italian standby, is a variety of chicory, sending up a tall stalk to produce seed. Before it does, enjoy masses of bright blue flowers.

Collect seed heads when dry, drying further indoors, rubbing between the hands to release seeds into a bowl. Dry another week before storing in screw-top jars. No need to separate different types of lettuces if they will grow in your microclimate through summer and winter. Sprinkle seed mix three or four times a year.

MELONS (*Cucumis melo*)

Companion: bush beans. Use horse manure compost. Melons probably originated in Africa but found their home in Central Asia. Hami, near the Turpan Depression in Xinjiang, is known as melon heaven, thanks to ancient irrigation methods and plenty of sunshine. Afghanistan also once grew and exported beautiful melons.

Easily grown from seed in early spring, indoors. Plant out when danger of frost is over. Melons dislike cold nights, so choose a warm spot. Select cantaloupe or green-fleshed honeydew, or heirloom varieties from the Amish, Ukraine, France, or Israel. For a Hami melon, you need a long summer, hence the need to germinate seed under glass. Yet the melon called "Collective Farm Woman" ripened in Moscow. If you tried growing melons and failed, seek out seed to complement your climate. They need CMC, B&B, and good drainage.

To create a warm plot, dig a pit, fill it half with compost, plant melon seedlings, and cover with an old glass door or rigid plastic held down by bricks. Provide ventilation and open up on warm days. Or make a small plastic poly tunnel. Check drainage. Commercial growers use black plastic to warm up the earth and plant seedlings in punched holes. As the vines grow, apply B&B monthly or old chicken manure between plants. Sprinkle lime to deter snails and slugs.

Either grow vines on a wire trellis, supporting melons in net bags, or put planks under rambling melons to stop rot. When ripening, protect melons with cages or cloth bags against rats and possums. In my dam-watered garden, melons stood up to brackish water longer than most other vines. Harvest melons with a piece of stem. If you run out of warm weather, use immature melons for a honey and yogurt desert with roasted sesame seeds. See also Watermelons (page 270).

MIBUNA
(*Brassica rapa* var. *japonica*)

Sow just a pinch of seeds late summer and late winter. This is a quick-growing hot salad green from Japan, widely used in restaurants. Pick leaves from the bottom up. Let one plant set seed.

MIZUNA
(*Brassica rapa var. japonica*)

Sow autumn to spring. From Japan. In its small form, a salad plant, but the larger mizuna, or Japanese endive, is a deeply indented green-leaved plant for cool weather. In summer, it bolts easily. Rather than space out seeds, grow one densely seeded patch so plants shade each other, don't dry out quickly, and, provided you pick twice a week, continue to provide tender leaves instead of bolting to seed. Add young leaves to a tossed salad for their peppery flavor. Use mature leaves as a steamed vegetable to accompany baked pumpkin or carrots, or mix into a stir-fry.

MUSTARDS (*Brassica juncea*)

Sow all seasons, but cool weather preferred. Will grow in acid soil. Natives of Asia and Europe. Giant red (see page 250), Chinese, black, white (*Brassica alba* or *Sinapis alba* syn. *Brassica hirta*). For others, consult the Seed Savers Exchange website (see page 317). All have yellow flowers. Easy and hardy. Mixed with legumes, they assist fruiting trees, vines, and tomatoes. Grow yellow mustard as a quick green crop after vegetables; dig in before flowering. Mustard is

grown as a vegetable in many countries, as well as for oil and condiments, being a prolific seed producer. They can grow to 4 feet with dinner-plate-sized leaves. Collect enough for your kitchen and the Wild Greens (Horta) Plot (page 180). Don't be without these fast-growing, maintenance-free, tasty, and healthy additions to meals.

ONIONS (*Allium spp.*)

Sow autumn, early winter, and spring, depending on whether they are early or late onions. Companions: carrots, nettle, parsley, tomatoes, and violets. (Onions and garlic are not always compatible with peas and beans, but are pest repellents where aphids cause problems.) From Western Asia. The Egyptians grew them in 3000 BCE.

Enrich soil with compost. For acidic soil, sprinkle lime three weeks before planting out. Choose from brown, white, or red salad onions, shallots, and green onions. Grow heirloom varieties from bulbs. Since onions need a long growing and drying off time, consider growing them in boxes to maintain a faster rotation of vegetables in your square. Or, dig an onion square. Or, plant a row of shop onions to sprout along a path and pick green straps for half a year!

Sowing onions directly and then thinning them out is a waste, unless you replant the thinnings. Better to punch holes in a margarine container, fill with fine soil, and sow enough seed to cover. They come up like a forest! From a whole packet, you may obtain a 3⅓-yard onion row. Calculate how many containers to sow for half a year's supply. When seedlings are 4 inches high, make trenches with a hand trowel, pushing the earth higher on one side. Place seedlings at intervals the size of an onion along the low side of the trench, then fold in the high wall of earth. They will straighten up in a week. Water well.

Since onions look like grass, weed carefully. Top dress with CMC plus straw. Sprinkle OF. As they grow, heap compost around bulbs poking above ground. Pick greens sparingly for salads and stir-fries. Begin harvesting as tops shrivel. Most onion varieties store for several months, braided on a rope and hung in a cool dark place. See Chives (page 246) for more onion material when stored onions run out.

Onions have one mystery habit. Some grow nice greens before drying off prior to harvest. Others set seed, handsome balls of white or mauve sparklers. If the onion is a good size and you want to save seed, let it happen. Seed growing will completely waste the bulb. Harvest seed when the stem goes yellow. Alternatively, snap flowering stems to let bulbs develop. Why do some onions set seed and others not? Different varieties are sensitive to planting time, too early or too late, and behave accordingly. As your garden's mini-climate needs to be factored in, you do best to follow general rules and experiment from year to year until you know what your onions tend to do where you are. This is what "knowing your onions" means.

I adore heirloom Welsh bunching onions (*Allium fistulosum*) from Germany, where *welsche* means "foreign," as they arrived there from Siberia. Also known as Japanese bunching onions. Each bulb planted grows a bunch of elongated small onions. They can be propagated from seed or root division. Potato onions also bunch and grow from divisions. Pick green straps sparingly. Find them in markets or at heritage seed outlets. Grow shallots from bulbs. The Egyptian onion, or tree onion, grows a bunch of minute onions, no bigger than your pinkie nail, at the top of the stem. I've never quite known what to do with these. I have pickled them, but peeling so many midgets puts me off. They can probably be roasted in the skin like garlic.

ORACH (*Atriplex hortensis*)
Sow in spring, summer, or autumn. Known as mountain spinach, it is native to Western Asia and Eastern Europe.

Grows like amaranth. A decorative red or yellow vegetable that stands hot or cold weather, grows to 6 feet high, and provides plentiful spinachy leaves.

PARSNIPS (*Pastinaca sativa*)

Sow in autumn. Companions: carrots, radishes. From Southern and Central Europe. Add some old chicken manure and lime to the soil a few weeks prior to sowing. Sow parsnips like carrots. Pull the biggest ones to make room for little ones to grow. The main problem with parsnips is that the seed does not remain viable very long. Buy seed in a foil packet and sow soon thereafter. Let one parsnip go to seed—the beautiful umbrella head of flowers attracts beneficial insects. Sow new seed straight away; wrap excess seed in foil after drying, and store it in a jar in the bottom of the fridge. Use as soon as convenient.

Slice parsnips and carrots in a baking tray, cover with red onion slices, orange or lemon slices, ground coriander seed, sprinkle with sesame oil and olive oil, and bake under foil in medium oven until al dente. Remove foil to brown. Serve with noodles or sweet or mashed potatoes and a green salad.

PEAS (*Pisum sativum*)

Plant September to November and again in early spring. Companions: turnips, potatoes, parsnips, carrots, radishes, and beans. Cultivated as long as 10,000 years ago in Western Asia. Today, most peas are shelled and frozen, but snow peas and sugar snaps are eaten fresh in the pod. The latter two need climbing support, but a bush variety of sugar snaps is available.

Dig in old horse manure and lime. Don't use a high-nitrogen fertilizer. For climbing peas, rig up poles, wire tower, tepee, or trellis (see Hardware in the Food Garden on page 105). Plant peas ½ inch deep and 2 inches apart in a shallow ditch and press earth down by hand. If you have rodents digging up germinating seeds, raise peas indoors in toilet paper tubes. Plant outside when roots hang out the bottom. Tuck in seedlings with compost and cover with leaf mulch, grass clippings, wood ashes, compost, or a mix of all these. Add B&B if plants are slow to develop.

Podded peas are best for freezing and can be used in many decorative ways, in almost any dish you care to prepare, as well as be served as an instant green vegetable when you've run out of greens.

PEA SHOOTS (*Pisum sativum*)

Similar to bean sprouts, but grown outside. Easily harvested from peas left in pea straw. Cut them when 4 inches tall and use in curries, stir-fries, and salads. Pea straw peas are called fodder peas but are common podding peas quite suitable for human consumption.

POTATOES (*Solanum tuberosum*)

Plant when no frost is expected for four to five months. Companions: nasturtium, corn, or grow after a fava bean crop. Potatoes date back to 11,000 BCE. Their homeland is Peru, where some 3,000 varieties are still being grown on family farms. That's biodiversity! That huge collection may be needed in the future, if today's artificial farming methods smite one after another potato with blight, causing a new-age potato famine.

As quite a few plants are inhibited by potatoes, even its cousin the tomato, there is a case for growing potatoes somewhat separate. As potatoes are an important staple food—used baked, mashed, in snacks, soups, salads, and as wedges—it is vital to grow heirloom potatoes to keep strong old strains in the system. Source them from the Seed Savers Exchange (page 317). Potatoes return your investment tenfold. Choose from yellow, white, red, and purple varieties, each with its own flavor and properties for cooking, baking, or salads. Select shop- or market-bought tubers you like, grow them, then test how well they keep. Try another variety the following year.

If you can eat potatoes, you are lucky. People with arthritis may not want to eat the fruits of the Solanaceae family (see An A–Z of Vegetable Families on page 224). Do make sure growing potatoes stay underground, for any exposed to light develop green patches, a sign of the toxic alkaloid solanine. Do not eat potatoes with green patches: they are toxic, especially for little people.

Growing potatoes in straw: if you have it, grow potatoes in soil, as friable as possible. Potatoes do not like lime. But you can grow them by spreading a thick layer of wet newspaper and a very thick layer of pea straw over a rocky hump where nothing else will grow. Make gutters in the straw and fill with compost, then bury cut potatoes or peelings, covering again with straw and sprinkling B&B. When plants are big and healthy, stick your hand under the straw, feel around, and steal the biggest potatoes for dinner without the plant even noticing. Keep covering this arrangement with more compost and straw. It's a different potato game from the wholesale ripping out of plants on commercial farms, after all tops have been sprayed to die off simultaneously. Eventually, your plants will flower and stop growing. Harvest all and replant baby spuds. Do not plant potatoes in the same place year after year. Make a fresh plot or tub each time. Store potatoes in a cool place away from light after rubbing off any eyes.

Growing potatoes in tubs or wire cylinders: This method also works in winter, as it elevates potatoes above the frost line. Use a plastic or wooden tub, or make a chicken-wire cylinder lined with thick layers of wet newspaper. Or, use old buckets without bottoms or the body of an old washing machine. Place in a warm spot on high ground or stack between biscuits of straw.

For the tub, cut one potato with eyes into pieces, place in the bottom of the tub, and cover with old manure and straw. When plants appear, surround the plants with more soil and straw, or add soft weeds and non-invasive grass clippings. Repeat as the plant grows up inside the tub. In a cylinder, do the same, making sure plants get no more light than in a tub. In other containers, fill up as soon as plants appear, because they will reach for the light faster. If your soil gets waterlogged in winter, grow potatoes on higher ground or use the above methods. If you expect true wet seasons, harvest all before the onset. Never plant in low-lying pockets.

Convert lawn to a food plot by laying small potatoes on one 3-foot square of lawn and cover with manure and thick straw mulch. As plants appear, add more mulch. The grass becomes potato food, and, after harvest, you can plant other vegetables. May not work with some grasses.

PUMPKINS (*Cucurbita* spp.)

Sow in spring. Dates back to 7000 BCE in Mexico. Also see Squash on page 266. The variety of pumpkins is stunning. In our shops, you mainly buy pie pumpkins and yellow butternut (not a true pumpkin) because these have long keeping qualities. But, generally, blue and green ones are the keepers, while yellow and orange ones are for eating soon. If you see an unusual pumpkin, buy it, dry the seeds indoors for a month, then refrigerate overnight. Rub off the silvery membranes before storing in an airtight container. If you have mice, don't leave pumpkin seeds uncovered; they'll bring the clan to devour them. Growers' markets, small seed companies, and the Seed Savers Exchange (page 317) are sources for varieties of pumpkin seed suitable for all climates. There are also mini pumpkins for singles and giant pumpkins weighing in at hundreds of pounds for the whole clan.

Start seed early under glass to allow for a long warm season. Dig holes one spade deep and fill with manure, soft weeds, grass clippings, and compost, adding lime for acidic soils. When this sinks down, add more compost and mulch and plant seedlings in a depression when all danger of frost is over. Although pumpkins survive dry days, to get results, a daily watering at the roots is needed.

After a year's gardening, you may find pumpkin plants coming up in the compost. These are strong and viable. Leave them in place, or transplant them with a clod of earth attached. One of our keeper pumpkins had begun to rot, and I didn't want to insult the chickens with it. Thrown on the compost heap in autumn, it dissolved in winter rains, but in spring, there were scores of dark green seedlings ready to transplant.

Mini pumpkins and butternuts are for small gardens, but most pumpkins need to sprawl. If you hope to limit your food garden to one or two squares, plant them on the edge to sprawl over, or make a pumpkin station somewhere else. Dig a bag of manure into a backyard corner (as long as the hose can reach it), raise a compost mound on top, and plant seedlings in a circle, protected by bottomless yogurt tubs. When they grow over the edges, remove protectors.

Pumpkin aficionados will pinch out the tips of pumpkin vines to encourage production of less but bigger fruit. When pumpkins are half grown, pinch every vine and carry the tips, complete with two or three furry leaves, flowers, and embryo fruit, to the kitchen. Steam lightly, toss in coconut cream, and serve hot. From mid-summer on, discourage the formation of more fruit by picking flowers. As a side dish, quick-fry these in batter, with or without vine tips, and sprinkle with parmesan.

Pumpkins carry male and female flowers on the same plant and are pollinated by bees. Observation tells gardeners that, according to weather and temperature, pumpkins will, in some seasons, produce all male flowers for a long time, whereas ideally female flowers bloom simultaneously. Yet when male and female flowers are in attendance but the weather is dark and cloudy, bees don't leave the hive. Then, the gardener should consider hand-pollinating. Every morning, pick freshly opened male flowers (slender stem) and rub their pollen onto the stamen of the female flowers (swollen stem base), until the sun and bees return. Also do this when bees become scarce.

Pumpkins benefit from pruning in late summer to help maturing fruit. Cut vines to the nearest maturing pumpkin. Do this carefully, as half-grown pumpkins hide under leaves and you'll really regret cutting off a one-pound junior. Now all the nutrients that course through the vines benefit pumpkins that will make the end of the season. If in doubt whether a small pumpkin has time to ripen, consider that even an unripe pumpkin makes good soup if you spice it up with onions, garlic, coriander, and cumin.

Maddeningly, when cool weather arrives, the vines go into production again! With autumn on the doorstep, new tips with tiny pumpkins appear everywhere! Have another meal of steamed tips in coconut cream, or toss tips into an end-of-season stir-fry with the last beans, broccoli shoots, or whatever is about to be pulled up, and some Thai curry paste. Serve with rice—so healthy!

By autumn, the vines take up a lot of space, yet they need to dry off before you should cut away the fruit with a short stem. Sometimes, when short of space, I carefully separate vines to clear space between them without disturbing the pumpkins. After filling the space with new compost, I may grow a quick crop of lettuce or radishes, even cauliflowers that stay after the pumpkins are harvested. Or, I'll pick up the end of a vine and coil it like a rope around its root, being careful to lift each attached pumpkin by hand. There they can sit—on a paver or plank—until they're done.

When the vines are dry, or if rains threaten to rot pumpkin tops, cut fruit with 2 inches of stem and place in a dry place, preferably in full sun, to harden off. In North India and Nepal, you see pumpkins drying on roofs, holding down the thatch. If your harvest season is damp, harden them off in a covered area. Hardy varieties will keep from several months to one year, so that you could be eating the last one when the new crop is getting ready. Occasionally, a rat or possum will attack a pumpkin with a soft top, but well-hardened pumpkins are usually left alone. Not all varieties harden off like Queensland blues and butternut, so store others in a cool room. The mini pumpkin "golden nugget" keeps well, too.

A friend saw one pumpkin vine climb her apple tree in autumn and flower. "Silly old thing," she thought and left it to its endeavours. Mid-winter, while weeding, she found a perfect pumpkin on a dried-up vine, gently sinking down in the grass.

If you have grown a colorful variety of pumpkins, squashes, and zucchinis, pile them artistically on a garden table, take a photo, and send copies to friends. If they are astonished at your productivity, send them seed! Make yourself a batch of pumpkin *pakora*. Mix besan (chickpea flour) with your favorite spices and popped mustard seed into a thin batter. Leave standing while cutting pumpkin into thin wedges. Dip into batter and deep-fry until golden. The gardener's reward.

RADICCHIO (*Cichorium intybus*)
Sow in spring and autumn. Companions: beets, carrots, and onions, which all provide root shade in summer. From Asia

Minor. Also see Lettuce on page 254. Italian growers achieve amazing red to purple coloration of the leaves by leaving them out in the cold, then digging them up, balancing them above water, and covering plants with black plastic. On cold nights, all that may happen spontaneously, except for the long curling shoots. Heirloom chicories from Italy are radicchio for the salad bowl. What Italian cooks do not do with radicchio is not worth mentioning. The leaves can be shells for Waldorf salads with olives, or covered with steaming bean soup, served with antipasto, or grilled with olive oil.

RADISHES (*Raphanus sativus*)

Sow in all seasons. Companion: nasturtium (one seed will do!). Probably from the Mediterranean, but had dispersed to Egypt by 2000 BCE, thence to China and Japan. Choose from small round red, long red, red and white, European black, giant daikon or Japanese white, or the bulbous Chinese red radish (I wondered what people did with those). Sow small ones in spring and most of the year, big ones in autumn. Salad radishes grow so easily that kids can do it. Big ones need deep soil, or a deep box, tub, or cylinder.

There may be as many types of radishes as there are chilies, and with luck, or carelessness, you may create a new variety. Years ago, I grew my first daikons alongside round, red table radishes. Plants of both went to seed and the bees must have cross-fertilized the daikons. The next year, using saved daikon seed, I harvested monstrous round red radishes. They were good to eat, some hot, some mild, but there were buckets of them. I saved their seed, calling it "Lolo radish."

During a stay in Singapore, we lunched at a hawker's stall with our hostess. "Try carrot cake," she advised, "it's my favorite." We thought of European-style carrot cake, and decided we'd rather have spicy noodles. Days later, when looking for tea and cake, we saw a sign announcing carrot cake. This time, I was in the mood for it. We ordered, sat down, and waited. After a while, the hawker brought tea and a large plate of steaming something. "I ordered carrot cake," I pointed out politely. The cook looked annoyed. "This is carrot cake," he said decisively, pointed at the dish and walked away. We took a spoonful each. It was yummy and we began to analyze it. Scrambled egg and green onions were easy to identify, but it took a sly walk past the hawker's stall to see that the unidentified ingredient was grated daikon, the large white radish. Perhaps it was translated as "white carrot."

So, I started to make Chinese carrot cake at home with my monstrous round reds. It is a great feed. Asian cookbooks have more recipes, but try rolling grated daikon into patties with besan (chickpea flour), and spices, then deep-frying. Grated daikon gives new flavor to old stir-fry combinations. Try it in soups, and use it to thicken sauces. But dig your soil very deep, or the daikon will push up and turn green up top. Cut off any green parts before using.

Daikon prefers cool weather, winter being best. Like all root vegetables, it should not grow in manured soil. Deep good earth with compost, topped with straw, is just fine. Tie a red ribbon or yarn on the best one and let it flower. The giant plant produces hundreds of white or pinkish mauve flowers visited by beneficial insects. Flowers turn into fat green pods. You don't need all of these for seed. Pick smaller pods while fresh and green, parboil a few minutes, drain, pack in small jars, and cover with vinegar and a spoonful of oil. Large pods take time to fill out before seed is dry. Prune the bush down to what you want to save. To sow seed next year, break open the pods to release the seeds—this may have to be done in a mortar and pestle. Grow daikon sprouts by sowing seeds thickly in a pot. Harvest white stems with two green cotyledons at 2 or 3 inches for soups and salads. Or sprout seed like mung beans.

Finally, try grated apple and white daikon salad with a dressing of sweet-and-sour or spicy plum sauce. Daikon is useful in many dishes, produces bountiful seed, and attracts good insects. Do grow a few.

RHUBARB (*Rheum rhabarbarum*)

Plant rhizomes in autumn in well-manured soil topped with compost. Water well when stalks form in spring and summer. From Manchuria and Siberia; traded along the Silk Road in early times. The deep red or pale green rhubarb leaves are toxic, but if you have a bug problem in the garden, spread rhubarb leaves around affected plants. Only the stems are edible. Red rhubarb has the looks, but the green ones also taste fine.

For a yummy dessert, cook rhubarb, sweeten, and beat in cream cheese. Top with mint leaves and a strawberry. Or bake a rhubarb bread pudding.

RUTABAGAS (*Brassica napus*)

Frost tolerant, sow spring to autumn. Companion: elderberry (spread branches around rutabagas to discourage borers). Keep mulch away from roots. There are Chinese, Japanese, English, and American rutabagas. These firm bulbous roots are sweet and juicy when eaten raw and young, or grated in salads. They can taste a bit earthy when cooked, but are great in soups, absorbing other flavors. Like radishes, they grow easily and rapidly, and are well worth cultivating. Fork soil lightly, but don't fertilize if they follow a previous crop of gross feeders. Do not plant after brassicas. Some LS for the seedlings should be enough.

SALAD GREENS

Salads start with lettuces, but the young leaves of many other plants can add interest, flavor, and more nutrition to the bowl. Some are found in mesclun mixes, but not often in the shop selection. Farmers' market mesclun may be more on the wild side, as they are in France, where these salads originated.

Pick young leaves to 4 inches of amaranth, beet, bok choy, borage, fava beans, buckwheat, chervil, chicory, Chinese cabbage, collards, cilantro, cress, dandelion, endive, kale, mibuna, mizuna, mustard, nasturtium, peas, arugula, salad burnet, salsify, chard, sorrel, spinach, rutabaga, tatsoi, and turnip. Check edible flowers under Flowers on page 285. For salad dressings, see page 154.

SALSIFY (*Tragopogon porrifolius*)

Sow direct in spring 4 inches apart. Also known as oyster plant (not the ornamental variety). From the Mediterranean. The tapered white salsify root has a delicate taste when boiled or baked and served with butter sauce. Leaves are edible and good in salads. As salsify grows

deeper than carrots, cultivate soil two spades deep. Apply CMC between plants, which can grow to over 3 feet tall. See also Scorzonera (below).

SCARLET RUNNER BEAN (*Phaseolus coccineus*)

Plant in spring. Strong climber, but appears not to like hot, dry climates, although it originated in Mexico's mountains. Mine succeeded at an elevation of 1,600 feet with cool nights. Stringy green pods up to 12 inches contain pink-spotted black beans. String, then thinly slice beans prior to cooking. It has gorgeous scarlet flowers and is prolific under the right conditions.

SCORZONERA (*Schorzonera hispanica*)

Sow direct in spring 4 inches apart. Also known as black salsify. From Southern Europe. The tapered root, of delicate taste, is similar to salsify, though dark brown. Cultivate like salsify. If the top of the root is cut off and replanted, it grows a second harvest of smaller spears.

SORREL (*Rumex acetosa*)

Any season. A perennial from the European mountains from Italy to Germany. A wild plant usually bought as a potted herb, but prolific enough to be classed a vegetable. Seed is available. Sorrel is related to dock, a giant cousin producing thousands of seeds per single stem, sinking roots to the center of the earth. Sorrel doesn't do that.

Depending on the soil, sorrel forms a migrating, self-seeding clump or is content with one fifth of a square, which is all you need. Water like lettuce. Not fussy and needs no fertilizer. Come winter, the plant goes mostly dormant. I grow mine in a box.

Pick sorrel for a fresh sour flavor in salads. Sorrel soup is a delicacy. Sauté sorrel leaves and blend with stock. Serve with black pepper and a teaspoon of cream. Add to kale, cabbage, and spinach. The French also put sorrel into leek-and-potato soup for *la difference*.

SPINACH (*Spinacea oleracea*)

Plant in part shade to make it last. Sow in autumn with B&B and compost. English spinach. Originally from Iran. It thrives only during the cool months. A perennial spinach related to chard (*Beta vulgaris*) grows virtually all year round in a clump and tastes truly spinachy. Pick the large, light green leaves. When it goes to seed, let the best stalk have its head. Keep picking. Cut the clump down after harvesting seed, spread CMC around it, and water well to encourage new growth. Spinach likes nitrogen, so add B&B occasionally. Next season, cultivate new clumps from seedlings.

See also Amaranth on page 230. Chinese spinach (*Amaranthus gangeticus*) can grow several feet high. Other plants going by the common name of spinach in their places of origin are Ceylonese spinach (*Basella rubra*) on long creepers, and Indian spinach named *saag*, which is popular in Indian cooking. Pick these vegetables from the bottom up, as needed.

English spinach is a delicious accompaniment for young potatoes and baby carrots in butter, spicy tofu with noodles, or in a real spinach quiche. For the baking of spinach loaves, triangles, pies, and similar weekend food, grow perennial spinach and gourmet chard. They take little space and shrink less than English spinach.

SQUASH (*Cucurbita*)

Sow in spring. Companion: nasturtiums. Also see Pumpkins on page 260. Squashes come in colors, stripes, and shapes from buttons to giants. For the square-yard principle that inspired this book, look at baby squash, also called button squash or "patty pan." You see them in baskets at gourmet greengrocers—toy flying saucers with scalloped edges in bright yellow, white, green, or striped. Expensive to buy, yet they grow readily.

Start two or three seedlings in toilet paper tubes under glass. Plant on one quarter when danger of frost is over, definitely before the first day of summer. They may need support. They benefit by having their roots in a shallow trench or earth saucer to hold the daily watering. Smaller squashes climb on wire netting. Female flowers need to be fertilized through bees or human hand to set fruit. They crop quickly and produce into autumn. At the height of the season, you'll pick several each day.

Pick patty pan when 4 inches across or smaller, then cover with water, simmer until a fork goes in, drain, and slice in wedges. Serve with mustard, lime pickle, or homemade apple and rosemary chutney to retain the delicate texture and taste. Dice leftovers in a garden salad. Particularly good is sliced button squash grilled or baked and served with garlic, ginger, and herb butter.

To pickle patty pan, pick fruit small—about 2 to 3 inches. Parboil until a fork just goes in with resistance. Drain and keep covered in a tea towel. Boil half water, half vinegar with a rosemary twig and bay leaf, remove herbs, and when liquid has cooled, pack buttons in jars, pour liquid to ½ inch under the lid, and close tightly. Leave for a month. Eat all once jar is opened.

For large appetites, the Hubbard squash (*Cucurbita maxima*), which is really a pumpkin, comes highly recommended. It keeps several months if stored in a dry, airy place. This ungainly fruit, resembling a retired football, has fine orange flesh and large white seeds that can be roasted, after saving some for replanting. And if you have too many, do what the Shakers did. They peeled, thinly sliced, and dried pumpkin flesh, then ground it into flour for pumpkin bread.

SWEET CORN (*Zea mays*)

Companions: beans, potatoes, pumpkins, squashes (see the Aztec Plot on page 182). From South America. Many varieties, including popping corn, are available from small seed companies and the Seed Savers Exchange (page 317). Grow only one variety per season if you save your own seed. Maize is more starchy than the juicy corn on the cob and is grown for the processed food industry and as stock feed.

This ancient plant loves warmth and sun. Frost kills it. Plant late spring and be prepared to sow again if a cold spell hits. Sweet corn needs five months to mature. Plant as late as June if your summers are long. Several weeks before planting, dig in manure and an organic nitrogen and phosphorus-rich fertilizer. Add lime or wood ash to acidic soil. See the Starchy Staples Plot (page 199). Sweet corn can grow with less water than dark green leafy plants, but the cobs are bigger and better if watered well. Deep mulch around the plants reduces water needs.

Plant sweet corn in a square and hammer in strong, tall stakes at the corners. Place corn seeds in pairs inside a protector (PVC pipe ring or bottom-less yogurt tub) to prevent night prowl-ers digging them up. Push in a piece of screening for good measure and don't remove either until the seedling pushes against the wire. By then, the seed is no longer attractive to prowlers. Apply LS. As stalks grow, wind a rope around the stakes to keep plants upright in the wind. Plant a short variety if you live in a stormy place. Don't plant sweet corn in a long row; they need close proximity for cross-pollination. Once stalks are up and away, apply chicken manure, OF or B&B, mulch with straw, and water well.

When the silken tassels on the tops turn brown, the cobs are ripening. Strip down one cob leaf to see whether kernels have filled out and ooze milky sap when pinched. Don't let them stand too long; they get tough and starchy. Each kernel is attached to one silken thread in the tassel, so that a thin tassel means part of the cob has not filled out.

To foil rats, make collars under the cobs from large waxed paper plates, cut to the center to fit around the stems like umbrellas. Staple the cut, then wrap the stem with a cloth strip to hold the plate up.

Freeze ripe cobs. No need to blanch. Peel and pack into the freezer. Eat corn on the cob with butter, after boiling in plenty of water. Barbecue, or roast cobs at picnics.

The usefulness of the sweet corn plant does not end there. Tassels are used in basket weaving or decorative loom weaving, and dried leaves make bread and fruit baskets. Leaves and stalks are used as fodder for domestic livestock, and cobs can also be dried for kindling.

SWEET POTATO (*Ipomoea batatas*)

Plant late spring after frost. Probably from Mexico and now a staple food in the Pacific Islands, Africa, and Asia. Sweet potatoes are generally larger than ordi-nary spuds and not related. The white, yellow, orange, or purple tubers are a staple food in Papua, New Guinea's highlands, where the soil is volcanic and every afternoon at 4:00 p.m. the rain pelts down for an hour.

Sprout a sweet potato on top of the fridge. Cut off pieces and grow in pots indoors until warm weather allows planting outside. Mulch thickly and keep moist. As they need five months to develop, you may have to bring them in again later.

Having sprouted a sweet potato, take side stems of no more than 8 inches with a heel (the bit that attached them to the main stem) and root them in a glass of water. This way you make more plants to grow outside when summer arrives.

In Papua New Guinea, we boiled sweet potatoes in coconut milk, made by squeezing grated coconut in warm water, or baked it with bananas in an earthen oven. Following local custom, we ate the heart-shaped leaves on tender vines as a tasty spinach, also steamed in coconut milk. Sweet potatoes are delicious boiled, baked, roasted, or fried. In Hong Kong, they are prepared with sugar, nuts, ginger, nutmeg, and cinnamon, and served as a sweet.

TATSOI (*Brassica narinosa*)

Sow late summer or autumn. Companion: bush beans. Favorite Asian greens. A flat, dark green rosette with an endearing flavor. Loves cool weather. Pick outer leaves while it grows on. Lends a distinct flavor to salads and stir-fries. Plant a quarter, because it shrinks like spinach.

TOMATILLOS (*Physalis ixocarpa*)

Solanum genus. Sow in spring. Companions: same as for tomatoes (asparagus, garlic chives, young mustard, parsley, stinging nettle). It is the cousin of Cape gooseberry. From Mexico. Drought tolerant. Grown like tomatoes, they produce small yellow or purple fruit in papery lanterns. Used for salsa with garlic and onions, and in sauces and salads.

TOMATOES (*Lycopersicon esculentum*)

Sow in spring. Plant out after frosts cease. Companions: asparagus, garlic chives, young mustard, parsley, stinging nettle. From Mexico. Tomato plants protect gooseberry shrubs from insect attacks. Organic gardening author Peter Bennett grows a green crop of barley before planting tomatoes to provide phosphorus. When I planted four cherry tomatoes, the one with self-seeded onion, nettle, and young cabbage as neighbors grew to more than double the size of the others. The onion also looked better than its mates.

Choose bush or climbing, big beefy fruit or cherry size, in colors from red, orange, pink, and yellow to black Russian. Look to seed companies or the Seed Savers Exchange (page 317) for heirloom gourmet varieties. Prepare soil with organic matter low in nitrogen, no chicken manure, and a little lime for acidic soil. When the staked plants stand tall, drooping with bright orange globes, the heart swells. There are as many tomato experts as there are tomato growers. The tomato is the food gardener's pride.

Unless you want to make tomato sauce, you need just one good cropper on a stake, or two cherry tomatoes or bush tomatoes, or one of each. Start seed in toilet paper tubes under glass in early spring. Plant out when all risk of frost has gone. Douse with LS. A pot of garlic chives nearby prevents wilt.

Save your own seed from a ripe tomato, wash off the pulp in a sieve, then place seeds on paper towels ½ inch apart each way. Let this tomato towel dry thoroughly indoors before storing in a paper bag. Next spring, cut off as many seeds on paper as you want plants, lay each one on soil in a toilet paper tube, sprinkle with ½ inch of fine soil, water daily, and raise behind glass. The paper disintegrates.

Freeze cherry tomatoes for use in sauce, juice, or stir-fries. Let them ripen to a good red, wash, and drop the daily handful in a freezer container. For pasta sauce, sauté garlic and onions, oregano, basil, or parsley in plenty of olive oil before adding defrosted or fresh diced tomatoes. Add pepper and salt, but little or no sugar. Use wine vinegar to the degree of acidity you want. Bottle hot. Once a bottle has been opened, keep it in the fridge. Alternatively, make a Balti sauce—see Fenugreek (page 283).

TURNIPS (*Brassica rapa* var. *rapa*)

Frost tolerant. Plant spring to autumn. If soil is acidic, fork in a little lime three weeks prior to sowing. Companion: elderberry (spread branches around plot to discourage borers). Described in Alexander the Great's time, and probably from the Middle East and Iran. Cultivate like rutabagas (page 264). They deserve better.

Plant after a well-manured crop, but not brassicas. Apply LS regularly. Choose white, yellow, green, or purple top. Roots and edible tops are best when grown quickly and eaten young. Make several sowings during spring and summer, and see whether they will grow all year in your microclimate, for turnips are actually biennial. They provide a pithy taste to soups and stews and bulk up other dishes when sliced, cubed, or grated raw. Stir-fry the leaves, serve with mustard and soy sauce. Tenzin Palmo, the Buddhist nun who lived fourteen years in a Himalayan cave, grew turnips all summer as the roots kept well into winter. Middle Eastern pickled turnip makes a good condiment. Use one part vinegar to two parts water, a quarter part salt, and add sliced beets or garlic cloves.

WATERMELONS (*Citrullus lanatus*)

Plant in spring. Companion: a compost heap! Originally from Africa, watermelons have spread themselves around the globe for about 3,000 years. Mini watermelon seed is available. A farmer I know, who began growing watermelons as a boy, saved the seed from the biggest melon every year to plant the next. His watermelons became bigger and bigger, and by the time he was a young man, his biggest watermelon was 36 × 18 inches! That is what farmers have always done in imitation of natural selection. This farmer raises money for charities every year with his champion watermelons.

Our friend Maureen has always been besotted with watermelons. Whenever we went camping—when we were young and restless—she would keep her eyes peeled for watermelon signs in roadside villages, uttering a bloodcurdling cry when spotting one. She always bought a whole melon the size of a giant's football. Seeing Maureen eat watermelon was beholding pure happiness. When she married fellow camper John, who bought many a watermelon to woo her, they set up house and garden, and Maureen continued to eat watermelons. Great was her joy when told that the little plants with scalloped leaves springing up in her compost heap were watermelon seedlings from the pips she'd spat out! Soon, she harvested her own watermelons. That is lasting happiness! In China, they roast the seeds, full of protein and unsaturated oil, to nibble. We are wasteful when it comes to pumpkin and melon pips.

Watermelon seeds germinate readily. They like rich soil and some lime. Horse manure preserves the moisture that melons need. They must grow plump in full sun, needing a long, warm growing season. Start them off in toilet paper tubes, indoors or under glass, then harden seedlings off outside during the daytime. Plant out when weather is warm. Cultivate like pumpkins (page 260).

WATER VEGETABLES

There are a number of edible plants that grow in pots sunk into a pond, or in a big water pot—like lotus and water chestnut. Consult catalogs of small seed companies or specialty nurseries.

ZUCCHINI (*Cucurbita pepo*)

Companions: young nasturtiums, but zucchini will be retarded if growing near chard, which could be a good thing. From Central America. Called courgettes when picked young. Zucchinis belong to the family of gourds, squashes, and pumpkins in the genus *Cucurbita*. They are green, white, or black, smooth or ribbed. They like rich soil with some lime. Plant in a depression to hold water. It is said that growing zucchinis is easy: all you have to do is turn your back. This, for once, is true. One summer, it rained a few days. When I looked again, there was a zucchini 18 inches long of commensurate width. I juiced it for a week at one glass per day. If you make juice, you will cope with more than one plant. Delicious with apples, carrots, and ginger.

Most families need just one or two plants. A container of seedlings better be shared around. Or, plant two seeds in toilet paper tubes. Pick zucchinis young and regularly.

Zucchinis, like pumpkins, produce male and female flowers on thin and swollen stems to be pollinated by bees. If your garden has no bees, plant bee-attracting herbs and pollinate by hand the first year by picking a just-opened male flower and pushing it into an open female flower, rubbing carefully. You feel you're invading their privacy. Place the used male flower in a tiny vase in the kitchen.

When zucchini plants have produced their first spectacular burst of fruits, they start looking like giant green centipedes lying with their feet in the air. Suddenly, there are but few flowers and hardly any fruit. Rejuvenate them by pruning. Cut off all leaves from the beginning of the main stem up to where the fruit is forming, leaving enough leaves to shade new fruit. This enables plants to put all nutrients into a second production run, not as boisterous as the first, but satisfyingly regular. In late summer and early autumn, let fruit grow to full capacity. The skin hardens, and it becomes a gourd to keep for a while and save seed from.

There are more recipes for zucchini than anything else. If all you have ever tried is fried zucchini, battered male zucchini flowers (only in the zucchini and pumpkin world is it the males who get battered), and zucchini soup, become adventurous. Try sliced male zucchini flowers in an omelet, bake zucchini cake and bread with marigold petals, or grate zucchini into lettuce with herbs, oil, lemon, and soy sauce. You can grill zucchini with tomatoes, garlic, cheese, and basil, serve zucchini sandwiches with chutney or grilled cheese and mustard, and make velvet zucchini soup with arugula, coriander, cumin, and lemongrass. Or stir-fry zucchini with green beans and broccoli or tomato chutney, and make up your own zucchini relish, jams, and pickles. My favorite salad is grated zucchini and carrots with chopped celery or grated apple and a dressing of Dijon mustard, curry powder, olive oil, and balsamic vinegar. Pure health.

MORE VALUE *from* POPULAR VEGETABLES

THE SOLANUM FAMILY of plants is now ubiquitous, but the ones we eat most originally came from Central and South America only five centuries ago after Columbus sailed the wrong way. Europeans first eyed them with suspicion, and they weren't half wrong! Solanum plants are recognizable by their five-petaled flowers—white, mauve, or other—and pronounced yellow pistil. The family includes potatoes, tomatoes, red peppers, eggplants, chilies, and a number of other edible plants. Those five are the mainstay of fast-food outlets; the potatoes so filling, the others so colorful and tasty. There are solanums indigenous to other continents, such as goji berries from Asia and kangaroo apple from Australia (see An A–Z of Vegetable Families on page 224).

When buying seeds and plants, check labels for solanum or Solanaceae, as these plants contain solanines that, in small amounts, do not bother most people, but can aggravate certain forms of arthritis. One has to make dietary choices sometimes, but if you are not able to eat these summer favorites, you are free to indulge in other exotic vegetables: "Darling, I'd be stricken if I ate your beautiful solanum salsa, but I brought my own avocado and mango pickle, is that all right?"

Solanums and many other vegetables can have extended usage when grown at home (see Preserving and Using Home Produce on page 307).

ARUGULA (*Eruca sativa*)

Grows in winter. Save seed to re-sow in autumn. Perennial or wild arugula (*Diplotaxis tenuifolia*) grows through summer, dies down and reappears in the same spot in spring. Both make delicious pesto. In the blender, reduce a bowl of leaves to a pulp while drizzling in a little olive oil and a tablespoon of lemon juice, gradually adding a cup of pine nuts (or walnuts or cashews), and blend. Add two cloves of garlic, 2 tablespoons of grated Parmesan cheese, and blend. Drizzle in more olive oil, if needed. Pack in small containers and freeze for instant, delicious pasta and dips.

BEANS

Dry on the bush, remove seeds from pod, and store.

BROAD BEANS (*Vicia faba*)

Eat whole young pods, up to 4 inches, picked around the bottom of the plant. Do not cut off ends, but lightly cook whole pod. Pick large pods as they form from bottom up, and shell. Enjoy fresh beans and freeze surplus by immediately packing portions in the freezer, without blanching. Keep picking and freezing as the pods mature. Can be dried.

BROCCOLI (*Brassica* spp.)

The chopped young leaves are delicious sautéed in olive oil with garlic, lime leaf, and sprigs of sage, thyme, and rosemary. From six plants, pick two leaves each occasionally. Broccoli seed heads, flowers, and stems are eaten while tender, raw in salads, or tossed in olive oil.

CARROTS (*Umbelliferae* family)

Can be stored stuck upright in a box of sand. Grows all year as well. Cook surplus carrots to a mash, spice with salt, cumin, and green herb of choice, like tarragon, roll into rissoles, and freeze in portions.

CAULIFLOWER (*Brassica* spp.)

Eat leaves as from broccoli. The taste is quite different but good.

CHILIES (Solanaceae family)

Treat as eggplants and red peppers. Dry on a string in a shady veranda. Or, cut plants at soil level when most chilies have turned red and hang upside down in an airy, shady place. This allows nutrients to flow into the fruit from the stems.

EGGPLANTS (Solanaceae family)

If your microclimate is not too cold, cut plants to 8 inches after harvest and cover with bottomless plastic bottles for overwintering. They may shoot again in spring, becoming perennial. Or, overwinter in pots in the sunroom. Can be sliced and dried or pickled.

FENNEL
(*Foeniculum vulgare* var. *azoricum*)

Also known as *finocchio*. This beautiful plant has many uses. Grow for the edible bulbs, but serve them raw to retain vitamins and minerals. Keep at least one plant to grow up and flower. It survives a long time during which you use the ferny leaves in cooking, added to soups, omelets, the greens pot, mixed stir-fries, rice pilaf, risotto, cooked and served warm, or sparingly in salads. The aniseed taste is strong, so experiment with quantities. Let seed heads develop, and harvest green seeds for curries. Dried seeds keep a long time. Ground to powder, a pinch of fennel lifts just about any dish, fry, or soup. Indispensable in Indian cooking.

MELON SEEDS (Cucurbit family)

The Chinese, and others on the vast Asian continent where melons grow, save seeds of melons, dry and toast them, and sell them in little bags. You split them open between your teeth to find a delicious little flat kernel inside. This habit may never catch on in fast-moving societies, although it does alleviate stress! When we have melon, I sometimes save a saucer of rinsed seed and put it by the computer. Makes me write better.

MUSTARD (*Brassica* spp.)

A refreshing instant pickle from Japan is made with a bunch of young mustard leaves, parboiled for seconds to a bright green. Chop finely, sprinkle with a little sea salt and lemon juice. Serve cold as a side dish. Young flower heads of mustard plants can be added to salads, steamed with soy sauce, and drizzled with sesame oil. Mustard plants clean up the soil for other crops.

ONIONS (Allium or lily family)

Although onions are traditionally planted at Easter, you can plant whole onions from the shop any time to grow them for their fresh green straps. They start sprouting within weeks of finding themselves having a second life in real soil and reward you for many months. Buy a large bag of unsorted barbecue onions for a ridiculously low price—an opportunity for the grower to sell all of his crop, not just supermarket standard sizes. Plant these beautiful bulbs in borders of beds with kale and spinach. Once the green straps grow lustily, pick them for soups, salads, stir-fries, omelets, homemade pizza, and the pot that sautés your daily green leaves. When the bulbs are exhausted, they divide into small onions. How generous is that?

PEAS (Leguminosae family)

Can be dried on the bushes, shelled, and stored.

POTATOES (Solanaceae family)

Potatoes are cheap to grow and crop heavily. Source seed potatoes from cooler climates to avoid viruses. Or, select healthy spuds from a good shop and cut into pieces with "eyes." If you want large potatoes, remove all but one stem from the plant. Multi-stemmed plants produce more but smaller potatoes. Potatoes are full of vitamins and minerals. I was born into a potato culture. My favorite potato food, apart from real French fries, was spicy potato rissoles with herbs. Make them from mashed potato with corn or potato flour, parsley, nutmeg, five-spice, salt, pepper, and breadcrumbs. Fry in olive oil on both sides and eat hot. Great in a salad or with a bread salad. Potatoes keep for some time laid out on newspaper, not touching, in a cool, dark place.

PUMPKINS (Cucurbit family)

Eat the pumpkins, and most of the male flowers when enough fruit has set. Shred flowers on salads or dip in a thin batter and deep-fry. When vines get longer and fruit is growing, harvest tips and side shoots of young leaves to steam in coconut cream. When harvested—always with 2 inches of stem—harden off pumpkins on a table in the sun. When cooking, save the nutritious seeds. Set aside enough seed for replanting, dry and store. Dry the rest, rub off the silvery outer skins, and roast slowly in a low oven. Watch them, as they can burn quite suddenly. Roasted pumpkin seeds can be chewed if you don't mind a little roughage, or spitting. Or grind them in a spice grinder and put through a sieve to obtain a nutty flour to add to cake and biscuit dough. Mix cooked, mashed pumpkin into dough; add sugar or five-spice, or both, to make pumpkin scones and loaves. Pumpkin soup freezes well.

RED PEPPER
(*Capsicum* spp., Solanceae family)

One red pepper plant grown with plenty of manure and great care once produced as many as 100 fruits! Overwinter as for eggplants. Can be dried, or roasted, then pickled—or frozen raw.

SPINACH (*Chenopodiaceae family*)

Most people think Swiss chard when spinach is mentioned. But real spinach is more delicate and tender with a taste all its own. It gave old Popeye his legendary strength to defeat adversaries, and, in my youth, all children were told they would never grow if they didn't eat their spinach. This wonderful vegetable grew profusely in the damp grey atmosphere of pre–global warming Holland and England. When Mama came back from the greengrocer with a large, light-weight bundle wrapped in newspaper, I knew we'd be sorting spinach. The bright green bunches were soaked in a tub of water to let bits of soil and manure sink to the bottom, since all vegetables were organic. Then, we'd lift each bunch and check it for seeds. Spinach seeds are not unlike three-cornered jacks, and you don't want to find them on your tongue, not even cooked! After reducing spinach briefly on high heat in water that clung to the leaves, Mama drained it before serving mixed with butter and breadcrumbs.

English or European spinach is a delicious accompaniment for young potatoes and baby carrots in butter, or spicy tofu with noodles, or in a real spinach quiche. Spinach shrinks dramatically during even the briefest of cooking, so you need a field to get your fill. But perennial spinach can be picked frequently and will soon regrow, throughout hot weather and cold. Keep picking large leaves and, when it goes to seed, let the best stalk have its head, while gradually stripping the rest for meals. When the clump has been pruned down and dried seed harvested, spread composted manure and compost around the plant and water well for new growth and seedlings. Spinach likes nitrogen; feed it B&B. After a year, cultivate new clumps from spontaneous seedlings. Small seed companies carry spinach seeds from many countries: New Zealand, Egypt, Sri Lanka, and more. A fleshy type is French Viroflay spinach, while Indian saag is my comfort food.

TOMATOES (Solanaceae family)

One summer, I grew four different heritage tomatoes, three climbers and one bush. You learn a few things by comparing.

The Amish brandywine tomato is a phenomenal climber, rising 10 feet, therefore flowering late. When it does, it is advisable to prune off all branches not carrying flowers. The puckered fruit is enormous. One fruit fills the palm of my hand; one whopper filled both hands. The fruit tends to split along the creases. Not one fruit ripened on the vine, probably because of our altitude with cool nights and misty mornings, our late springs, and our early onsets of autumn. Also, a fat 2-inch-long whitish green worm eats big holes into brandywine. I brought the fruit in as soon as it started coloring, to ripen indoors to a smooth pinkish orange. Even totally green fruit ripened indoors. The taste is exceedingly good. A childhood memory taste. Given full sun most of the day, brandywine produces great tomato volume for sauces, chutneys, salads, salsas, and frozen tomato soup.

The Russian black climbed on an 8-foot wire tower, its tomato the size of a large ping-pong ball. It intertwined with the Russian black cherry tomato, the size of big cherries. These two were the first to flower and set fruit and cropped over two months. The black cherry tomatoes are the most prolific, akin to similar cherry tomatoes in the regular red-orange range. Both black Russians taste like childhood on a stick, absolutely delicious. One of my visiting sons tasted one from a handful placed with crackers, biscuits, and nuts set out at coffee time, and soon was popping them into his mouth like peanuts.

The fourth tomato I grew was yellow pear, because my daughter fancied taking cocktail platters to parties. She planned to mix red, yellow and black tomatoes, arranging them on kebab sticks. The yellow pear does not climb, it sprawls. This is another small tomato to pop whole in the mouth, ideal for kids' lunchboxes and party plates. With two bushes I simply didn't know what to do with the volumes of yellow pears produced. I preserved some in malt vinegar and olive oil. As there is still frozen brandywine and black Russian paste in the freezer, this year I'm growing only one variety. Black Russian cherry is my little champion!

ZUCCHINIS (Cucurbit family)

Eat them young before making curried zucchini rice soup, zucchini/coconut/green pea soup, zucchini rissoles with onions, garlic, oregano, and cheese, grated drained zucchini pancakes (add flour, eggs, seasoning, and crumbly cheese), zucchini relish with tomato, zucchini slice, zucchini bake, zucchini loaf, zucchini bread, zucchini salsa. Next year, plant only one zucchini seed.

COMMON HERBS:
HOW *to* GROW *and* USE THEM

HERBS INCLUDED have culinary values and/or properties to ward off pests or promote plant health. Many are listed as companions to vegetables in List of Common Vegetables (page 230). Some suggestions for using herbs in the kitchen are included.

Plants carrying *officinalis* as their second botanical name have medicinal properties. To discuss these properties is beyond the scope of this book—see References and Further Reading (page 314) for further information.

General Growing Notes

Wherever it is recommended to grow an herb in a pot, either because its roots are invasive or to act as a mobile pest controller, make sure to water regularly, as pots dry out. Place potted herbs with invasive roots on a tile to prevent roots anchoring the pot. Herbs that like full sun, gritty soil, and being well drained are mullein, sage, and thyme. Mints, lemon balm, and other soft-leaved herbs prefer part shade and moisture-holding soils, compost, LS, or B&B. Woody herbs tolerate poorer, stony soil. Try grouping plants accordingly.

HERBAL TEAS

Those herbs indicated as suitable for making herbal tea can be picked fresh for pot or cup, dried and mixed, or dried separately.

NATIVE HERBS

Many regional plants are suited for culinary use. Check with local nurseries or a guide book what will grow where you are, as they may be location-sensitive.

PEST-REPELLING HERBS

All aromatic herbs will repel one pest or another. For good health in and around the food garden, start collecting basil, chamomile, feverfew, various mints, pennyroyal, rue, rosemary, sage, southernwood, tansy, and thyme. Plant these in large pots to be moved among vegetables. Plant some as edgings and hedges.

List of Common Herbs

ARUGULA (*Eruca sativa*)
See Arugula on page 231.

BASIL (*Ocimum basilicum*)

Sweet basil. Sow spring to summer when cold weather has fled. Companions: tomatoes and beans (although the marriage may benefit basil more than the beans). From India, this tropical herb is an annual in non-tropical areas. When basil grows lush in summer, you can afford to make pesto for pasta. Pinch out tips to encourage leaf growth. Try sacred basil for Thai cooking, bush basil, purple basil, and flavored basils. Although I'd rather combine basil with lemon juice then use lemon-flavored basil, I could be wrong. Freeze basil in airtight bags at summer's end before cold nights kill off the plant, or bring it indoors in a big pot.

Basil mint has a good enough basil flavor, combined with the hardiness of mint, although you can lose it in a hard winter.

BAY LAUREL (*Lauris nobilis*)

A slow-growing small tree. In Roman times, emperors, senators, and victorious generals wore bay-laurel wreaths on their curly heads. Fresh leaves flavor soups and sauces, but must be removed before serving, as they are not edible. Use in a bouquet garni with thyme and parsley. Leaves can be dried and stored for years. A little bay goes a long way, so, if you're pressed for space, just buy a packet. But for elegance in a big pot, she's your babe.

BORAGE (*Borago officinalis*)

Prefers cool weather, sow late summer or late winter. Companion: strawberries. A soil improver. Originally from Italy. This proud herb with medium-size, light green, hairy leaves, faintly tasting of cucumber, bears masses of tiny, star-shaped, bright blue flowers. Young leaves and petals are nutritional additions to salads or steamed vegetables. Mix finely cut leaves with cream cheese or yogurt. Sprinkle salads with borage flowers, minus the black seeds, or freeze flowers and tiny leaves in ice cubes for summer drinks.

Borage adds delicate beauty to the food garden and becomes a sight for weary eyes when mixed with marigold or nasturtiums. Grow borage to attract bees to pollinate pumpkin, squash, and zucchini flowers. Geese love borage, and what they eat is good for you, too. Let old plants decay—they return more to the soil than they took out. A must-have companion plant.

CARAWAY (*Carum carvi*)

Sow in autumn. Probably from Asia. White to pinkish flowers. The seeds are used in bread and cakes. Added to boiled or fried cabbage, they prevent bloat. Use leaves in salads and soups. Caraway attracts beneficial insects. Save an umbel of seed for next year, or let plants self-seed. Grind seeds with coriander for a nuts-and-spices pilaf. A versatile spice.

CATMINT (*Nepeta* spp.)

From England's hedgerows. Choose between the large, sprawling, white-flowering catmint and the elegant gray rosettes with mauve flowers, known as Persian catmint, which makes a delicious tea. They seed themselves and grow rootlings. Good insects visit the flowers, and their scent keeps troubles away. Water during dry spells.

CELERY HERB
(*Apium graveolens* var. *secalinum*)

Sow in autumn. From Europe, but known in Asia as Chinese celery. Prefers cool seasons, setting seed in summer. Collect seed and prune stalks to the ground for new growth. May only last a few seasons, therefore sow again next autumn, or if you have mild summers, in spring. It is a versatile clumping plant providing aromatic leaves for soups, stews, stir-fries, omelets, and sandwiches. The stalks are not tender enough to eat, but the leaves add celery flavor in cooking. Root divisions grow readily and make a nice present in a generous pot. If growing real celery seems too much trouble, grow celery herb.

CHAMOMILE (*Anthemis nobilis*)

Sow in spring and autumn. The wild plant has been widely known in Europe, North Africa, and temperate Asia, and many varieties are bound to exist. Keeps surrounding plants healthy, attracts good insects, and repels white cabbage moths. Make chamomile tea with the flowers. Recent research confirms that chamomile boosts the immune system and relaxes muscles.

CHERVIL (*Anthriscus cerefolium*)

Sow late summer or early spring. Needs shade in summer. From Asia Minor and the Caucasus. Chervil takes up little space, but needs to be re-sown in most climates. A much underrated small herb for fine food and egg dishes. Make chervil butter for artichokes, carrots, pastas, and cheese dishes.

CILANTRO (*Coriandrum sativum*)

Sow thickly in autumn in one quarter. Probably from the Mediterranean. Best grown during winter. Fallen seeds germinate any time of the year, so a cool location makes it an all-rounder. Prepare soil with B&B and CM. This unmistakable herb with its peculiarly pungent taste is easy to grow. Put a dishwashing rack over the plot until plants are 2 inches, to prevent wild things raiding the seeds. Start picking leaves when stems are 12 inches. Flowers and roots are edible.

Let several plants produce seed from the exquisite white-grayish-pink flowers beloved by dragonflies and lacewings. Or, let all the crop set seed, harvest seeds when dried on the stalk, then strip, and store. The seeds are coriander, a fragrant spice, and lack the pungency of fresh cilantro that some writers have called fetid but that most people find an absolute nostril-pleaser.

CRESS (*Lepidium sativum*)

Also known as garden cress. See also Arugula on page 231. Cress seed is sown thickly in shallow trays for mustard-and-cress sandwiches. As cress takes longer to germinate, sow mustard three days later in another tray and hope they synchronize. Although both prefer cooler seasons, by sowing them in trays in a sheltered spot or in the kitchen, you can grow them all year round. Watercress (*Nasturtium officinale*) needs clean running water, something difficult to come by in many locations, and land cress (*Barbarea verna*) also needs lots of water to become edible.

CUMIN (*Cuminum cyminum*)

Sow in autumn. From Egypt and the Mediterranean. White to pink tiny flowers. Seeds are more pungent than caraway. Used in Indonesian, Mexican, and Indian food, curries, pickles, and sauerkraut. Self-seeds and attracts good insects.

DILL (*Anethum graveolens*)

Sow for autumn or spring, or in dappled shade in summer. From Western Asia and Southern Europe. Let some go to seed, for the yellow umbrellas are beloved by beneficial insects. Use foliage in cooking and baking; use seeds for pickling dill cucumbers, dill vinegar, dill butter, and dill bread.

DOGBANE (*Plectranthus ornatus*)

Plant for autumn or spring. A deep green succulent needing little care, it makes a dense patch with purple flower spikes resembling Italian lavender. This is another pest-repellent plant to shift to trouble spots, not for eating. Some say it stinks, others love the pungent odor of crushed dogbane leaf. Dogs apparently avoid it. I lost mine in a garden move and have yet to find another plant in a nursery, as seed appears unavailable. Old-fashioned gardens may be a source.

FENNEL (GREEN) (*Foeniculum vulgare*)

Sow late winter. There is also a bronze fennel. For Florence fennel see page 249. From the Mediterranean.

Grow your own in a garden or orchard, but control the spreading of seed. Whether you grow common fennel or the elegant bronze variety—a mystical sight on a misty morn—you have to collect all seed heads as they ripen, or cut the plant down. If fennel seeds spread on the wind, the neighborhood may be less than pleased with you. Fennel is not easy to dig out after growing to teenage size undetected, but the taste of fresh fennel greens and the seed make it a wonderful herb, and the golden flowers attract thousands of beneficial insects. Do not plant fennel among vegetables, as it inhibits other plants. If you have an herb garden, plant fennel with invincible vegetation like mints or crab apple.

Fennel is an ingredient in fine liqueurs. Grind seeds for a new gourmet flavor in plain soups and stews. Fennel bread and hot fennel buns are easy achievements, the seed used whole. Toasted fennel seeds stave off hunger. In India, from luxury hotels to humble roadside eating shacks, toasted fennel seeds are served after meals to clear the palate and prevent flatulence. Sometimes, they are mixed with sugar—delicious, but bad for dental health. One plant provides a year's supply.

Fresh foliage, green or bronze, makes a fragrant bed for arrangements of cheeses, olives, tomatoes, and slices of red onion and orange.

Red valerian and bronze fennel in a border adjoining the vegetable plot.

FENUGREEK
(*Trigonella foenum-graecum*)

From Western Asia and the Mediterranean. Easy to grow, it stands clay and dry conditions and will germinate in any season, so experiment. Begin by sowing a teaspoon of seed in autumn. Seeds are sprouted for a spicy addition to soups and salads. Store-bought seed may grow plants but not sprout well, whereas home-grown fenugreek does so readily. Sickle-shaped pods contain the ochre seeds, an ingredient in curry powder.

In the 1980s, the *National Farmer* newspaper, inspired by British research, touted fenugreek as a promising new crop because of its birth-control potential, but also advocated it as a high-quality stock feed—presumably not on stud farms. It promised to become a forage crop like Lucerne—a high-nitrogen, legumous cover crop, oil producer, sprouting vegetable, and more. The seeds contain oil, high protein, gum, and resin, and the plant contains high levels of carotenes. Seeds can also be roasted for use as a coffee substitute.

Fenugreek leaves are indispensable in a popular one-pot meal called the Balti—from Baltistan. The Balti originated in Himalayan fields and contains what shepherds have on hand or carry in their bags, supplemented with wild garlic, herbs, and vegetables from the fields. You can design your own Balti at home.

Gather up literally any food at hand: vegetables, mushrooms, legumes, or any other protein food. Fry onions, garlic, ginger, and chili in oil or ghee until golden brown. In a separate pan, gently heat spice seeds—coriander, cumin, fennel, mustard, and a few peppercorns—for less than a minute (enough to release aromas) before grinding them up and mixing in some powdered turmeric, cinnamon, cumin, or paprika. Stir all into the onion mixture and fry for half a minute. Now, add the diced vegetables and mushrooms, the legumes, and

anything else that harmonizes. Diced tomatoes or tomato puree is added with a little water, and the pot is set to simmer. Meanwhile, cut up fresh fenugreek or cilantro leaves to stir into the Balti when the food becomes tender. Sesame seeds can be used ground or whole to add a nutty flavor. Serve with chapatis made with *atta* (whole wheat) flour, or rice.

Balti sauce—now available in some supermarkets—is easily made at home. Just fry in oil the onion and spice mixtures as above, adding a whole bay leaf and a cardamom pod. Add tomatoes or tomato puree with some water and simmer half an hour. Remove the bay leaf and cardamom pod. When cool, puree in a blender and bottle. This sauce keeps in the fridge for a week, or can be frozen. For quick meals, use Balti sauce on chunky salads, on parboiled, roasted, or barbecued vegetables, or with rice or bread in any form. Add fresh fenugreek leaves.

Grind fenugreek seeds for your own curry or spice blend for chutneys. Use leaves through winter and harvest pods in late spring. Spend an hour podding them in a deep bowl before drying the seeds for storage. They will jump open when bashed in a pillowcase or pounded, but I like podding them and seeing the ochre, squarish seeds lying inside. Having started with 2 teaspoons of supermarket seed, I now grow enough fenugreek for our needs. Restore a harvested vegetable plot by sowing fenugreek in autumn for a fragrant spring harvest.

FEVERFEW
(*Chrysanthemum parthenium*)

This medium-size plant with pungent serrated leaves is a garden insecticide. It carries heads of small white daisies with yellow hearts. Growing one in every vegetable plot removes the need for other insecticides, or grow it in a mobile pot. Feverfew self-seeds moderately and is easily transplanted to where it is needed. Root division is recommended, as plants may die after a few years.

FLOWERS

So many flowers are edible that it is impossible to list them all. Violets, borage, nasturtium, and calendula are used as garnish in restaurants. Elderberry, hibiscus, hollyhock, pumpkin, squash, and zucchini flowers are fried in batter. The shungiku yellow daisy is added to Chinese dishes. The yellow flowers of broccoli and Asian greens can be eaten with the vegetables. Many herb flowers can be added to salads or made into teas. Mauve garlic-chive flowers are garlic flavored. Lavender flowers enhance jams and biscuits, as do scented geranium leaves and flowers.

To protect people with allergies, always remove style and stamen from flowers before using. There are books on cooking with flowers. Avoid flowers of plants with toxic properties unless you know they have been tried and proven safe to eat.

GERANIUMS (*Pelargonium* spp.)

Plant cuttings anytime. Scented geraniums repel pests. Plant a low-but-tough hedge on the sunny side of the food garden, mixing peppermint, rose, nutmeg, coconut, lemon, and whatever other scented geraniums you find in friends' gardens and in markets. Apply mulch and water for great results. The flowers are unappreciated miniature beauties. Flowers and young leaves grace gourmet salads. Geraniums will put up with brackish water.

HORSERADISH (*Armoracia rusticana*)

Companion to none, horseradish tends to push out any other plant. An invasive plant that annually conquers neighboring territory, it is not advisable to grow horseradish in a vegetable garden unless you pound sheet iron 2 feet into the ground surrounding it.

An ancient root, probably from Western Asia and Southern Europe. The roots are dug up when the poisonous leaves dry off. All harvesting and cutting of tops has to be done on the plot itself, because any piece of the horseradish plant lost somewhere else will start the formation of a new squadron. The roots should be ground up in a meat mincer. Face mask and goggles are recommended when doing this as the fumes attack nostrils and eyes.

How do I know all this? Because we did grow our own, and after having pickled some in vinegar for a month, it made a divine condiment. After we moved, we chose to buy little jars from the supermarket, not half as good. Horseradish is the Genghis Khan of the vegetable world. We learned to keep our distance.

HYSSOP (*Hyssopus officinalis*)

Sow or plant early autumn. From Southern Europe. This was once a favorite culinary herb for plain cooking. It has a strong aroma, deep purple flowers, and is fairly hardy but can disappear in a heat wave. Worth reinstating.

LAVENDER (*Lavendula* spp.)

Sow in spring, plant cuttings any time. From Southern Europe. There are English, French, Italian, and Canary Island lavenders, and shades of mauve, purple, pink, and white. The old-fashioned lavenders from France and Italy have strong perfume. Lavender is a powerful insect repellent.

Plant a lavender and rosemary hedge on the north side of the vegetable garden, as they stand cold winds well. Lavender puts up with brackish water, but likes alkaline soil. Apply lime or place concrete rubble around plants. In a garden where two rows of lavender showed a marked difference in growth and health, although planted at the same time, the vigorous row edged a concrete path. Use leaves sparingly in salads, sauces, and jellies. Try apple-and-lavender jam, or lavender tea with honey and lemon.

LEMON BALM (*Melissa officinalis*)

Sow in spring, or plant root any time. Also known as bee balm. From the eastern Mediterranean. Fresh lemon balm leaves make an invigorating tea. Used sparingly in cooking for a hint of lemon. Beneficial in the food garden, as it attracts bees, but place it in a large pot, as it can be invasive.

LEMONGRASS (*Cymbopogon citratus*)

Grow from seed in spring and summer, buy a root, or try sticking a bunch from the market in good soil, cutting down the tops to 12 inches.

Indispensable for Southeast Asian dishes. A tropical plant tough enough to survive a chilly winter if protected by a bag or plastic on three sticks, or a mini hothouse of water-filled plastic bottles.

The base of the stem is used in cooking. The spiky leaves are cut and dried for lemongrass tea. A lemongrass marinade with olive oil, garlic, tamari or soy sauce, and lime or lemon juice will flavor many dishes.

MARIGOLD (*Calendula officinalis*)

Sow any time. Companion plant for all vegetables. The ruffled French marigold is said to be as good a companion plant as calendula due to its strong smell. Calendula does not have a strong smell but works in subtler ways.

Presumably native to Europe, but naturalized in India, where it is used to make garlands and votive offerings. Also called English marigold, calendula, or pot marigold. Orange or yellow, flat, daisy-like flowers. Also available are Himalayan marigold (*Tagetes lunulata*), if it likes your climate, and Mexican marigold (*Tagetes minuta*) growing to 6 feet with bronze-colored tufts. Both control nematodes (eelworms).

The Mexican's leaves look embarrassingly like marijuana, and whenever a helicopter or small plane hovered low over my second garden where they grew tall, I expected the drug squad to drop in for a chat. I looked forward to having them smell a leaf, as the plant is called "Stinking Roger" in Queensland where it was let loose. They never came.

Calendulas adorn every organic garden, as they attract good insects, need no maintenance, self-seed, and are easily pulled up when in the way. They are also a welcome addition to the compost. Calendula flowers (but not the others!) are edible and endowed with magic health qualities. Pick an uneven number, as magic never works with even numbers. Sprinkle petals on salads and gourmet platters and dry for baking cakes.

MARJORAM (*Origanum marjorana*)

Sow any time. Also known as sweet marjoram. Native to Portugal. More delicate than oregano. Plant in a large pot and move around to help vegetables. There are several varieties, some sweeter, some more aromatic.

MINT (*Mentha* spp.)

Plant any time. Native to Europe and North Africa, but now a global citizen. I picked mint in the Himalayan Spiti Valley. Grow in pots placed on tiles or planks to prevent roots invading the garden. I saw a food garden periodically left alone almost entirely overrun with mint. Although the roots go wide rather than deep, it is a big job to clean up the soil, as every tiny bit left behind grows again.

Move pots between vegetables, especially the cabbage family. Mints prefer temperate climates. In hot weather, I place mint pots in trays, or in a wheelbarrow with an inch or two of water, in the shade. There are many varieties.

Peppermint repels mice and makes a favorite tea, spearmint spells chewing gum, bunches of eau-de-cologne mint act as room fresheners. Bowle's mint is good in cooking, and ordinary garden mint can probably do all of those. Basil mint grows so fast, you can make basil mint pesto. Mint goes with peas, fruit salad, and yogurt.

MUSTARD
(*Brassica alba* and *B. nigra*)

Plant any season. Companion: tomatoes, protecting them from diseases they are prone to. See also Giant Red Mustard on page 250, and Cress on page 282. White mustard was a native of Europe, but mustards are widely cultivated everywhere for seed and oil. Start with a packet of mustard seed from a grocery spice rack. Sow a few mustard seeds between tomatoes, but when they grow taller, cut and leave the stalks lying around.

To recondition a bed of run-down soil where nothing grows well, sow mustard thickly and dig in when flowering. Grow mustard each year in a different plot to keep the garden healthy and free of nematodes.

Use green leaves for salads and stir-fries. Ambitions to make your own mustard? Thickly sow a square and let plants set seed. Cut dry pods into a pillowcase without holes. Let them dry a few weeks more, then slap the pillowcase from left to right on a table to separate the seed and chaff. To separate seed, read about winnowing in the chapter Saving Seed (page 129). As I haven't made mustard yet, you'll have to chase down a recipe.

NASTURTIUM (*Tropaeolum minus*)
Sow in autumn. Companion plant to just about anything, as it attracts good insects. Also known as *Nasturtium majus* or Indian cress. From Peru. Nasturtiums keep aphids away. Restrain nasturtiums by folding old plants under straw. Pick fat seeds just after petals have fallen, and pickle in vinegar for a peppery pseudo-caper. Use leaves and flowers in bean salads.

OREGANO (*Origanum vulgare*)
Sow or plant any time. Found in Asia, Europe, and North Africa. This is the wilder, more pungent sibling of marjoram. An essential herb in pizzas, pastas, and bouquet garnis. Grow in mobile pots as a companion plant.

PARSLEY (*Petroselinum crispum*)
Biennial. Sow in spring in part shade. Curly-leaved. Native to Europe. Italian parsley is flat-leaved and more frost resistant. Plant parsley in the flower border to aid roses. As parsley is not perennial, collect seed in the first year and dry in a paper bag. Cut stalks right

down and mulch for a second year's growth, while sowing seed in autumn for next year when the old root dies.

Parsley aids digestion, which may have given rise to the restaurant custom of decorating meals with a sprig. Unfortunately, most people push it aside. Parsley has also been pushed aside as a garnish by dill, cress, fennel, arugula, nasturtiums, and other fashionable herbs. Yet parsley remains an important food that is said to lower cholesterol. Grow plenty of parsley for tabouli, the Middle Eastern dish of chopped parsley, onions, and soaked bulgur wheat with lemon juice, olive oil, and pepper. If you can't eat wheat, use crushed buckwheat or coarse polenta. Tabouli makes a great meal with hot beans, just as a bean dish improves with parsley. In Europe, flat-leaved parsley roots are eaten as a vegetable.

Parsley, tansy, thyme, and rosemary keep struggling young fruit trees healthy.

ROSEMARY (*Rosmarinus officinalis*)

Sow spring or plant cuttings any time. From the Mediterranean. These aromatic evergreen shrubs should grace every garden. They are water-wise, low maintenance, and provide the greatest amount of herb for the least effort. Bees love the blue flowers. Add rosemary to a bouquet garni for gourmet chard. Pasta improves with finely chopped rosemary. Homemade drinks of lemon or other fruits benefit by a rosemary infusion. Apple-and-rosemary chutney goes with summer squash, rice, and beans. Rosemary tea helps the memory—mix the rosemary with purple sage. A rosemary rinse makes your hair shine. The list of rosemary's benefits goes on, and you simply should find space for *Rosmarinus officinalis* and then take cuttings. Cultivars have brighter flowers, but you want strongly fragrant foliage. Plant a rosemary hedge along the boundary of the food plot that faces the prevailing wind.

SAGE (*Salvia officinalis*)

Sow spring or autumn. From the Mediterranean. Repels cabbage moths and carrot flies. Although there are many sages with flowers, ranging from white and pink to night blue, *Salvia officinalis* is the culinary herb. Use sparingly in cheese and breads. Sage crispy fried in olive oil is good on pasta. Medicinally, sage makes a throat gargle and a tea to reduce fever. Pineapple sage (*Salvia rutilans*) is a great tea herb. Purple sage tea is said to aid the memory in old age.

SALAD BURNET
(*Poterium sanguisorba*)

Sow in autumn. From Europe. Also known as lesser burnet. A pretty, upright rosette of fine stems, with serrated tender leaves tasting of cucumber. Adds beauty to the herb plot. Sprinkle leaves on salads, or in *raita*, the Indian cucumber and yogurt dish.

SHUNGIKU
(*Glebionis coronarium*)

Sow in autumn. From East Asia. The leaves and flat yellow flowers are used sparingly in Asian cooking to add a distinct aroma and taste. Collect seed heads to sow annually.

SOUTHERNWOOD
(*Artemisia abrotanum*)

Sow spring to autumn, or plant cuttings any time. Also known as "lad's love." Native to Europe. Repels cabbage moths. Southernwood and Roman wormwood (*A. pontica*) are my favorite artemisia plants for their stimulating fragrance. Southernwood was once used to accompany marriage proposals, perhaps because of its sweet apple scent. It grows ferny upright branches up to 3 feet. Plant in a mobile pot and in hedges pruned annually with big shears. Not invasive. Use in wardrobes and drawers against moths.

STINGING NETTLE (*Urtica dioica*)

Sow spring to autumn. Companion plant for many crops to improve soil, compost, and you. Found in Asia, Europe, South Africa, North and South America, and Australia. Stinging nettle in the garden is a blessing.

Eat young nettles as spinach—they taste good, and the sting disappears when cooked. Make velvety nettle tea from fresh tops or dried leaves. Cook nettles like sorrel soup, blended and with a dollop of yogurt. Before supermarkets and greengrocers, Europeans ate stinging nettle in many dishes, as it is a nourishing, wildly profuse vegetable.

Let only one nettle set seed. Although plants are easily pulled up where not wanted, neighbors may complain if seeds blow across. To contain the seed, tie a paper bag over the top. In compost and liquid manure, nettle is a prime ingredient.

SUNFLOWER (*Helianthus annuus*)

A native of Peru. Not so much an herb as a food plant for its seed and oil.

Sunflowers make a great addition to food gardens as background and as windbreaks. Use them as live stakes for climbing beans. Handsome varieties come in golden yellow, brown, and caramel. Harvest seed heads, dry indoors, then lay them out one by one for birds during the hungry season on a squirrel-proof board hung from a tree branch.

TANSY (*Tanacetum vulgare*)

Sow spring to summer, plant rootlings anytime. Companion for fruit trees as an under-planting against various diseases. From Europe. Not recommended for cooking or baking nowadays, as the plant is somewhat toxic (19th-century English cooks flavored biscuits and cakes with tansy). Both flat-leaved and curly-leaved tansy carry clusters of golden buttons. The roots are invasive, but easily pulled up.

TARRAGON (*Artemisia dracunculus*)

Sow in spring. From the Mediterranean. French tarragon is lauded as the only one to use for cooking. There is also German tarragon. Mexican tarragon is a strong grower with a fresh aniseed taste—to be used by the branch rather than the single leaf. The Russian variety is called "false tarragon," even though it is an artemisia and has that artemian whiff about it. They're all good, just different.

THYME (*Thymus vulgaris*)

Sow spring or autumn. Companion to many vegetables. Repels cabbage moths. Known as "mother of thyme," as all varieties sprung from this common thyme of Southern Europe and then conquered the globe. It clings to Himalayan mountainsides in a blaze of mauve flowers. Essential when cooking with tomatoes, and in a bouquet garni. Use lemon thyme in pasta and caraway thyme in Indian cooking. Serve garlic and thyme butter with zucchini. Search markets and nurseries for flavored thymes or settle for one in a mobile pot, guarding a vegetable plot.

WORMWOOD (*Artemisia absinthium*)

Sow spring or autumn, plant cuttings when pruning after flowering. Native to the Northern Hemisphere. The sacred bitter herb of China used to ward off evil. A Southeast Asian artemisia is important medicinally against malaria. *Artemisia annua* is the wormwood that ekes out a living along farm fences, washed only by rain, with never a decent haircut. Wormwood makes a powerful pest-repellent hedge for an organic garden, but plant it several yards away from vegetables, as it tends to retard other plants. After flowering, cut it back by half for vigorous growth. The silver leaves are gorgeous in bouquets. Wormwood keeps chickens lice-free when planted near the coop.

YARROW (*Achillea millefolium*)

Sow spring to autumn, plant rootlings anytime. From Europe. White and cyclamen-pink yarrows are hardy. Cultivars come in pastels. Yarrow roots are invasive: a 3-foot square patch may result from one plant. This is a very good herb in the orchard, working as a pest repellent and growth promoter for other plants, especially apple trees. It is also an excellent compost starter. Yarrow tea, made with flowers and leaves, soothes the spirit when you are stressed or fatigued, or just had a hard day in the garden.

EASY-CARE FRUIT TREES *and* BERRIES: HOW *to* GROW *and* USE THEM

READ THE chapter Easy-Care Fruit Trees (page 49) before making your selection from the list on page 295. Trees marked with an asterisk (*) are super easy to grow.

General Growing Notes

CULTIVATION

Fruit trees need care in their first three years while making deep roots. After that, they continue to need manure and/or fertilizer with mulch in spring, and lime and deep mulch in autumn. If you grow dense herbs under a fruit tree, little mulch is needed, but it does need food to produce well. Many trees can survive without watering after the first summer, or just three deep waterings per summer, depending on your climate.

DISEASES AND PESTS

When planting new trees, consider heritage varieties, as many are more disease resistant and have better nutritional properties—see Useful Addresses (page 317) and organic gardening magazines. By spraying fruit trees with liquid seaweed early in spring and the root area in autumn, you may prevent diseases. Grow companion herbs under fruit trees (see List of Common Herbs on page 279) to prevent infestations and attract predators. Mix borage, comfrey, fenugreek, and feverfew with recommended companion plants for each fruit tree. Nettle is very beneficial. With chickens in the orchard, only deep-rooted herbs like yarrow, lemon balm, and tansy survive and must be protected while establishing themselves. If you live in an area frequently affected by fruit fly, do inform yourself on how to prevent it, as it is a serious pest that destroys susceptible crops in a wide area. Organic gardening magazines carry advertisements for fruit fly prevention products.

DWARF FRUIT TREES

Ask your nursery. Another space saver is a "fruit salad tree" with a number of stone fruit, or citrus, or apple varieties grafted onto the same trunk.

ERADICATING WEEDS AND GRASSES

Always keep soil around young trunks weed free. Chicken tractors are small A-frame cages, half timber, half wire netting, housing a few chickens to dig up grass and weeds. Move around the tree as needed. Chickens are perfectionists. Without chickens, consider a fence-to-fence herbal carpet after eradicating competing weeds and lawn grasses by other means. Alternatively, spread large flattened cardboard boxes in autumn— ask the electrical goods store. Or spread weedmat through three summer months.

ESPALIERED ORCHARD

Save space, increase production, and keep fruit within reach by espaliering fruit trees. Apart from the common fruit trees, I have espaliered mulberry, fig, and quince. Citrus varieties probably produce more as freestanding trees. See Espalier on page 50.

GRAFTING

With permission, cut buds from a neighbor's different fruit tree and graft onto yours, pome to pome and stone fruit to stone fruit, in mid-autumn. If this interests you, borrow a library book on budding and grafting, as it is easy to learn.

IF YOU HAVE LITTLE TIME

Plant the fruit you love best in the first year, your second love in the second year, and so on. It is better to prepare an excellent hole for one tree, look after it, see it flourish, and be proud, than to bang in six to see them flounder for lack of attention and feel sorry. Most trees take a few years to fruit, but berries produce in their first summer, black mulberry and loquat in the second.

PLANTING

Fruit trees are best planted in very late winter when dormant, unless otherwise indicated by the supplier. Citrus trees should be planted when soil is still warm.

Dig a hole much larger than the root ball. Fill hole with water two days before planting. If the water drains away, it's a good spot. Put a spadeful of rubble, gravel, or broken tiles and clay pots in the bottom to prevent wet roots. Spade in compost mixed with old manure. Cover well with more compost for the root ball to sit on. Place the tree so that the graft (the knobbly bit above the root ball) is well above ground level. Fill in with good soil. Mulch and top dress with B&B after planting, and water well to settle roots. Do a foot-stomping dance around the trunk to compact the earth. If the level sinks and forms a saucer, level this out with mulch, keeping the graft above it.

PRUNING

To prune espaliered trees, see Easy-Care

Fruit Trees (page 49). For freestanding trees, keep pruning simple:

1. Prune when trees are dormant. Shaping is your choice.
2. Prune away dead wood and crossing branches.
3. Prune trees to keep fruit within reach.
4. Prune away excess growth in summer.

SEEDLING TREES

Seedlings of apple, quince, plum, and nectarine may bear good fruit, sometimes better suited to cooking or juicing. Such trees show strong growth and disease resistance. Worth trying with any seed, if you have space. I've had excellent fruit from seedling nectarines, plums, and apples.

List of Easy-Care Fruit Trees and Berries

APPLE* (*Malus domestica*)

Companions: yarrow, chives, apple mint, self-heal (*Prunella vulgaris*), and nasturtium. All apples originate from *Malus sieversii* in the Tien Shan, the Heavenly Mountains range in Central Asia, where they survive in the wild. They love cool nights.

Apple trees are amazing. They can grow without being watered or otherwise tended, even in often drought-stricken regions. Yet young nursery-raised trees may die in a bad year. We inherited three apple trees in acidic, non-wetting soil, which blossomed and annually produced good fruit. We have newly inherited a cathedral of an old apple tree that has survived on rain. Its fruit is only fit for pies, yet its presence and shade are immense. I have had good fruit from a sucker, grown from an excellent old tree that produced good eating fruit. I've also nurtured self-seeded trees whose apples were good enough for chutney, apple stew, and sauces for the freezer. Apple trees love growing in hedgerows, where their roots are protected by herbs and shrubs.

Apples from a sucker off an old-fashioned nameless apple tree. They were good to eat and to cook.

Fruit fly and codling moth are the apple tree's enemies. See An A–Z of Pests and Problems (page 94).

APRICOT* (*Prunus armeniaca*)

Companions: feverfew and garlic—keep cutting garlic tops for best results. Also chives, comfrey, tansy, and yarrow. From China, cultivated worldwide, and a main crop in Pakistan's Hunza Valley. The earliest stone fruit to set fruit. Hardy and moderately drought tolerant. Apricot trees can be espaliered. Taste ripe home-grown apricots straight from the tree! Apricots can be dried, preserved, stewed, frozen, or devoured instantly. Team with cream cheese, cinnamon, or polenta, one at a time.

AVOCADO (*Persea americana*)

From Central America. Some varieties will stand a few degrees of frost. A nutritious food of proven benefit to arthritis sufferers. Before buying a tree, taste test varieties. There are distinct differences in flavor and texture. Take your favorite avocado from a shop to your local nursery and discuss its growing needs.

Since the avocado does not ripen on the tree, but after it has been plucked, it may be worth trying to grow one no matter your climate. I saw my first avocado tree in fruit outside our hotel window in Kandy, Sri Lanka. Later, I beheld the same sight through the window of my Adelaide dentist as I lay open-mouthed in the chair. The dentist said the fruit wasn't ripe yet. Although I tried to convince him to pick it all the same, he wouldn't. He moved to another building, and that avocado may still be hanging there.

Plant an avocado where it gets shade from other trees, yet receives warmth. Prepare soil with lots of organic matter for moisture and essential drainage. If drainage could be a problem, dig deeper and put a layer of rocks in the hole before planting. Mulch heavily. A shade cloth may be necessary, or a shady courtyard. It will be several years before you see fruit. Sprouting seeds make lovely house plants.

BERRIES*

The brambles: raspberries (*Rubus idaeus*), blackberries (*R. ulmifolius*), boysenberries (*Rubus* spp.), loganberries (*R. loganobaccus*), and youngberries (*Rubus* spp.). Other brambles are tayberries and lawton berries. See below for blueberries, gooseberries, and currants. Companions: try borage mixed with non-invasive herbs without overpowering aromas, like chamomile, dill, and nasturtiums.

Northern Hemisphere natives. Take cuttings in autumn or spring. Should these fail, take cuttings in the optimum growing season in your area. Soak cuttings in water with honey for one hour, then plant immediately, providing water and shade until rooted. Cuttings must never dry out. Thornless blackberry and youngberry are available

Having grown all of the above, the youngberry proved to produce not only large, delicious, and firm fruit, but was the only one to survive a searingly hot summer with temperatures in the sun around 110 degrees on many days. The canes sprouted back to see another summer. All berries do best in cooler climates. Imitate their natural environments with a mulch of old leaves, or twiggy compost with straw. Check the pH of the soil—they don't do well under 6 or over 7, and 6.5 is just right.

Brambles are best grown on a wire trellis, preventing the formation of wild, rambling thickets and allowing access from two sides to pick fruit. An espalier wire arrangement between droppers or posts will do. Position the trellis north-south to make the most of the sun. Plant cuttings or canes under the wire and, when they lengthen, gather them up (with gloves), and twist and wind them around droppers, posts, and wires to tie up. Louis Glowinski writes that tying them in a fan shape gives the best crop. If you only plant three to five canes, place them around a wire tower (see Hard-

ware in the Food Garden on page 105). Glowinski also describes other hybrid varieties.

Improve soil with CMC to retain the moisture essential for all berries. In the wild, they thrive in dark, muddy glens. After harvesting, prune out the canes that bore fruit, as next season's fruit appears on new canes. Add young leaves of raspberry and blackberry to any tea for fragrance and health.

BLUEBERRIES (*Vaccinium spp.*)

From North America. A thornless bush. They like it cool and can stand half shade, although full sun increases production. Wind protection is important. Grow blueberries if you have acid soil and can make it drain well by digging in loads of organic matter. Lime in the soil will inhibit blueberries. They must never dry out, so mulch thickly with pine needles, sawdust, leaves, or shredded branches. Ask your nursery to provide two different plants for better pollination. Be prepared to fuss over blueberry bushes like a brown bear would. Be prepared to wait for first fruit.

CAPE GOOSEBERRY (DWARF)* (*Physalis peruviana*)

Companions: mine happily rambled among fifty vegetables and herbs, productive and self-seeding. From northeastern and Central America. This medium-size plant is easily grown from seed. The sweetly tart yellow berries are sheathed in a paper Chinese lantern. No kidding. Arthritis sufferers reconsider; this fruit belongs to the *Solanum* genus.

CITRUS

Companions: lavender, sage, self-heal (*Prunella vulgaris*), tansy, and yarrow. Citrus includes kumquat, grapefruit, lemon, lime, mandarin, and orange. All need excellent drainage, a warm spot, and the protection of other trees from cold winds. They like neither frost nor high humidity. Plant in the ground, if you live in the right part of the country, otherwise in tubs.

There are more stories about the success or failure of individual citrus trees than any other fruit tree. I've grown citrus on a stony hill where they fruited, and in a hotter place where they ailed. In desperation, I applied commercial citrus food, and still they died. But a Tahitian lime planted next to a banana palm—in a great heap of compost, manure, and straw, situated between three water tanks reflecting heat and tempering cold night air—was just beginning to set fine fruit when we moved. Everyone agrees drainage is vital, compost and animal manures important, and peeing around them is possibly the secret of success!

My best citrus was an ugli (I kid you not—see the 1997 edition of *The New Oxford Book of Food Plants*), which was the rootstock of a failed kumquat. It bore plenty of sweetly tart fruit, lovely in salads. The backyard lemon tree is similarly unpredictable. If your neighbors have a great lemon tree, your soil may support one, too, or arrange a fruit swap.

With citrus, the message is location, location, location, translating as drainage, drainage, drainage. Dig an enormous hole and partly fill with gravel and rubble before adding compost and planting the tree. After the first winter, give it morning urine once a week, diluted 1:10 with water. Many other fruit trees also benefit from our sterile, mineral-laden by-product.

Oranges are ever popular—there are sweet and sour varieties, and all are beautiful trees with fragrant flowers. The fruit can take up to a year to ripen, but is not bothered by birds.

Mandarins crop heavily in the right spot. Consult your local nursery.

Grapefruit trees appear to need even more water than other citrus until established. I fill up a slowly leaking watering can every day and put it by one of my four citrus trees, then give the grapefruit a hose watering as well.

Kumquats are lovely eaten raw from the tree, although people insist on preserving them in brandy, which as good as spoils the taste.

Lemons can be preserved by rubbing the fresh fruit with petroleum jelly and placing them, not touching, on newspaper in a dark, cool place. To preserve in salt, cut in quarters, rub with salt, and pack into glass jars. Or, squeeze the juice and pour into ice cube trays in the freezer; one cube equals the juice of half a lemon. Grate the zest off the skins and store in a plastic container in the freezer to scoop out with a fork, as much or little as needed, for lemon cake or lemon sago. Or, dry the peel on trays in a hot place (but not in the sun). When thoroughly dry, store in airtight jars. To use, chop finely or grind.

CURRANTS

Companions: try tomato plants and the same herbaceous mix as for berries, although they can go it alone. Northern Hemisphere natives. Red (*Ribes rubrum*) and white (*R. sativum*) currants are small shrubs; the black currant (*R. nigrum*) grows taller.

The red currant produces fruit on old wood, just to be different. Even in my Uncle Wim's garden in overcast Holland, the currant bushes grew in the shade of a massive walnut tree, where light was dappled. They like it cool and need a winter and regular waterings. Uncle Wim applied plenty of old poultry manure.

Black currants grew wild on the sandy heights of the heather in full sun between his village and ours. They grow fruit on last year's wood, so take care in pruning. They can be espaliered. As children, we filled small buckets while stuffing ourselves with this curiously winey-tasting fruit. Mostly, black currants were made into jam, liqueur, and genever. Add the young leaves from currant bushes to herbal or black tea for fragrance and health.

ELDERBERRY* (*Sambucus nigra*)

Sow in spring, or plant cuttings in autumn or anytime. A tall shrub of the honeysuckle family from England, but there are blue elderberry (*S. caerulea*), American black elderberry (*S. canadensis*), and an elderberry panax (*Tieghemopanax sambucifolius*) with blue edible fruit. I have only grown what I assume to be the self-pollinating English one.

The fruit should not be eaten raw. Leaves, bark, roots, and seeds are toxic, yet the English elderberry provides food and drink, as well as pesticide. The tall shrub grows fast if treated with CMC and watered when stressed. Plant 18 inches apart for a dense windbreak. Leave some gaps to prevent turbulence.

Elderberry exudes a pest-repellent substance due to its glycoside content. Cut branches for vegetable seedlings under

Elderberry flowers make a distinctive cordial. Elder branches and leaves can be spread where there is a pest problem. A young loquat, producing first fruit of spring, stands in the background.

attack. In autumn, prune shrubs back to 6 feet. In spring, the shrub will be laden with umbels of creamy flowers which precede the black elderberries that can be used to make the famed elderberry wine, jam, or pies (remove the seeds).

Before berries form, pick trays of elderflowers to dry and store. Fragrant elderflower tea acts as a decongestant. Finely chopped flowers can bulk up scones, cakes, and biscuits. Make cordial by boiling flowers in water with sugar. Keep in the fridge and dilute for a refreshing drink. Adding ¼ cup citric acid per ½ gallon of water and a few sliced lemons makes it keep longer. The

English make an elderflower and gooseberry preserve, as well as elderflower fritters in a batter of flour and egg. Any berries I leave are eaten by birds who didn't read these notes. Despite the toxicity of the plant and some of its parts, elderberries have been used for centuries, cooked or processed. Elderberry varieties may play important pest-control functions in future food gardens.

FIG (*Ficus carica*)*
The edible fig we know is one of the oldest cultivated fruits from Iran, Turkey, and Afghanistan. It starts as

a multiple-branched shrub that grows into a medium-size tree that can be espaliered. Fresh figs are purple ecstasy. Even fig haters eat fig jam or fig tart. Give the tree a good start with manure and mulch, water when the fruit is forming, but, apart from that, do not fuss. I picked five figs from a tiny fig tree, then espaliered and manured it, and the next year picked almost 100 figs.

GUAVA (*Psidium guajava*)*

From Central America. There are several varieties, and it is best to ask your nursery what does well where you are. This medium shrub is easy to grow and the fruit is a vitamin C bomb. Strawberry guava is said to have the best flavor. I've tasted wonderful guava from the cool Dandenongs in Victoria, while Louis Glowinski claims his Melbourne guava taste like blotting paper. The guava is reputed to be a pharmacy for a raft of serious but common diseases and able to grow in most soils. They don't like heavy frost—although my little guava survived it unscathed—but make a good hedge on the warm side of the garden. All parts of the tree are used.

GOOSEBERRY*
(*Ribes grossularia*)

Companions: tomato plants, chives. These low-growing, thorny shrubs originate in Europe. An infusion of chives is supposed to stop gooseberry mildew, so try growing chives as companions. Oak-leaf mulch also helps. My Uncle Wim grew them on the sunny side of his walnut tree, and we only ever picked them fully ripe with a red blush, sweet and succulent. Fork in poultry manure and mulch heavily. If you want a row of gooseberry bushes, layer low branches. Scoop out soil, bend a branch into the trench, cover with soil, and pin down with a bent wire. When it has grown roots, cut it from the mother plant and plant it independently. Make sure you have access on both sides. Gooseberry does not like brackish water.

GRAPE (*Vitus vinifer*)*

Companions: floribunda bush roses. I have found grapes to be about the easiest fruit to grow, but that may be due to my garden's climactic conditions. An open position where the wind blows through, even a western wall, has produced grapes for me on mere cuttings from friends' grapevines, and without mildew attacks. But in my third garden, half a dozen bare-rooted vines from a nursery all died in acidic soil with brackish dam water.

Grape cuttings are inexpensive, and, if they take, they bear in the second year. Cuttings should be 15 inches and have two buds. Dry dark grapes for raisins, light grapes for sultanas, and, if you can get it, the small seedless black grape is suitable for drying as currants. Stop watering after the plants set flower.

Established vines can go it alone on rain, if mulched. To grow a vine on a pergola (protecting the fruit from birds), let the main stem grow up and spread branches across the structure. Prune bush vines back to two buds after harvest. In spring, make dolmades—young grape leaves stuffed with rice.

LOQUAT (*Eriobotrya japonica*)*

Drought tolerant. Bantam chickens love roosting between the broad leaves, fertilizing the soil underneath. From the Himalayas, but will grow in subtropical and Mediterranean-type climates, tolerating moderate neglect. Often starts bearing in the second year. Prune after harvest to keep fruit at reaching height. Each year, the crop will increase, ripening gradually over two months.

If space is a problem, prune loquats to stay small. Unpruned, they become grand, shady trees. As urban gardens become smaller, loquat trees disappear. Yet, we should not lose such a long-bearing tree. Plant it, prune it, and rave about fresh loquats, the first fruit of spring, and the ideal fruit for an al fresco dessert. Pick a branch of fruit and lay it on the garden table. Eat loquats skin and all or peel. Serve with sour cream or yogurt dip with a drizzle of honey. Then, pop a few big seeds in pots to grow loquat trees for friends. Loquats are seldom available in shops, as they bruise readily. They contain beta-carotene.

MULBERRY (*Morus nigra*)*

The black mulberry. From Iran (Persia) or Africa. Given its head, the mulberry tree forms a beautiful spreading canopy loved by children. But with increasing urbanization, this big tree is also heading for extinction in our cities. Only the black mulberry is worth growing for fruit. It bears in its second year. The white mulberry produces insignificant fruit, while another variety is grown for its leaves to feed silkworms doomed to die for the luxury rag trade.

Although I have espaliered mulberry, I'd much prefer to grow the untamed tree. My first mulberry tree still sits on its stony hillside twenty years after planting, and although it has not received any attention and is not very big, the new owners say it bears fruit reliably.

NECTARINE*
(*Prunus persica* var. *nectarine*)

Companions: chives, garlic, and tansy (keep garlic cut to release its odor). The name is derived from nectar, the food for the gods that the Romans didn't have. Nectarines are an exhilarating fruit.

They are related to peaches, but are smooth-skinned and have a more decisive flavor. Small tree, easy to grow, and can be espaliered. A seedling grown from a nectarine stone can bear fruit true to type. Bury a few stones in compost in an area where you won't need to transplant them. When birds start pecking the still-unripe fruit, it is excellent for jam making. Protect with netting to ripen fruit. The bane of nectarine growers is curly-leaf affliction in early spring. If neglected, it can reduce the crop considerably because the tree feels sick, unable to function through its leaves.

OLIVE (*Olea europaea*)*

Companions: mixed herbs to imitate meadows. Olives grow on stony hillsides in Mediterranean countries. Drought tolerant. Another tree that has survived, despite neglect, for some 10,000 years. Their leathery leaves don't wither in the blazing sun. The fruit is tough and bitter and needs pickling, or processing into olive oil.

My olive tree literally fell from the back of a truck. It lay on the road in its black tube, the top broken. When planted, it grew. We moved house and it moved with us and grew. Then a lost cow broke it in half, and it regrew!

Italian urban gardeners are known to prune their single olive tree to within an inch of its life each winter, for bumper crops to pickle. My recipe: soak black olives in strong brine for one week. Rinse and steep another week in fresh strong brine. Rinse and make a weak brine (2 tablespoons of salt per ½ gallon of boiled water). Put olives in wide-mouthed jars interspersed with bruised garlic cloves, chopped celery, and oregano. Leave to mature one month. If you have no space for an olive tree, ask your Mediterranean greengrocer to get you a case of black olives in autumn.

PASSIONFRUIT (*Passiflora edulis*)

This vine from Brazil is not long-lived. Many legends of success and failure exist about this plant. I grew my first passionfruit in a square foot of soil surrounded by concrete near an east-facing back door. It stormed up the wall, spread several yards along the gutter in a glory of bright green leaves, produced a bucket of sweet purple fruit, and died. Rather like a Brazilian carnival. Next, I planted passionfruit facing north with organic material, nitrogen, and a trellis. Three times. None survived.

If you love passionfruit, ask your local nursery for the hardiest variety and growing advice. Once established, the plant needs a couple of handfuls of B&B in spring and likes sulphate of potash, something I was ignorant of when I lost my passion for growing passionfruit.

PAWPAW (*Carica papaya*)

Sow late spring and protect into winter. Presumably from Mexico. Although a tropical fruit, I include this to encourage experimentation. If you live in one of the country's sub-tropical regions (roughly the space between southern California and Florida) and have a southerly-facing skylight or greenhouse, you can try growing tropical fruit. I grew a banana plant in a tank yard, heat bouncing off iron tanks and shed, keeping out winds and ameliorating night temperatures.

Pawpaw is the easiest tropical fruit to germinate. *The New Oxford Book of Food Plants* calls it a "tree-like herb," which shakes up our perceptions about what an herb is. The seeds are chewed by travelers with dysentery, and the pulp prevents fresh wounds from becoming infected. This "herb" shapes up to be a tree of 6 to 30 feet, depending on circumstances. In Papua New Guinea's highlands, where nights can be cold, pawpaw trees grow simply from discarded pips. There are male and female trees, but also self-pollinating ones. Hoping for the latter, I bought a pawpaw at the market, scooped out the seed, and within weeks had fifty seedlings. I potted some to give away as pot plants with attractive foli-age, but kept some in the greenhouse at a 1,600-foot elevation. One produced a reasonable-size fruit.

The mountain pawpaw (*Carica candamarcensis*) comes from the Andes. When sowing seed in the 1980s, I found it was not prolific in germination, and I ended up with just one viable tree: a non-fruiting male. But it was a beauty—surviving at 1,600-foot elevation and backed by native forest bathing in sun all day. The fruit-bearing life of the tree is evidently not long, and the fruit has to be cooked. Small seed companies may still carry this seed.

PEACH (*Prunus persica*)

Companions: chives, garlic, and tansy (cut garlic tops during fruiting to release odor). See An A–Z of Pests and Problems (page 96) for treatments of curly leaf. Originally from western Tibet, where we bought some small but sweet fruit from a valley farmer, and the Tien Shan mountains of Central Asia. Peaches reached Europe via Iran (Persia).

Peaches can be dried, preserved, stewed, frozen, or eaten daily as they ripen. Trees are small and can be espaliered. A sun-warmed peach straight off the tree is a treat. If they like your place, they crop impressively. If not, they're still a thrill. White or yellow flesh, find your preference at the greengrocer.

PEAR (*Pyrus communus*)*

Companions: catmint, rosemary, sage, and yarrow. From the Tien Shan mountains. Hardy and prolific. They like a cold winter, but seem to take heat better than apples. A full-grown pear tree spreads a shady canopy. If space is limited, prune your pear each winter to manageable size, or espalier. They start bearing within a few years, if there is another pear tree in the neighborhood for pollination. If not, buy the self-pollinating Williams pear for its big, juicy fruit and prolific crop. For pear slug on the leaves, see An A–Z of Pests and Problems on page 98.

PLUM (*Prunus* spp.)*

Companions: chives and tansy. From Europe and Japan. Many varieties, hybrids, and colors. Carefree trees, hardy, prolific, fast growing. Apply dolomite. One early and one late plum may overwhelm a family, so get one special plum instead. Greengage is special but bears only every other year and needs another plum for pollination. Do you want a firm or juicy plum, to eat, dry, or preserve? For drying, choose Prune D'Agen.

POMEGRANATE (*Punica granatum*)*

From Iran. Tolerates dry climates and some neglect once established. Not choosy about soil. A tree-size shrub with deep orange flowers and red fruit, although dwarf varieties do exist. Seeds are surrounded by juice, which has been rediscovered as a health drink. Children love pomegranates. Serve whole for dessert at a garden lunch.

QUINCE (*Cydonia vulgaris*)*

Companion: yarrow. From the Caucasus, this shrubby tree grows wild near some abandoned settlements. The shell-pink petals of quince flowers in velvet leafy rosettes herald spring. One of the earliest fruit trees to blossom, but the last fruit to ripen. Autumn's fragrant harvest suggests quince paste and jelly, preserves, salads, desserts, and perfumed juice. They need cooking, but even the cooking water is divine!

Espaliered quince laden with ripe fruit in its fourth year.

The hard pomes will keep in a cool place for several months while you eat your way through stewed quinces and quince crumbles. To peel a quince, lop off top and bottom, stand fruit upright on a board, and with a sharp knife, shave the skin off all around. Then chop pieces off the fruit until reaching the core. Much easier than trying to quarter them, as the core is stubborn.

STRAWBERRIES (*Fragaria spp.*)*

Sow from seed in spring or plant runners in late autumn. Companions: borage, bush beans, lettuce, and spinach. The cabbage family is not a favorite of strawberries and the Solanaceae family (potatoes, tomatoes, etc.) should be kept at a distance. Wild ancestors such as alpine strawberries do best in cool to cold areas, and wild strawberries are native to all Northern Hemisphere woodlands. I was once smitten by the sight of North American alpine strawberries flowering in May along Mount Washington's icy mountain streams.

The appearance of cultivated strawberries is a story of wild reluctance, chance encounters, and a persistent English horticulturalist. Despite growing as far north as Finland, strawberries do well in southern climates (think of the woody giants in every grocery store!), fruiting from spring to autumn.

Buy certified virus-free roots and prepare your plot generously with CMC and B&B. Slightly raise rows or small hills for essential drainage, and mulch with clean straw mixed with pine, spruce, or fir needles. Adjust soil to a pH of 6—if acidic, add lime. Apply LS regularly for disease resistance.

In autumn, the plants throw out runners to take root in nearby soil. Prepare a new plot. Cut and transplant runners from autumn to spring, manuring and mulching as above. Clean up the old bed by removing any dead leaves. To prevent disease build-up, don't keep any bed longer than three years. Protect with netting or a cage and pick off slugs and snails. Water at the roots to avoid fungal problems. Strewth! Yet they are easy to grow.

Strawberries are loved by all wildlife. In my forest garden, the occasional snake came for dessert, as did bandicoots. We never had better-tasting strawberries than those reared near the forest's edge, mulched with rotting fallen apple pulp. Visitors would rave at tasting a long-lost memory. With strawberries, it's the plant food that determines the taste.

White strawberries are also available. They taste good and reputedly don't attract birds, but millipedes are color blind.

PRESERVING *and* USING
HOME PRODUCE

"S ETTING BY" it used to be called. "I'm setting by some pickles," the prudent mother would say, wiping her hands on her flower-print apron in a kitchen redolent with green aromas and the sharpness of mustard, wine, and vinegar. Before refrigeration, "setting by" was part of providing for the family. It was regulated by the seasons. Harvest at summer's end was the busiest time for preserving home produce. Traditional methods of keeping fruit and vegetables for future use are drying and pickling, which need care to succeed, and preserving in vinegar, brine, or sugar to kill bacteria that normally make food go off. Refrigeration has added freezing as a marvelous method.

Drying

Apples and pears are cored and cut in slices. Dunk apples in water with vinegar to prevent them going brown, then string up in a dry place, out of the sun and dust, in your attic or shed.

Broad beans, borlotti beans, other fat beans, and peas can be dried on the plant. When thoroughly dry but not blackened, pick, pod, and dry for another week indoors before storing in glass containers. All dried pulses need to be reconstituted by soaking overnight before cooking.

Chilies look decorative strung up to dry under the eaves.

Coriander can be let go to seed before picking stalks and hanging to dry further indoors. Strip off seeds and store in glass in a dark place. Do the same with other seeds you can grow, such as caraway, cumin, and mustard. Cut off coriander roots and freeze in a container between baking paper so that you can peel off one root at a time to flavor your cooking.

Eggplant and bell peppers can be dried slowly in a low oven.

Fenugreek, my favorite herb for Indian cooking, can be left on the plant till the sickle-shaped pods are dry. Bring inside to dry off, pod them, and let the seeds dry for another week before storing in glass in a dark place.

Garlic is hung in bunches in a dry, dark place, keeping for up to six months.

Herbs dry quickly, hung in small bunches in a dry place. For tea, dry lemon balm, mint, nettles, sage, tarragon, and yarrow, and mix for a taste sensation. Vamoose fatigue! For cooking, dry mint, oregano, rosemary, sage, and tarragon. When thoroughly dry, rub leaves off stalks, rub till fine, store in glass jars, and place in a dark cupboard. For herb vinegars, stuff bottles with herbs like fennel, lemon balm, lemongrass, mint, oregano, sage, tarragon, or thyme, pour on white vinegar, and let stand for a month before using.

Onions, should they all ripen at once, can be divided in two lots. Spread half in a dark, dry place on newspapers for gradual use, hoping they won't sprout. Any that sprout can be planted back in the garden to produce green straps for several months, plus a clutch of small onions. (Make sure to crop rotate onions every year and not leave them in the ground for more than their growing season.) Peel and slice the other onions thinly, spread on oven trays and dry at a low temperature. This can take days and may perfume the house, but having dried onions on hand is handy in winter. Or, do it on trays outside during a heat wave.

Prunes (from the tree named Prune d'Agen) or plums, cut in halves and pits removed. Dry at low temperature in the oven for a long time, maybe more than one day. Dry indoors for a week before storing in jars.

Sweet corn loses sugar when dried, becoming starchy. Don't bother.

Freezing

I would be loathe to keep a separate large freezer, unless I lived on a remote station or was cooking for crowds. The freezing compartment of standard family fridges can hold a large amount of well-stacked meal-size packages and is often underused except for ice and ice cream.

Solid vegetables freeze well: beans, broad beans, broccoli, carrots, cauliflower, corn-on-the-cob (for a short period), and peas. Freshly picked, not blanched, into the freezer within 15 minutes from harvesting. Quarter tomatoes and red peppers so they can be frozen tightly packed for cooking purposes. Pick in the morning—on a weekend, if you work full-time. Eggplant and red peppers can be fried in oil in julienned strips with red onions and garlic, then frozen in containers to pull out for an impromptu lunch—great with Italian bread and avocado. Or purée eggplant, adding salt and pepper, and freeze for later use.

Freeze beans with ends still on, slice carrots, break cauli and broccoli into florets and thinly peel the delicious stem, remove leaves from cobs, pod peas, and beans. Don't wash vegetables, wipe if necessary. Pack in plastic containers of meal-size portions. I heard from an Italian cook that you can blanch radicchio and freeze it, but haven't tried. She said to dip the vegetable into water just off the boil, shake and pat dry, and then freeze.

Freezing also enables you to process vegetables you could not otherwise keep for long. Process arugula (Italian in spring and wild in autumn) to make pesto (see More Value from Popular Vegetables on page 273). Frozen soups are a great standby. Make surprise soups by putting leftovers from the daily pot into a container and freeze. It may be a few spoonfuls of vegetables, a few beans, some lovely cooking juice, or a handful of pasta. Defrost and blend with a dash of sauce, spice, and fresh herbs for an easy meal of soup with grilled cheese and red onion on bread.

Process a tomato glut into thick tomato, parsley, and onion soup, and freeze. Anything else you can turn into a favorite soup when plentiful in the garden, such as zucchini and potato and leek spiced up with curry, or Siberian kale, is great to have on hand in the lean season.

Remember: using big containers means using up all the contents after defrosting, because refreezing is a no-no due to proliferating bacteria. Collect meal-size containers.

Clever use of the freezing compartment above your refrigerator allows a host of ways to make from-scratch menus. If you think of a menu the day before, you can take one or more items out of the freezer to defrost overnight— in the fridge. Frozen foods have most of their nutrients to benefit you, but make sure you eat from the freezer on a regular basis, so that there is turnover and things don't become too ancient.

That said, we just had dessert of two-year-old persimmons with store-bought custard and it was divine! My freezer has just been defrosted, very quickly so that none of the contents had time to thaw, and looks almost empty due to space previously taken up by built-up ice. The half-empty freezer compartment presently contains the following two-person meals:

- 9 packets of podded broad beans

- 3 containers of cooked eggplant with garlic

- 2 large containers of tomato, onion, and garlic pasta sauce

- 2 containers of plain tomato paste

- 2 containers of arugula pesto

- 1 container of hummus

- 2 containers cooked beet salad

- 2 containers of stewed quince

- 2 containers of fried tofu

- 3 large containers of lentil soup

- 2 containers of pumpkin soup

- half a bar of homemade cake

- 1 bag of frozen peas from the shop

All these delicacies, except the last one, were frozen at different times, when I was cooking and made too much, or purposely made more to freeze for later. Defrosting by placing a container in a bowl of hot water to dislodge the contents, then transferring it to the cooking pot, is a much-used method in this household when friends arrive who don't mind a scratch lunch. The soup is dressed with freshly chopped parsley, the pesto needs a pasta, broad beans and peas go with anything, hummus on pita bread or crackers, heat the beet salad and serve warm, and quinces for dessert with a dash of maple syrup. Defrosted cake with coffee concludes the scratch meal from the freezer.

There is, of course, one joker in this pack of possibilities, the electricity utility that keeps the fridge running. Living in the bush, we were early converts to solar power, and when we saw the lights go out in a distant town, we read our books by solar-generated electricity. Now, we are semi-urban in a semi-rural environment where the electricity generated by our roof panels goes into the grid, and when there is a blackout, we are also in the dark. When the first company we sold electricity to only gave us paper credits for overproduction, we changed to a company that sends a check. To buy candles.

Quince tree two years after being espaliered.

Pickling

Pickling in vinegar is something anyone can do. Pickle small gherkins with dill and peppercorns, cucumber chunks with dill or fennel. Both need draining. Sprinkle with salt and stand overnight. Dry with a clean dish towel before pickling. Radish seedpods and nasturtium pods are pickled straight into plain vinegar. Vinegar may be diluted with boiled water 3:1. But the less vinegar, the more chance of mold developing. Check jars periodically.

Eggplant and red peppers can be pickled as slices in more olive oil than balsamic vinegar, with garlic. Yum. Making tomato sauce is a form of pickling, although with less vinegar, as the fruit contains acid—and some sugar, salt, and onion. There are many home recipes for tomato sauce. Every one is the best!

I love piccalilli, traditionally a summer mixture of cauliflower, carrots, peas, broad beans, green beans, gherkins, cucumbers, and shallots in a spiced mustard sauce with vinegar. Read this recipe to collect what you need before starting. It is fun to make piccalilli with children. Let them wash a number of glass jars with lids in warm water with baking soda to remove any contaminating substances. Let jars dry upside down on a clean rack. Next, the children can clean and cut a couple pounds of vegetables. Make florets from a small cauliflower, slice carrots, cube cucumbers and drain, slice gherkins and shallots, and pod peas and beans. While they are busy doing this and placing vegetables in a big pot, you can mix into a smooth paste 2½ ounces dry mustard, 1 teaspoon salt, 2 teaspoons each of ground cumin and ginger with a little

vinegar from a liter bottle (you'll need the rest of the liter later). Taste and add a dash of anything you feel it needs, maybe a teaspoon of honey? Bring the rest of the one liter vinegar to a boil in a separate pot, add the spice paste, and cook about five minutes. Meanwhile, dunk the vegetables in boiling water for five minutes, strain and pat in a dry dish towel, then cook the vegetables in the mustard sauce for another five minutes. The children set the jars in a clean tray of hottish water so they won't crack when receiving the hot piccalilli. When ready to fill, set jars on a towel or bread board, pour in the well-stirred piccalilli, and seal with lids. Pick up jars with oven gloves and turn upside down to remove vacuum, then screw the lid tight once more. While jars cool, the kids write labels with the correctly spelled name and date of this refreshing pickle! Attach when cold.

Pickling in brine: Olives are pickled in strong brine for a week. Drain, repeat for one week, drain. Then, place olives in a weak brine of 1 tablespoon of salt per two quarts of boiled water. While filling jars, add crushed garlic, bay leaf, and sprigs of celery, rosemary, sage and marjoram between layers—or any herb you like. Tarragon is good; so is oregano and fennel. Be creative. Stand for one month.

Enjoy your meals!

Notes

1. United States Environmental Protection Agency, "Demographics," *Ag 101*, epa.gov.
2. Julian Cribb, "Perspective," ABC Radio National Australia (March 5, 2007).
3. Colin Tudge, *The Time before History* (New York: Scribner, 1996), 278.
4. *Encyclopaedia of Lands and People* (London: Kingfisher, 1999).
5. *Permaculture International Journal*, No. 74 (March–May 2000).
6. Andrea Gaynor, *Harevest of the Suburbs: An Environmental History of Growing Food in Australian Cities* (Perth: University of Western Australia Press, 2006), 119.
7. *Bush Telegraph*, ABC Radio One, May 17, 2010.
8. *Organic Gardener* (November–December 2007), 11–12.
9. Chris Alenson, "The Use of Nitrogenous Fertilizers and Their Effects on the Health of Plants, Animals and Humans" in "Barraclough's Backyard," *Green Connections*, Issue 31 (September–October 2000).
10. *Organic Gardener* (Summer 2000), 59.
11. Hogan Gleeson, *Organic Gardener* (Spring 2002), 47.
12. Esther Dean, *Esther Dean's Gardening Book: Growing without Digging* (Sydney: Harper and Row, 1977).
13. Colin Tudge, *So Shall We Reap: What's Wrong with the World's Food—and How to Fix It* (London: Penguin Books, 2004), 46.
14. Ernest L. Bergman, "Vegetable Farming in China" in *Oriental Herbs and Vegetables: A Handbook*, Plants and Garden Series, Brooklyn Botanic Garden Record, Vol. 39, No. 2, (Summer 1983), 37–38.
15. "Man Battles for Life after Eating Slug Infected with Rat Lungworm," news.com.au (May 13, 2010).
16. Round Table 2004 report, Environment Protection Authority, Adelaide, 2004.
17. Felicity Lawrence, *Not on the Label* (London: Penguin Books, 2004), 61.
18. See websites grain.org and fao.org
19. Ibid.
20. geneethics.org.
21. banterminator.org.

22. Seed Savers Network, *Seed Savers Network* Newsletter, No. 37 (Spring 2004); Seed Savers Network Newsletter, No. 39 (Spring 2005).

23. J. Chatto and W. L. Martin, *A Kitchen in Corfu* (London: Weidenfeld and Nicholson, 1993), 29.

24. Gaynor, *Harvest of the Suburbs.*

25. Seed Savers Network, *Seed Savers Network Newsletter*, No. 37 (Spring 2004).

26. Alan D. Cook, "Supermarket on a Stalk" in *Oriental Herbs and Vegetables: A Handbook*, Plants and Garden Series, Brooklyn Botanic Garden Record, Vol. 39, No. 2 (Summer 1983), 42–43.

References and Further Reading

Ashworth, Suzanne, *Seed to Seed: Seed Saving and Growing Techniques for Vegetable Gardeners*, Seed Savers' Exchange, 2002. (See Useful Addresses, page 317, for contact details.)

Bergman, Ernest L., "Vegetable Farming in China" in *Oriental Herbs and Vegetables: A Handbook*, 37–38. Brooklyn, NY: Brooklyn Botanic Garden Record, Vol. 39, No. 2, Summer 1983.

Bartholomew, Mel, *Square Foot Gardening.* Emmaus, PA: Rodale Press, 1981.

Baxter, Lynette, *Balti: The Complete Cookbook.* USA: Greenwich Editions, 1998.

Bissell, Frances, *The Scented Kitchen: Cooking with Flowers.* London: Serif Publishing, 2007.

Bittman, Mark, *Leafy Greens: An A–Z Guide to 30 Types of Greens Plus More than 120 Recipes.* New York: Macmillan, 1995.

Buchanan, Rita, *The Shaker Herb and Garden Book.* New York: Houghton Mifflin, 1996.

Dean, Esther, *Esther Dean's Gardening Book: Growing without Digging.* Sydney: Harper and Row, 1977.

Donaldson, Stephanie, *The Shaker Garden: Beauty through Utility.* Newton Abbot, UK: David and Charles, 2000.

Foster, David, and Foster, Gerda, *A Year of Slow Food: Four Seasons of Growing and Enjoying Food in the Australian Countryside.* New South Wales: Duffy and Snellgrove, 2001.

Fukuoka, Masanobu, *The One-Straw Revolution: An Introduction to Natural Farming.* New York: New York Review Books Classics, 2009. (A classic on true organic growing.)

Gaynor, Andrea, *Harvest of the Suburbs: An Environmental History of Growing Food in Australian Cities*, University of Western Australia Press, Perth, 2006

Grieve, Margaret, *A Modern Herbal: The Medicinal, Culinary, Cosmetic and Economic Properties, Cultivation* and *Folklore of Herbs, Grasses, Fungi, Shrubs, and Trees with All Their Modern Scientific Uses.* New York: Penguin Books, 1980. (First published 1931. Still the herb bible, although classifications may have changed for some plants.)

Hadidian, John, *Wild Neighbors: The Humane Approach to Living with Wildlife.* Humane Society of North America, 2005. (A useful book for urban householders.)

Hemenway, Toby, *Gaia's Garden, Second Edition: A Guide to Home-Scale Permaculture.* White River Junction, VT: Chelsea Green, 2009.

James Jr., Theodore, *Cultivating the Cook's Garden.* Tulsa and San Francisco: Council Oak Books, 1998.

Klaus, Carl H., *My Vegetable Love: A Journal of a Growing Season*. New York: Houghton Mifflin, 1996. (About the pain and the ecstasy of growing food!)

Lanza, Patricia, *Lasagna Gardening for Small Spaces: A Layering System for Big Results in Small Gardens and Containers*. Emmaus, PA: Rodale, 1998.

Larkcom, Joy, *The Salad Garden*. Sydney: Doubleday, 1984.

Lawrence, Felicity, *Not on the Label: What Really Goes into the Food on Your Plate*. London: Penguin Books, 2004.

MacDonald, Janet, *The Ornamental Kitchen Garden*. Newton Abbot, UK: David and Charles, 1994.

McClure, Susan, *Preserving Summer's Bounty: A Quick and Easy Guide to Freezing, Canning, and Preserving and Drying What You Grow*. Emmaus, PA: Rodale, 1998.

Mobbs, Michael, *Sustainable House*. Dunedin, New Zealand: University of Otago Press, 1998.

Mollison, Bill, and Holmgren, David, *Permaculture One: A Perennial Agriculture for Human Settlements*, Melbourne: Transworld Publishers, 1978.

Mollison, Bill, *Permaculture Two: Practical Design for Town and Country in Permanent Agriculture*. Tasmania: Tagari Community, 1979.

Mollison, Bill, *Permaculture: A Designer's Manual*. New South Wales: Tagari Publications, 1988.

Mollison, Bill, and Slay, Reny Mia, *Introduction to Permaculture*. New South Wales: Tagari Publications, 1992.

Nearing, Helen, and Nearing, Scott, *Living the Good Life: How to Live Sanely and Simply in a Troubled World*. New York: Schocken Books, 1970.

Nearing, Helen, and Nearing, Scott, *The Good Life: Helen and Scott Nearing's Sixty Years of Self-Sufficient Living*. New York: Schocken Books, 1979.

Nicholson, B. E., Harrison, S. G., Masefield, G. B., and Wallis, M., *The Oxford Book of Food Plants*. Oxford, UK: Oxford University Press, 1969. (Superb pictures and text—there were many reprints until a wholly new edition appeared, see Vaughan and Geissler.)

Norberg-Hodge, Helen, and Gorelick, Steven, "Bringing the Food Economy Home." localfutures.org

Philbrick, Helen, and Gregg, Richard, *Companion Plants and How to Use Them*, Old Greenwich, CT: The Devin-Adair Company, 1982.

Phillips, Karen, and Dahlen, Martha, *A Popular Guide to Chinese Vegetables*. Singapore: MPH Bookstores Publication, 1985.

Pollan, Michael, *In Defense of Food: An Eater's Manifesto*. New York: Penguin Books, 2008, 2009.

Pollan, Michael, *The Omnivore's Dilemma*. London: Bloomsbury, 2006, 2007.

Roberts, Paul, *The End of Food: The Coming Crisis in the World Food Industry*. London: Bloomsbury, 2008.

Schwenke, Karl, *Successful Small-Scale Farming: An Organic Approach*. North Adams, MA: Storey Publishing, 1991.

Starcher, Allison Mia, *Good Bugs for Your Garden*. Chapel Hill, NC: Algonquin Books, 1995.

Stewart, Amy, *The Earth Moved: On the Remarkable Achievements of Earthworms*. Chapel Hill, NC: Algonquin Books, 2004.

Till, Antonia (ed.), *Loaves and Wishes: Writers Writing on Food*. London: Virago Press, 1992.

Tudge, Colin, *So Shall We Reap: What's Wrong with the World's Food and How to Fix It*. London: Penguin Books, 2004.

Vandana, Shiva, "Terra Madre: A Celebration of Living." banterminator.org and geneethics.org.

Vaughan, J. G., and Geissler, C. A., *The New Oxford Book of Food Plants*. London: Oxford University Press, 1997.

Wickham, Cynthia, *Common Plants as Natural Remedies*. London: Frederick Muller Limited, 1981.

Woodward, Penny, *Pest-Repellent Plants*, Melbourne: Hyland House, 1997.

Useful Addresses

ORGANIC GARDENING magazines carry lists of organizations, publications, nurseries, seed companies, new products, and service providers. If you are interested in growing native food and fruit, consult your nursery and library.

NON-HYBRID SEED COMPANIES

Native Seeds | SEARCH
(Southwestern Endangered Aridland
Resource Clearing House)
3061 North Campbell Avenue
Tucson, AZ 85719
520-622-5561
nativeseeds.org
(*An essential resource for anyone living in a hot, dry part of the country, but worth learning more about wherever you live on account of the amazing work they do to preserve and perpetuate the agricultural traditions of peoples indigenous to the Southwestern United States.*)

Territorial Seed Company
PO Box 158
Cottage Grove, OR 97424
541-942-9547
territorialseed.com

Seeds of Change
PO Box 4908
Rancho Dominguez, CA 90220
888-762-7333
seedsofchange.com
(*The company that supplied the seeds for the 2009 White House Organic Garden!*)

Seed Savers Exchange
3094 North Winn Road
Decorah, IA 52101
563-382-5990
seedsavers.org

Baker Creek Heirloom Seed Company
2278 Baker Creek Road
Mansfield, MO 65704
417-924-8917
rareseeds.com

ORGANIZATIONS

Biodynamic Association
1661 North Water Street, Suite 307
Milwaukee, WI 53202
262-649-9212
biodynamics.com

MAGAZINES

Heirloom Gardener
theheirloomgardener.com

Rodale's Organic Life
rodalesorganiclife.com

WEBSITES

**Multilingual Multiscript
Plant Name Database**
www.plantnames.unimelb.edu.au
(*A fantastic site that allows you to search
plant names in over 60 languages and 20
scripts.*)

SHARING A GARDEN

Seeds for Africa
seedsforafrica.org
(*Works to provide developing communities
in Africa with diverse and indigenous plants
and growing practices to start their own
food gardens. Contact for information or to
donate.*)

COMMUNITY GARDENS

If you don't have a garden, join a community
garden near you. Consult your city
council, library, or resource center, or
visit the American Community Gardening
Association, which supports gardens in
both the United States and Canada, online
at communitygarden.org.

EVENTS

Slow Food Movement, Italy, holds an
annual Terra Madre (Mother Earth)
exhibition and coming together of
traditional food growers from all over the
globe. A major aim is to prevent loss of food
diversity. To discover what is happening
with the Slow Food Movement in North
America, visit slowfoodusa.org or
slowfood.ca.

Acknowledgments

PRIMARY GRATITUDE goes to my mother and grandmother, excellent plain cooks with the ingredients available to them. They put all their efforts into my survival during the famine in western Holland that became known as the Hunger Winter of 1944–1945. By a miracle, they themselves survived to cook again. Uncle Wim shared out vegetables from his small farm until that severe winter closed down the earth. He was my gardening teacher from the moment I could toddle, introducing me to his beloved pole beans, currant bushes, and happy chickens.

I thank all vegetable-growing friends for stories that found their way into this book. Special thanks go to Chris Watters and Daryn Howell, who helped design and run an eight-week course in Strathalbyn about growing vegetables on one square yard. We charged a nominal fee of one dollar per session for potting soil and seeds to give participants hands-on experience in raising their own. Chris, passionate tomato aficionado, introduced us to mixed salad boxes. Daryn, who grew carrots in his driveway, was a mine of horticultural information. Both shared their food gardens with the participants, some of whom returned to do the repeat course. Thanks also to Jane Henderson who demonstrated vegetarian gourmet cooking, and Thelma and Mario Ielasi for sharing their skills in preserving home-grown produce. Percy McElwaine allowed me to photograph his food garden and bequeathed me his portable plastic roof. Else Jansen started a kitchen garden just when I needed more photos. My first herb, a yarrow, came from Mrs. Moss, whose pioneering herb nursery at Mount Barker spawned most subsequent herb nurseries, including my tiny Middle Hill Herb Nursery. Gratitude goes to three gardeners, Louise, Jeff, and Vivienne, who, over the decades, helped out with the ornamental gardens on a regular basis, allowing me more time to experiment with vegetables.

Three authors who profoundly influenced my thinking about food growing at home were Mel Bartholomew, author of *Square Foot Gardening*, more recently Colin Tudge with *So Shall We Reap*, and Michael Pollan with *In Defense of Food* and *The Omnivore's Dilemma*.

At Wakefield Press, Michael Bollen acted as the devil's advocate every non-fiction book needs, and Bethany Clark edited the text with tender care and much enthusiasm. I accept that any errors or omissions may well be mine, but regret having let go of some elaborating little chapters. All the same, neither time nor effort was spared by all involved in producing this book to make it the most accessible grow-your-own text for food gardeners born and yet to be born.

As the North American edition goes to press, my thanks go to Matthew Lore at The Experiment for his enthusiasm for the concept and emphasizing the organic method that underlies the book, while Elisabeth Watson deserves credit for extended research on specific American issues, the White House food garden story, providing plants with their American names and turning *chooks* into *chickens*.

Special thanks go to Batya Rosenblum for undertaking the task of splicing gardening sections from *Outside the Magic Square: A Handbook for Food Security* into the best garden plots from the original *One Magic Square*, to come up with the best magic book for food gardeners old and new.

Lastly, a very special thanks to my partner Burwell Dodd, computer and compost specialist, who turned a spade when I couldn't, put in posts for fences and espalier fixtures, and has eaten the results of my food-growing experiments without a murmur.

Index

For quick information and tips about growing particular vegetables, herbs, fruits, and berries, refer to the alphabetical lists in Part Four.

Note: Page numbers in italics indicate photographs.

codling moths, 95–96

colanders, 108

cold composting, 35

cold frames for seedlings, 45, 117

collards, 246

commercial seeds, 42

community, garden as, 21

companies, seed, 41–42

companion planting, *52*, 52–54, *53*

Compositae family, 222

compost

    about, 34

    in-bed, 37–38

    lawnmowers, riding, for making,
      36–37

    making, 34–40, *35*

    paper in, 38

    Shaker, 34

    tree, 38

    turning, 36

    worms and worm farms, 38–39, *39*

    See also composting

composting

    beginning, 26

    in bins, 35–36, *39*

    hot versus cold, 35

    seedlings and, 38

    time management, 18

    See also compost

composting toilets, 58

container gardening, 146

Convolvulaceae/morning glory family,
  223

Cook, Alan D., 236

cooking, 135–36

cool weather salads, 153

coriander, 307

corn, sweet, 199, 267–68, 308

corporations, multinational, 4, 5

cost of food production, 8–9

cress, 283

Cribb, Julian, 3

crop rotation

    about, 76–78, *77*

    1, 2, 3 method, 79–81

    1, 2, 3, 4 method, 79

    scenarios for, 78–79

crops

    fruiting, 127

    green, 81

    nitrogen-fixing, 81

    root, 127

    See also specific crops

Cruciferae family, 222–23, *223*

cucumber and yogurt soup, 197

cucumbers, 246–47

Cucurbitaceae/gourd family, 223

cucurbit family, 130–31

cumin, 283

cupboard self-sufficiency, 139–43

curly leaf, 96–97

currants, 300

Curry Plots

    about, 162

    autumn and winter, 162–63

cylinders, wire, 113, 259–60

D

dahl, 141

daikon, 263–64

glyphosate, 90

gooseberries, 297–98, 301

goosefoot family, 223

gourd, bitter, 235

gourd family, 223

grafting, 294

grains, 143

grapefruit, 298

grape residue, 71

grapes, 301–2

grasses, eradicating, 294

grass family, 224

grasshoppers, 98

gravel, 71

Great Potato Famine, 76

green crops, 81

green fennel, 282–83, *283*

green manures, 64–65

green rules, 21–22

greens, leafy, 127

greens, salad, 265

"green slurry" stir-fry, 74

gross feeders, 61–62, *62*, 67

Guangdong Province, China, 76–77

guavas, 301

gypsum hardpan, 65

H

hands, washing, 92

hand watering, 55–56

hardware, 105, 105–6

   See also specific types

hardy vegetables, 46–47

hay, 71

hay bales, 65

haybox, Oma's, 141–42

heat, and seed saving, 129

heirloom seeds, 41

herbal teas, 279

herbs

   all-season, 228

   drying, 308

   growing notes, general, 279

   herbal teas, 279

   list of, 279–92

   native, 279

   pest-repelling, 91–92, 279

   See also specific herbs

herb stalks, 71

herb vinegars, 155

heritage seeds, 41

Hippodamia, 88

holes, eating, 91

Holmgren, David, 55, 124

horse manure, 32

horseradish, 285–86

horta, 180–81

Horta Plot, 12–13, 180–81

hospital gowns, 108

hot composting, 35

hot frames for seedlings, 45–46

Hubbard squashes, 267

humidity, 129

humus, 65

hunger, 6

hyssop, 286

I

ice-plant family, 222

imported food, 2

plantains, 85

plant food, 63–68

planting

    biodynamic calendar, 44

    companion, *52*, 52–54, *53*

    density of, 13

    fruit trees and berries, 294

    by the moon, 44

    seeds, 44–45

    waterwise, 58

Plant Patent Act of 1930, 131, 132

plants, grouping, 67–68

Plant Variety Protection Act of 1970,
    131, 132, 133

plastic, black, 70

plastic bottles, 110, *110*

plastic lids, 110–11

plastic tubs, 111

plums, 306

Poaceae/grass family, 224

polenta, 142

poles, 111

pollutants, 31

Polygonaceae/buckwheat family, 224

poly pipe, 111

poly tunnels, 111

pomegranates, 305

population growth, 4

portable roof, Percy's, 109, *109*

possums, 99

potash, 67

potatoes, 199, 259–60, 275–76

potato onions, 43

pot scrubbers, 111

predators. *See* pests

preserving, 307–11

pride, 136

prunes, 308

pruning, 74, 294–95

Pumpkin Plot, *211*, 211–12

pumpkins, 74–75, 260–62, 276

PVC rings, 111

Q

quince, *305*, 305–6, *310*

R

rabbits, 99

racks from old fridges/ovens, 112

radicchio, 262–63

radishes, 263–64

rainwater tanks, 57

raised beds and trenches, 58–59

rat lungworm disease, 92

recipes

    Balti sauce, 284

    borscht, 196

    Cabbage Ribs and Co., 137

    cabbage soup, 196

    chai tea, 139

    chard, 244

    Chinese cabbage, 245–46

    cucumber and yogurt soup, 197

    cucumbers, 247

    dahl, 141

    easy party dip, 139

    eggplant (aubergine), 247

    falafel, 248

    fava beans, 248

recipes
  fenugreek, 284
  French onion soup, 196
  garam masala, 139
  garlic soup, 196–97
  gazpacho, 197
  gherkins, 250
  globe artichokes, 252
  horta, 180–81
  leek and potato soup with sorrel, 197
  lemon sago, 142–43
  parsnips, 258
  patty pan, 267
  polenta, 142
  potatoes, 275–76
  rudjak, 154–55
  Siberian kale soup, 197, 253
  sorrel, 266
  summer soups, 197
  tomatoes, 270
  turnips, 270
  winter soups, 196–97
  yogurt-based salad dressings, 155
red clover, 81
red currants, 299
red peppers, 276
reserves, food, 2
rhubarb, 214, 264
rice, 143
rock, 72
rocket. *See* arugula
rocky soil, 31
rodents, 99
Rodriguez, Francisca, 133
roof, Percy's portable, 109, *109*

Root Crop Plot, 176–77
root crops, 127
roots, 43, 83
rosemary, 190, 191, 289
Rotating Mono-Crops Plot, 200
row covers for seedlings, 46
rudjak, 154–55
rules, green, 21–22
Russian black tomatoes, 277–78
rutabagas, 264–65

S

sage, 190–91, 289–90
sago, 142–43
salad burnet, 290
salad dressings, 154–55
salad greens, 265
Salad Plots
  about, 13, *14, 147,* 147–48
  cool weather salads, 153
  salad dressings, 154–55
  spring and summer, 148–51
  summer salads, 152
salsify, 265
sandy soil, 33
saving seed. See seed saving
savoy, *68*
sawdust, 72
scarlet runner beans, 265
Schmeiser, Percy, 132
scorzonera, 265
screening, 112
seasons, 116–18
  See also specific seasons

turnips, 270

twigs, 72

twine, baling, 106

U

umbrellas, 113

Umbrelliferae family, 222

United Nations Convention on
Biological Diversity, 133

urine, 27, 67

Urticaceae/nettle family, 224

U.S. Bureau of Labor Statistics, 2–3

U.S. Department of Agriculture
(USDA), 2, 5

U.S. seed saving law, 131, 132, 133

Utah State University, 88

utensils, 137–38

V

Vavilov, Nikola Ivanovich, 43

Vavilov Institute, 43

vegetables
all-season, 228
appearance of, 19–20
colors, 230
easy to grow, 126–28
families, 222–24, 273–78
growing and using, 230–78
growing notes, general, 229–30
hardy, 46–47
Japanese, 252
lime, 229
list of, 230–78
nitrogen, 229–30
officinalis plants, 229

organically grown, 5–6
price of, 5
sowing seasons, 230
staple, 230
summer, 127–28, 225–26
water, 272
winter, 227–28
See also specific vegetables

Via Campesina, 133

Victorian Department of Agriculture,
27

Vietnamese mint, 191

vinegars, 155, 310–11

W

waste, garden, 21

water and watering
about, 13
composting toilets, 58
drip irrigation, 58
envirocycle systems, 58
hand watering, 55–56
length of watering, 57
microclimate and, 120
morning versus evening watering, 57
nozzles, 56
position of food plot and, 56
raised beds and trenches, 58–59
shade and, 56
water requirements, 55
water storage, 57–58
waterwise planting, 58

watermelons, 270–71

water vegetables, 271

waterwise planting, 58

About the Author

After surviving World War II and a year-long famine in Holland, **LOLO HOUBEIN** emigrated to Australia at the age of twenty-four with her husband and children in 1958. In the 1960s and 1970s, she studied the literatures of Britain, Africa, Australia, and Oceania, in addition to anthropology and classical studies at the universities of Adelaide and Papua New Guinea, along with earning a teaching degree. She has written articles, food columns, and books of fiction and non-fiction, three of which have won awards. One Magic Square was awarded a Gourmand award in 2009 and made the short list of world's best food book for Le Cordon Bleu in 2010. She also compiled the first bibliography of ethnic authors in Australia.

With Burwell Dodd, her partner of thirty-five years, she co-founded Trees for Life, a movement devoted to re-vegetating South Australia with native trees, and recently registered the South Australian Land Protection Association, affiliated with Lock the Gate, to protect farmland from mining. She also started a state branch of the Sydney-based movement Wrap with Love that unites thousands of knitters in making blankets for cold people around the world. Lolo lives and gardens in the Adelaide Hills of Southern Australia.